WRITING THROUGH MEDIEVAL HISTORY

Level 2

"*Cursive Models*"

A Charlotte Mason Writing Program
"Gentle and Complete"

Medieval History
400 AD – 1600 AD
From Saint Augustine to Shakespeare

Historical Narratives, Primary Source Documents, Poetry, and Cultural Tales

BOOKS PUBLISHED BY BROOKDALE HOUSE:

The Writing Through Ancient History books
Writing Through Ancient History Level 1 Cursive Models
Writing Through Ancient History Level 1 Manuscript Models
Writing Through Ancient History Level 2 Cursive Models
Writing Through Ancient History Level 2 Manuscript Models

The Writing Through Medieval History books
Writing Through Medieval History Level 1 Cursive Models
Writing Through Medieval History Level 1 Manuscript Models
Writing Through Medieval History Level 2 Cursive Models
Writing Through Medieval History Level 2 Manuscript Models

The Writing Through Early Modern History Books
Writing Through Early Modern History Level 1 Cursive Models
Writing Through Early Modern History Level 1 Manuscript Models
Writing Through Early Modern History Level 2 Cursive Models
Writing Through Early Modern History Level 2 Manuscript Models

The Writing Through Modern History Books
Writing Through Modern History Level 1 Cursive Models
Writing Through Modern History Level 1 Manuscript Models
Writing Through Modern History Level 2 Cursive Models
Writing Through Modern History Level 2 Manuscript Models

The Fun Spanish Level 1

Sheldon's Primary Language Lessons
(Introductory grammar workbook for elementary students)

The Westminster Shorter Catechism Copybook
(Available in the following font styles: traditional, modern, italic, and vertical, both print and cursive)

The Geography Drawing Series
Drawing Around the World: Europe
Drawing Around the World: USA

Easy Narrative Writing

ISBN: 9 78-1-64281-017-2

Table of Contents

Introduction	v
Definitions—Narration, Copywork, Studied Dictation	vii
Scheduling	x

Chapter I — Historical Narratives

Alaric the Visigoth	394 – 410 AD	I-3
Attila the Hun	434 – 453 AD	I-9
Clovis	481 – 511 AD	I-15
Justinian the Great	527 – 565 AD	I-21
Mohammed	570 – 632 AD	I-27
Charles Martel and Pepin	714 – 741 AD	I-33
Charlemagne	768 – 814 AD	I-39
Egbert	802 – 837 AD	I-45
Alfred the Great	871 – 901 AD	I-50
Rollo the Viking	died 931 AD	I-56
Canute the Great	1014 – 1035 AD	I-62
El Cid	1040 – 1099 AD	I-67
Edward the Confessor	1042 – 1066 AD	I-73
Peter the Hermit	1050 – 1115 AD	I-78
William the Conqueror	1066 – 1087 AD	I-83
Frederick Barbarossa	1152 – 1190 AD	I-88
Henry the Second	1154 – 1189 AD	I-93
Marco Polo	1254 – 1324 AD	I-99
William Tell and Arnold von Winkelried	14th Century	I-104
King Robert Bruce	1306 – 1329 AD	I-109
Edward the Black Prince	1330 – 1376 AD	I-114
Henry V	1413 – 1422 AD	I-120
Joan of Arc	1412 – 1431 AD	I-125
Gutenberg	1400 – 1468 AD	I-130
Warwick the Kingmaker	1428 – 1471 AD	I-135
Christopher Columbus	1435 – 1506 AD	I-141
Vasco da Gama	1469 – 1524 AD	I-148
Sir Walter Raleigh	1552 – 1618 AD	I-155
Galileo	1564 – 1642 AD	I-161

Chapter II* — Primary Source Documents

The Confessions of Saint Augustine (excerpt)	354 – 430 AD	II-3
Of The Greatest Good (excerpt) by Boëtius	475 – 525 AD	II-7
Institutes of Justinian (excerpt) by Justinian the Great	529 – 534 AD	II-12
A Letter from Alcuin to Charlemagne	796 AD	II-17
The Life of King Alfred (excerpt) by Asser	888 AD	II-21
Pope Urban II Plea for a Crusade 1095 (excerpt)	1095 AD	II-25
How Can the Absolute Be a Cause? (excerpt) by Aquinas	1226 – 1274 AD	II-29
The Decameron (On the Black Death) (excerpt)	1350 – 1353 AD	II-33

*Note: While some stories may be legends, the dates indicate the estimated lifespan of the main character.

The Imitation of Christ (excerpt) by Thomas à Kempis	1418 AD	II-39
Joan of Arc (from transcript of trial)	1431 AD	II-45
Dedication of the Revolutions of the Heavenly Bodies	1543 AD	II-48
Martin Luther before the Diet of Worms	1483 – 1546 AD	II-54
The Autobiography of St. Ignatius (excerpt)	1555 AD	II-59
Columbus to the Lord Treasurer of Spain	1493 AD	II-64
Queen Elizabeth's Address to her Army	1588 AD	II-68

Chapter III+ Poetry from/about ancient times

All Glory, Laud, and Honor	820 AD	III-3
Arnold von Winkelried	1386 AD	III-6
The Glove and the Lions	1515-1547 AD	III-11
Hamlet's Soliloquy	c. 1599 – 1601 AD	III-14
The Ladder of St. Augustine	354 – 430 AD	III-17
Polonius' Advice by Shakespeare	c. 1599 – 1601 AD	III-21
Saint Bernard's Hymn	1091 – 1153 AD	III-24
The Sermon of St. Francis by Longfellow	1182 – 1206 AD	III-27
The Slaying of Owain by Aneurin	6th Century AD	III-31
The Vesper Hymn of Abelard	1079 – 1142 AD	III-34
Where to Find True Joy by 'Boethius'	849 – 901 AD	III-37

Chapter IV++ Cultural Tales

The Gods of the Teutons	Norse myth	IV-3
The Nibelungs	Norse myth	IV-9
Siegfried, the King's Son	Norse myth	IV-16
The Story of the Merchant and the Genie (pt. 1)	Arabian Nights	IV-21
The Story of the First Old Man and of the Hind (pt. 2)	Arabian Nights	IV-27
The Story of the Second Old Man and Two Black Dogs (pt. 3)	Arabian Nights	IV-32
The Fairy	Charles Perrault	IV-37
Little Red Riding Hood	Charles Perrault	IV-42
The Master Cat or Puss in Boots	Charles Perrault	IV-47
Mr. and Mrs. Vinegar	English Tale	IV-53
The Three Wishes	English Tale	IV-59
Schippeitaro	Japanese Tale	IV-63
A Tale of a Penny	Medieval tale	IV-68
As You Like It	Shakespeare	IV-72
King Lear	Shakespeare	IV-78

Appendix

Oral narration questions	2
Grammar Guide	3
Models from Chapter I Historical Narratives	6
Models from Chapter II Text Excerpts from Primary Source Documents	16
Models from Chapter III Poetry from Medieval History	21
Models from Chapter IV Folktales from Various Cultures	26

+Note: **Chapter III is in alphabetical order. Search for the time period or topic that will best fit your history schedule.**
++Note: **The publication dates for Chapter IV are not included. These are very old tales with many variations published at various times.**

Introduction

Writing Through Medieval History Layout

Writing Through Medieval History is a writing program that teaches grammar, spelling, and history—all at once. This volume covers medieval history, from 400 AD to 1600 AD—the second year of a 4-year cycle.

Writing Through Medieval History, L2 teaches writing the Charlotte Mason way for upper grammar stage students, third through fifth grade. It is divided into four chapters: short stories, text excerpts from primary source documents, poetry, and cultural tales. For Chapter I, short stories that give insight into people, places, and events during medieval times have been selected. Chapter II contains excerpts from primary source documents including, but not limited to, historical essays reflecting medieval philosophy and church history. Chapter III contains poetry from and about medieval times. Chapter IV contains folk tales.

In all four chapters, the reading selection is followed by a practice model, which is used for copywork and dictation. There are more than 60 selections included in *Writing Through Medieval History*.

To coordinate *Writing Through Medieval History* with your history topics, refer to the Table of Contents, which also serves as a timeline. Use the timeline provided to determine which selection would be the best fit for that week's history lesson. Historical narratives will primarily come from Chapters I and IV. Feel free to move around the book.

In the Appendix, you will find two models for each reading selection. The first model is the same as the copywork model which followed the reading selection. The second model, which is in italics, is also from the reading selection. It has been added for use by those that like to use a separate model for dictation.

Because *Writing Through Medieval History* was written for grades 3–5, some selections will be too long for some students. Simply reduce any of the models by drawing a line through the unneeded portion. Sometimes you will have to break the model in the middle of a sentence. In that case, stop at a semi-colon (;) or coordinating conjunction (", and" ", or" ", but" ", nor" ", for" ", so" ", yet") to make the selection shorter. Semi-colons and coordinating conjunctions are used to separate main clauses—those with a subject and a predicate. If you must break the model into a shorter sentence, modify the new selection by adding a period at the end and ensure that you have a grammatically correct model. Explain to your student the use of semi-colons and coordinating conjunctions and why the change is being made. This is an excellent opportunity to reinforce and explain the grammar rules involved.

Note: Many of the works included were taken from the public domain; many have been edited for Writing Through Medieval History.

Note: Although titles of books and ships would normally be italicized in texts, they are underlined to teach children that these names are underlined in handwritten works.

Most of the principles in *Writing Through Medieval History* are based on the work of Ms. Charlotte Mason. She advocated that children of the grammar or elementary stage practice narration, copywork, and dictation as their primary method of learning to write. But because Ms. Mason's methods have been interpreted differently over the years, I have included alternative suggestions on how to implement *Writing Through Medieval History*. So to begin using *Writing Through Medieval History* as your child's writing program, please read all of the introduction, pages v–ix, before your student begins.

Additional Information

Reading Levels

Chapters II and III contain excerpts from historical documents and historically relevant poetry that may be well above the reading level of some grammar and even logic stage students. I recommend that these advanced selections be read to your student. If you would like to stretch your student, ask him to read all or part of the selection back to you. These reading selections offer great opportunity to cover new vocabulary as well as new ideas.

Appendix "Models Only"

The Appendix lists all of the models by chapter. The first model is in normal typeface while the second model is italicized. Only the first model follows the reading selections. The second models were added to give the students a different model for dictation. For the sake of organization, the Appendix contains a copy of the models to assist the instructor with copywork and studied dictation.

Getting Started

On the following page, I have covered each area of the program: Narration, Copywork, and Dictation. I have also provided a guide suggesting how to incorporate grammar into the program. Please read these in their entirety.

Correcting Work

Correcting writing, whether written summations, copywork, or dictation, is always difficult. Ms. Mason advised teachers and parents to correct the student's writings occasionally. This makes perfect sense when realizing that Ms. Mason's methods did not require the need for extensive corrections. She consistently emphasized that work be done correctly the first time. She believed that a student should not be allowed to visually dwell on incorrect work. When a child made a mistake during dictation, Ms. Mason had stamps or pieces of paper available to cover the mistakes so that the mistakes were not reinforced visually.

When a child made a mistake during narrations, she withheld correcting him. I believe that she used the time after the oral narration was finished to discuss the material that had been narrated.

When corrections are needed, it is good to practice the principle of praise before correcting children. Find out what is right with what they've done. Be impressed. Focus on their effort. Build them up. Ephesians 5:29 of the King James Bible says—

Let no corrupt communication
proceed out of your mouth, but
that which is good to the use of edifying,
that it may minister grace
unto the hearers.

The hearers are our students—our children. And the words we say will either minister grace or condemnation. We must encourage them and free them from the fear of our frustrations and negative feedback as we correct them.

Definitions

Personal Narrations –the act of retelling

Ms. Mason believed narrations should be done immediately after the story was read to the student or by the student. Narrations are very simple, yet very effective in teaching writing. The act of narrating helps children to internalize the content of the reading material they have been exposed to and allows them to make it their own. In order to narrate, students must listen carefully, dissect the information, and then express that same information in their own words. It is a powerful tool, but very simple to put into practice.

Oral narrations Read all or part of the story only once before requiring the student to narrate! It will require him to pay attention. Simply ask your student to tell you what he has just heard or read.

If your student has trouble with this process, show him how to narrate by demonstrating the process for him. **Read a selection yourself and then narrate it to him. Ask him to imitate you.** If he continues to draw a blank, use the list of questions below to prompt him. (See the removable list of narration questions in the Appendix, page 2, for daily use. The Appendix also contains questions for poetry and primary source documents.)

Besides all of the previously mentioned benefits, oral narrations teach students to digest information, dissect it, and reorganize it into their own words while thinking on their feet. This practice helps students to develop the art of public speaking. This formal process will force them to express their ideas without a written plan. It strengthens the mind. And over time, their speech will become fluent and natural. (I sometimes have my children stand as they narrate. It makes the process more formal.)

If your student has difficulty with narrations, ask some or all of the following questions:

1. Who was the main character?
2. What was the character like?
3. Where was the character?
4. What time was it in the story?
5. Who else was in the story?
6. Does the main character have an enemy?
   (The enemy may be another character, himself, or nature.)
7. Did the main character have a problem? If not, what did the character want?
8. What does the main character do? What does he say? If there are others, what do they do?
9. Why does the character do what he does?
10. What happens to the character as he tries to solve his problem?
11. Is there a moral to the story? If so, what was it?
12. What happens at the end of the story? Or how does the main character finally solve his problem?

Written Summations Around the age of 10, students were required by Ms. Mason to write down their narrations for themselves. Many students can do this earlier. Written summations will allow your student to develop this skill. If your student is able, have him write as much as he can, as perfectly as he can, even around the age of 8.

At the end of each oral narration, ask your child to summarize the reading selection by identifying the beginning, the middle, and the end. He should be able to do this in about three to six sentences—fewer is best. Younger students will sometimes begin each sentence with "First,..." or "At the beginning,..." This is okay. But once the student masters the summation, ask him to summarize without these types of words. Tell him to begin with the subject or the time.

Ex: When Louisa May Alcott was a young girl, she was very happy because she spent her time playing with her sisters and writing in her diary.

The benefits of written summations are manifold. They will help your student to think linearly from the beginning of the reading selection to the end. They also provide the right amount of content for the reluctant writer. Additionally, the act of summarizing teaches students to identify the main thread or central idea of a passage. (Even though your child begins to write his written summations, have him continue his oral narrations without limit. These will help him to internalize and learn the historical content of the stories in *Writing Through Medieval History* as well as develop his public speaking skills.)

Copywork and Grammar—copying a passage exactly as written

As your child copies the model before him, stay near so that you are able to correct any problems immediately.

Before your child begins, discuss the model with him. Point out the grammatical elements that he is learning. Have your child identify the part of speech in the model and circle it with a colored pencil. See page 3 of the Appendix for a grammar guide. (Spend approximately one month on each new part of speech.) When using the grammar guide, continue to review by including all previously learned work in the current lesson. For the second month, he is to identify both nouns and verbs. The third—nouns, verbs, and pronouns.

Ms. Mason recommended the formal study of grammar at about 4th or 5th grade. If you opt to add a formal program for your upper grammar stage student, that would be worthwhile. If you do so, you may omit the grammar study in this program.

Grammar
If you would prefer that your student study grammar with his copywork, see the grammar guide in the Appendix page 3. It focuses on the 8 parts of speech as well as fundamental punctuation. The process involves the student identifying the parts of speech and color-coding the copywork selections according to the guide. The process is cumulative in that students should roll the new grammar concept in with the old. By of the end of the year, students should be identifying all eight parts of speech in their copywork.

Studied Dictation—the act of writing from an oral reading

Once again, Ms. Mason's ideas are simple, yet effective. The goal in dictation is to teach your child to write correctly and from memory the sentences or clauses he has just heard. Ms. Mason let the child study the dictation for a few minutes. She wrote down any unknown or difficult words for him on a board. She then erased the board and read each passage only once. From this one reading, the child wrote; however, if the child made a mistake, she covered the mistake instantly so that the student was not allowed to visualize and internalize it.

For the child who has never done dictation, start by reading as many times as necessary so that your child memorizes the sentences. Work down to one reading per 2 or 3 sentences or main clauses. This is an advanced skill and may require time to achieve. Be patient, but consistent. (If needed, allow your student to repeat the model back to you before he writes. Some students may need this reinforcement; others may not.)

After you write the model on the whiteboard, discuss it, in depth, with your student. An example of the process follows.

MODEL

"Mary, did you spill the ink on the carpet?" asked Tom.
"No, Tom," answered Mary. "Did you, Will?"
"I did not, Mary, but I know who did," said Will.
"Who was it, Will?"
Will did not answer in words. He pointed a finger at Fido, and guilty little Fido crept under the sofa.

QUESTIONS TO ASK:

1. What are the names of the people in this story? How does each name begin?
   The names of people always begin with capital letters.
2. Study this model, telling what words begin with capitals and why; which words are indented and why; what marks of punctuation are used and why.

FIRST PARAGRAPH

3. Why is Mary indented in this paragraph.
4. Why is Mary capitalized? Why are the names capitalized?
5. Why is there a comma to separate "Mary" from the rest of the sentence?
6. Why are there quotation marks around certain words?
7. Why does the quoted sentence end with a question mark?
8. Why do some sentences end with a period?

SECOND PARAGRAPH

9. Where does the second paragraph begin?
10. The paragraph begins with someone speaking. How do we know this?
11. Why is the word no capitalized?
12. Why is there a comma after no?
13. Why is there a comma after Tom? After you?
14. Why is there a period after Mary and a question after Will.

DO THIS WITH EACH PARAGRAPH

If there are any questions that your student cannot answer, tell him the answers. Discuss the grammar with him, and work with him until he can narrate why the model is punctuated the way it is.

Do the same with spelling. Identify the words that your student doesn't know and discuss why that word is spelled the way it is.

To see an example of studied dictation, visit the youtube video at the link below:
https://www.youtube.com/watch?v=xoTACGomwsw

or search "Studied Dictation Demonstration" on youtube.
There I demonstrate this dictation process.

Scheduling Information

Listed below is a recommendation for the use of *Writing Through Medieval History*; however, this is **only a recommendation** and should be adjusted for your student's individual needs. **Further explanations and alternate methods** are included on the next page. Please feel free to adjust these methods to make writing as painless as possible for your student. Every child is different.

One Suggested Schedule:

Day 1 — **Reading, Oral Narrations, and Written Summations**
From the Table of Contents, choose a story from Chapters I or IV.
Either you or your student should read the story selection once.
First, have the student orally narrate the story back to you.
(If he has difficulty, use the narration questions listed in the Appendix.)
Second, ask the student to summarize the story in about three sentences to six sentences. If he is able, have him write one or more sentences from his summation. Write for him, if needed. **(For more on narrations, see page vii.)**

Day 2 — **Copywork and Grammar** Complete Model Practice 1 from Day 1's reading selection. Discuss/explain the grammar and punctuation in the model. Do a color-coded grammar study.
(For more on copywork and grammar, see page viii.)

Day 3 — **Studied Dictation** Complete Model Practice 2, using the additional model located in the Appendix, also from Day 1's reading selection. Follow the guidelines for studied dictation on page viii. Neatly write the italic model provided in the Appendix for your student on a separate paper or white board. Allow the student to study the model before writing. Erase the model and dictate.

Day 4 — **Oral narrations and Copywork**
From the Table of Contents, choose a selection from Chapters II or III.
Read all **or part** of the primary source document to your student. He may read the poem himself. If so, teach him to read with expression.
Discuss the complicated ideas in the document. Have your student narrate what he has learned. Complete Model Practice 1 using the copywork model.

Day 5 — **Studied Dictation** Complete Model Practice 2, also from Day 4's reading selection. Follow the guidelines for studied dictation on page viii. Neatly write the Italic model provided in the Appendix for your student on a separate piece of paper or a white board. Allow the student to study the model before writing. Erase the model and dictate.

If the models are too long

If the models are too long for your student, reduce them. Third graders, or even older reluctant writers, should not be forced to do more than they are able. See the bolded paragraph on page v for guidelines on reducing the models.

If your child isn't ready for dictation

Replace the dictation with copywork of the same model, or write the dictation model from the Appendix into the model practice 2 area. Have your student copy your written model in the model practice 3 area.

Optional Schedules

Charlotte Mason's Methods

Ms. Mason used narration, copywork, and dictation simultaneously throughout a young child's education. Narrations were done immediately after he had listened to or read the selection. Copywork was done from well-written sentences. And while many don't believe copywork to be valuable once a student learns to write from dictation, Ms. Mason believed that copywork was extremely valuable for many years alongside dictation. Dictation was a separate part of the process, mostly for the purpose of teaching spelling.

Ms. Mason allowed students to look at the dictation passages and study them before the student began writing. This process was helpful because it allowed the student to visualize how the passage should look. It taught him to study with intention. It taught him to focus on the words. After the passage was read once, the student wrote the passage from memory. This method improved a child's spelling and his grasp of correct punctuation as well.

But not everyone who follows Ms. Mason's methods follows each area of narration, copywork, and dictation in the same way. Below are some ways to incorporate some or all of these ideas into your child's learning adventure.

Different Copywork Passages Daily

Simply use *Writing Through Medieval History* as written, covering two stories per week. **Day 1**, pick a selection from Chapters I or IV. Read and have the student do an oral narration and a written summation. **Day 2**, do copywork and a color-coded grammar study of the model. **Day 3,** the teacher should write all or part of the italicized model from the Appendix onto the Model Practice 2 area, in ink. The student should copy the model and then do a color-coded grammar study of the model in the Model Practice 2 area. **Day 4**, pick a selection from Chapters II or III, a primary source selection or poetry selection. Do oral narration, copywork, and a color-coded grammar study of the model. **Day 5**, the teacher should write the italicized model from the Appendix onto the Model Practice 2 area, in ink. The student should copy the model and do a color-coded grammar study of the model in the Model Practice 2 area. This will provide your student with four different copywork selections each week from two different sources.

Copywork as Dictation

Day 1, pick a selection from Chapters I or IV. Read and have the student do an oral narration and a written summation. **Day 2**, do copywork and a color-coded grammar study of the model. **Day 3,** do studied dictation of the same model. Have your student write in the Model Practice 2 area. **Day 4**, pick a selection from Chapters II or III, a primary source selection or poetry selection. Do an oral narration, copywork, and a color-coded grammar study of the model. **Day 5**, do a studied dictation of yesterday's copywork. Have your student write in the Model Practice 2 area.

Copywork and Dictation

Follow the suggested schedule on page x.

Reminders and Helps

- Use *Writing Through Medieval History* in the best way possible to serve your student's needs. Adapt any area as necessary.
- Help students with spelling as necessary. Set your student up for success.
- In the case of dialogue, remind your student that each time a different character is speaking, a new paragraph is started via indentions. When he first encounters this, show him an example before requiring it of him.
- If the size of the selection is too large, **simply reduce it and require less.**
- Set your student up for success. He shouldn't be expected to know what he has not yet been taught.
- To sum up Charlotte Mason's methods:

Quality over quantity.
Accuracy over speed.
Ideas over drill.
Perfection over mediocrity.

Added Note on Paragraphing

For full-length written narrations (not summations, but the whole story)

You may want your student to occasionally write his narrations in place of the summation. Ms. Mason had children begin writing their narrations around the age of 10. This is equivalent to fourth or fifth grade, and it is a good time for most students. To make the transition to written narrations, have your student orally narrate first, then ask him to write down his narration. Eventually he won't need the oral narration.

In the actual writing of the narration, the difficult elements for most students will be punctuation, grammar, spelling, and paragraph breaks. Through the copywork and dictation, students actively learn correct punctuation, grammar, and spelling. And although they make mistakes, with practice in these areas, they will improve.

Paragraph breaks, however, are not often taught—in any curriculum. Many students intuitively learn when to begin a new paragraph because they read well-written literature. But this isn't always enough.

Paragraphing is easy to learn. Each time the who, what, when, where, why, or how of the story changes, a new paragraph is begun. Look at the following story—

The Penny-Wise Monkey
re-told by Ellen C. Babbitt
from More Jataka Tales

Once upon a time the king of a large and rich country gathered together his army to take a faraway little country. The king and his soldiers marched all morning long and then went into camp in the forest.
(who=king and soldiers, what=march and went, when=once upon a time, where=camp in forest, why=to take a country)

When they fed the horses, they gave them some peas to eat. One of the Monkeys living in the forest saw the peas and jumped down to get some of them. He filled his mouth and hands with them, and up into the tree he went again, and sat down to eat the peas.
(New paragraph, a change in the what, what=gave the horses peas, change in the when, when=feeding the horses, the monkey is introduced)

As he sat there eating the peas, one pea fell from his hand to the ground. At once, the greedy Monkey dropped all the peas he had in his hands and ran down to hunt for the lost pea. But he could not find that one pea. He climbed up into his tree again and sat still looking very glum. "To get more, I threw away what I had," he said to himself.
(New paragraph, a change in the who, the story is now focused on the monkey and not the king, who=monkey)

The king had watched the Monkey, and he said to himself, "I will not be like this foolish Monkey, who lost much to gain a little. I will go back to my own country and enjoy what I now have."
(New paragraph, a change in the who, who=the king, the story is now focused on the king again)

So he and his men marched back home.
(New paragraph, a change in the what, what=marched back home)

Also, when writing dialogue in a conversation, a new paragraph is started each time a different character is speaking.

Bonus Materials

To get additional educational resources, free and almost free, sign up for our newsletter at

www.brookdalehouse.com

or

scan:

CHAPTER I

Historical Narratives Covering Medieval History

Alaric the Visigoth

from Famous Men of the Middle Ages
by John H. Haaren, LL.D. and A. B. Poland, Ph.D.
394 - 410 AD.

Long before the beginning of the period known as the Middle Ages, a tribe of barbarians called the Goths lived north of the River Danube in the country which is now known as Romania. It was then a part of the great Roman Empire, which at that time had two capitals, Constantinople—the new city of Constantine—and Rome. The Goths had come from the shores of the Baltic Sea and settled on this Roman territory, and the Romans had not driven them back.

During the reign of the Roman Emperor Valens, some of the Goths joined a conspiracy against him. Valens punished them for this by crossing the Danube and laying waste their country. At last the Goths had to beg for mercy. The Gothic chief was afraid to set foot on Roman soil, so he and Valens met on their boats in the middle of the Danube and made a treaty of peace.

For a long time the Goths were at war with another tribe of barbarians called Huns. Sometimes the Huns defeated the Goths and drove them to their camps in the mountains. Sometimes the Goths came down to the plains again and defeated the Huns.

At last the Goths grew tired of such constant fighting and thought they would look for new settlements. They sent some of their leading men to the Emperor Valens to ask permission to settle in some country belonging to Rome. The messengers said to the emperor, "If you will allow us to make homes in the country south of the Danube we will be friends of Rome and fight for her when she needs our help." The emperor at once granted this request. He said to the Gothic chiefs, "Rome always needs good soldiers. Your people may cross the Danube and settle on our land. As long as you remain true to Rome, we will protect you against your enemies."

These Goths were known as Visigoths, or Western Goths. Other tribes of Goths who had settled in southern Russia, were called Ostrogoths, or Eastern Goths.

After getting permission from the Emperor Valens, a large number of the Visigoths crossed the Danube with their families and their cattle and settled in the country now called Bulgaria.

In time they became a very powerful nation, and in the year 394 they chose as their king one of the chiefs named Alaric. He was a brave man and a great soldier. Even when he was a child he took delight in war, and at the age of sixteen, he fought as bravely as the older soldiers.

One night, not long after he became king, Alaric had a very strange dream. He thought he was driving in a golden chariot through the streets of Rome amid the shouts of the people who hailed him as emperor. This dream made a deep impression on his mind. He was always thinking of it, and soon he had the idea that he could make the dream come true.

"To be master of the Roman Empire," he said to himself, "that is indeed worth trying for; and why should I not try? With my brave soldiers I can conquer Rome, and I shall make the attempt."

So Alaric called his chiefs together and told them what he had made up his mind to do.

The chiefs gave a cry of delight for they approved of the king's proposal. In those days, fighting was almost the only business of chiefs, and they were always glad to be at war, especially when there was hope of getting rich spoils. And so the Visigoth chiefs rejoiced at the idea of war against Rome, for they knew that if they were victorious they would have the wealth of the richest city of the world to divide among themselves.

Soon they got ready a great army. With Alaric in command, they marched through Thrace and Macedonia and before long reached Athens. There were now no great warriors in Athens, and the city surrendered to Alaric. The Goths plundered the homes and temples of the Athenians and then marched to the state of Elis, in the southwestern part of Greece. Here a famous Roman general named Stilicho besieged them in their camp. Alaric managed to force his way through the lines of the Romans and escaped. He marched to Epirus. This was a province of Greece that lay on the east side of the Ionian Sea. Arcadius, the Emperor of the East, now made Alaric governor of this district and a large region lying near it. The whole territory was called Eastern Illyricum and formed part of the Eastern Empire.

Alaric now set out to make an attack on Rome, the capital of the Western Empire. As soon as Honorius, Emperor of the West, learned that Alaric was approaching, he fled to a strong fortress among the mountains of North Italy. His great general Stilicho came to his rescue and defeated Alaric near Verona. But even after this, Honorius was so afraid of Alaric that he made him governor of a part of his empire called Western Illyricum and gave him a large yearly income.

Honorius, however, did not keep certain of his promises to Alaric, who consequently, in the year 408, marched to Rome and besieged it. The cowardly emperor fled to Ravenna, leaving his generals to make terms with Alaric. It was agreed that Alaric should withdraw from Rome upon the payment of 5,000 pounds of gold and 30,000 pounds of silver.

When Honorius read the treaty, he refused to sign it. Alaric then demanded that the city be surrendered to him, and the people, terrified, opened their gates and agreed that Alaric should appoint another emperor in place of Honorius.

This new emperor, however, ruled so badly that Alaric thought it best to restore Honorius. Then Honorius, when just about to be treated so honorably, allowed a barbarian chief who was an ally of his to make an attack upon Alaric. The attack was unsuccessful, and Alaric immediately laid siege to Rome for the third time. The city was taken and Alaric's dream came true. In a grand procession, he rode at the head of his army through the streets of the great capital.

Then began the work of destruction. The Goths ran in crowds through the city, wrecked private houses and public buildings, and seized everything of value they could find. Alaric gave orders that no injury should be done to the Christian churches, but other splendid buildings of the great city were stripped of the beautiful and costly articles that they contained. And all the gold and silver was carried away from the public treasury.

In the midst of the pillage, Alaric dressed himself in splendid robes and sat upon the throne of the emperor, with a golden crown upon his head.

While Alaric was sitting on the throne, thousands of Romans were compelled to kneel down on the ground before him and shout out his name as conqueror and emperor. Then the theaters and circuses were opened, and Roman athletes and gladiators had to give performances for the amusement of the conquerors.

After six days of pillage and pleasure, Alaric and his army marched through the gates, carrying with them the riches of Rome.

Alaric died on his way to Sicily, which he had thought to conquer also. He felt his death coming and ordered his men to bury him in the bed of the river Busento and place into his grave the richest treasures that he had taken from Rome.

This order was carried out. A large number of Roman slaves were set to work to dig a channel and turn the water of the Busento into it. They made the grave in the bed of the river, put Alaric's body into and closed it up. Then the river was turned back to its old channel. As soon as the grave was covered up, and the water flowed over it, the slaves who had done the work were put to death by the Visigoth chiefs.

Written Summation

One night, not long after he became king, Alaric had a very strange dream. He thought he was driving in a golden chariot through the streets of Rome amid the shouts of the people who hailed him as emperor. This dream made a deep impression on his mind. He was always thinking of it, and soon he had the idea that he could make the dream come true.

Model Practice 1 (adapted from the original)

One night, not long after he became king Alaric had a very strange dream. He thought he was driving through the streets of Rome amid the shouts of the people who hailed him as emperor. This

Model Practice 2

Model Practice 3

Attila the Hun

from Famous Men of the Middle Ages
by John H. Haaren, LL.D. and A. B. Poland, Ph.D.
434 - 453 AD

During the first half of the fifth century, the Huns had a famous king named Attila. He was only twenty-one years old when he became their king. But although he was young, he was very brave and ambitious, and he wanted to be a great and powerful king.

Not far from Attila's palace, there was a great rocky cave in the mountains. In this cave lived a strange man called the "Hermit of the Rocks." No one knew his real name, or from what country he had come. He was very old, with wrinkled face and long gray hair and beard.

Many persons believed that he was a fortune-teller, so people often went to him to inquire what was to happen to them. One day, shortly after he became king, Attila went to the cave to get his fortune told.

"Wise man," said he, "look into the future and tell me what is before me in the path of life."

The hermit thought for a few moments, and then said, "O King, I see you a famous conqueror, the master of many nations. I see you going from country to country, defeating armies and destroying cities until men call you the 'Fear of the World.' You heap up vast riches, but just after you have married the woman you love, grim death strikes you down."

With a cry of horror, Attila fled from the cave. For a time he thought of giving up his idea of becoming a great man. But he was young and full of spirit, and very soon he remembered only what had been said to him about his becoming a great and famous conqueror and began to prepare for war. He gathered the best men from the various tribes of his people and trained them into a great army of good soldiers.

About this time one of the king's shepherds, while taking care of cattle in the fields, noticed blood dripping from the foot of one of the oxen. The shepherd followed the streak of blood through the grass and at last found the sharp point of a sword sticking out of the earth. He dug out the weapon, carried it to the palace, and gave it to King Attila. The king declared it was the sword of Tiew, the god of war. He then strapped it to his side and said he would always wear it.

"I shall never be defeated in battle," he cried, "as long as I fight with the sword of Tiew."

As soon as his army was ready, he marched with it into countries which belonged to Rome. He defeated the Romans in several great battles and captured many of their cities. The Roman Emperor Theodosius had to ask for terms of peace. Attila agreed that there should be peace, but soon afterwards, he found out that Theodosius had formed a plot to murder him. He was so enraged at this that he again began war. He plundered and burned cities wherever he went, and at last the emperor had to give him a large sum of money and a portion of country south of the Danube.

This made peace, but the peace did not last long. In a few years, Attila appeared at the head of an army of 700,000 men. With this great force, he marched across Germany and into Gaul. He rode on a beautiful black horse and carried at his side the sword of Tiew.

He attacked and destroyed towns and killed the inhabitants without mercy. The people had such dread of him that he was called the "Scourge of God" and the "Fear of the World."

Attila and his terrible Huns marched through Gaul until they came to the city of Orleans. The people bravely resisted the invaders. They shut their gates and defended themselves in every way they could. In those times, all towns of any great size were surrounded by strong walls. There was war constantly going on nearly everywhere, and there were a great many fierce tribes and chiefs who lived by robbing their neighbors. So the towns and castles in which there was much money or other valuable property were not safe without high and strong walls.

Attila tried to take Orleans, but soon after he began to attack the walls he saw a great army at a distance coming towards the city. He quickly gathered his forces together, marched to the neighboring plain of Champagne and halted at the place where the city of Châlons (shah-lon') now stands.

The army, which Attila saw, was an army of 300,000 Romans and Visigoths. It was led by a Roman general name Aëtius (A-ë'-ti-us) and the Visigoth king Theodoric (The-od'-o-ric). The Visigoths, after the death of Alaric, had settled in parts of Gaul, and their king had now agreed to join the Romans against the common enemy—the terrible Huns.

So the great army of the Romans and Visigoths marched up and attacked the Huns at Châlons. It was a fierce battle. Both sides fought with the greatest bravery. At first, the Huns seemed to be winning. They drove back the Romans and Visigoths from the field, and in the fight, Theodoric was killed.

Aëtius now began to fear that he would be beaten, but just at that moment Thorismond (Thor'-is-mond), the son of Theodoric, made another charge against the Huns. He had taken command of the Visigoths when his father was killed, and now he led them on to fight. They were all eager to have revenge for the death of their king, so they fought like lions and swept across the plain with great fury. The Huns were soon beaten on every side, and Attila himself fled to his camp. It was the first time he had ever been defeated. Thorismond, the conqueror, was lifted upon his shield on the battlefield and hailed as king of the Visigoths.

When Attila reached his camp, he had all his baggage and wagons gathered in a great heap. He intended to set fire to it and jump into the flames if the Romans should come there to attack him.

"Here I will perish in the flames," he cried, "rather than surrender to my enemies."

But the Romans did not come to attack him, and in a few days he marched back to his own country.

Very soon, however, he was again on the warpath. This time he invaded Italy. He attacked and plundered the town of Aquileia (Aq'-ui-le'-i-a), and the terrified inhabitants fled for their lives to the hills and mountains. Some of them took refuge in the islands and marshes of the Adriatic Sea. Here they founded Venice.

The people of Rome and the Emperor Valentinian were greatly alarmed at the approach of the dreaded Attila. He was now near the city, and they had no army strong enough to send against him. Rome would have been again destroyed if it had not been for Pope Leo I who went to the camp of Attila and persuaded him not to attack the city.

It is said that the barbarian king was awed by the majestic aspect and priestly robes of Leo. It is also told that the apostles Peter and Paul appeared to Attila in his camp and threatened him with death, if he should attack Rome. He did not go away, however, without getting a large sum of money as ransom.

Shortly after leaving Italy, Attila suddenly died. Only the day before his death he had married a beautiful woman whom he loved very much.

The Huns mourned their king in a barbarous way. They shaved their heads and cut themselves on their faces with knives, so that their blood, instead of their tears, flowed for the loss of their great leader. They enclosed his body in three coffins—one of gold, one of silver, and one of iron—and they buried him at night, in a secret spot in the mountains. When the funeral was over, they killed the slaves who had dug the grave, as the Visigoths had done after the burial of Alaric.

After the death of Attila, we hear little more of the Huns.

Written Summation

The army, which Attila saw, was an army of 300,000 Romans and Visigoths. It was led by a Roman general name Atius and the Visigoth king Theodoric. The Visigoths, after the death of Alaric, had settled in parts of Gaul, and their king had now agreed to join the Romans against the common enemy—the terrible Huns.

Model Practice 1

Model Practice 2

Model Practice 3

Clovis

from Famous Men of the Middle Ages
by John H. Haaren, LL.D. and A. B. Poland, Ph.D.
481 - 511 AD

While the power of the Roman Empire was declining, there dwelt on the banks of the River Rhine a number of savage Teuton tribes called Franks. The word Frank means FREE, and those tribes took pride in being known as Franks or freemen.

The Franks occupied the east bank of the Rhine for about two hundred years. Then many of the tribes crossed the river in search of new homes. The region west of the river was at that time called Gaul. Here the Franks established themselves and became a powerful people. From their name the country was afterwards called FRANCE.

Each tribe of the Franks had its own king. The greatest of all these kings was Chlodwig, or Clovis, as we call him, who became ruler of his tribe in the year 481, just six years after Theodoric became king of the Ostrogoths. Clovis was only sixteen years of age, but he proved in a very short time that he could govern as well as older men. He was intelligent and brave. No one ever knew him to be afraid of anything even when he was but a child. His father, who was named Childeric (chil'-der-ic), often took him to wars which the Franks had with neighboring tribes, and he was very proud of his son's bravery. The young man was also a bold and skillful horseman. He could tame and ride the most fiery horse.

When Clovis became king of the Franks, a great part of Gaul still belonged to Rome. This part was then governed by a Roman general, named Syagrius (sy-ag'-ri-us). Clovis resolved to drive the Romans out of the country, and he talked over the matter with the head men of his army.

"My desire," said he, "is that the Franks shall have possession of every part of this fair land. I shall drive the Romans and their friends away, and make Gaul the empire of the Franks."

At this time, the Romans had a great army in Gaul. It was encamped near the city of Soissons (swah-son') and was commanded by Syagrius. Clovis resolved to attack it and led his army at once to Soissons. When he came near the city, he summoned Syagrius to surrender. Syagrius refused and asked for an interview with the commander of the Franks. Clovis consented to meet him, and an arrangement was made that the meeting should take place in the open space between the two armies.

When Clovis stepped out in front of his own army, accompanied by some of his savage warriors, Syagrius also came forward. But the moment he saw the king of the Franks, he laughed loudly and exclaimed, "A boy! A boy has come to fight me! The Franks with a boy to lead them have come to fight the Romans."

Clovis was very angry at this insulting language and shouted back, "Ay, but this boy will conquer you."

Then both sides prepared for battle. The Romans thought that they would win the victory easily, but they were mistaken. Every time that they made a charge upon the Franks, they were beaten back by the warriors of Clovis. The young king himself fought bravely at the head of his men and with his own sword struck down a number of the Romans. He tried to find Syagrius and fight with him; but the Roman commander was nowhere to be found. Early in the battle, he had fled from the field, leaving his men to defend themselves as best they could.

The Franks gained a great victory. With their gallant boy king leading them on, they drove the Roman's before them, and when the battle was over, they took possession of the city of Soissons. Clovis afterwards conquered all the other Frankish chiefs and made himself king of all the Franks.

Not very long after Clovis became king, he heard of a beautiful young girl, the niece of Gondebaud (gon'-de-baud), king of Burgundy, and he thought he would like to marry her. Her name was Clotilde (clo-tilde'), and she was an orphan, for her wicked uncle Gondebaud had killed her father and mother. Clovis sent one of his nobles to Gondebaud to ask her for his wife. At first Gondebaud thought of refusing to let the girl go. He feared that she might have him punished for the murder of her parents if she became the wife of so powerful a man as Clovis. But he was also afraid that by refusing he would provoke the anger of Clovis, so he permitted the girl to be taken to the court of the king of the Franks. Clovis was delighted when he saw her; and they were immediately married.

Clotilde was a devout Christian, and she wished very much to convert her husband, who, like most of his people, was a worshiper of the heathen gods. But Clovis was not willing to give up his own religion. Nevertheless, Clotilde continued to do every thing she could to persuade him to become a Christian.

Soon after his marriage Clovis had a war with a tribe called the Alemanni. This tribe had crossed the Rhine from Germany and taken possession of some of the eastern provinces of Gaul. Clovis speedily got his warriors together and marched against them. A battle was fought at a place called Tolbiac, not far from the present city of Cologne. In this battle the Franks were nearly beaten, for the Alemanni were fierce and brave men and skillful fighters.

When Clovis saw his soldiers driven back several times, he began to lose hope, but at that moment he thought of his pious wife and of the powerful God of whom she had so often spoken. Then he raised his hands to heaven and earnestly prayed to that God.

"O God of Clotilde," he cried, "help me in this my hour of need.

If thou wilt give me victory now I will believe in thee."

Almost immediately, the course of the battle began to change in favor of the Franks. Clovis led his warriors forward once more, and this time the Alemanni fled before them in terror. The Franks gained a great victory, and they believed it was in answer to the prayer of their king.

When Clovis returned home, he did not forget his promise. He told Clotilde how he had prayed to her God for help and how his prayer had been heard. He said he was now ready to become a Christian. Clotilde was very happy on hearing this, and she arranged that her husband should be baptized in the church of Rheims on the following Christmas Day.

Meanwhile Clovis issued a proclamation to his people declaring that he was a believer in Christ, and giving orders that all the images and temples of the heathen gods should be destroyed. This was immediately done, and many of the people followed his example and became Christians.

Clovis was a very earnest and fervent convert. One day the bishop of Rheims, while instructing him in the doctrines of Christianity, described the death of Christ. As the bishop proceeded Clovis became much excited, and at last jumped up from his seat and exclaimed:

"Had I been there with my brave Franks, I would have avenged His wrongs."

On Christmas day a great multitude assembled in the church at Rheims to witness the baptism of the king. A large number of his fierce warriors were baptized at the same time. The service was performed with great ceremony by the bishop of Rheims, and the title of "Most Christian King" was conferred on Clovis by the Pope. This title was ever afterwards borne by the kings of France.

Like most of the kings and chiefs of those rude and barbarous times, Clovis often did cruel and wicked things. When Rheims was captured, before he became a Christian, some soldiers took a golden vase from the church. The bishop asked Clovis to have it returned, and Clovis bade him wait until the division of spoils. All the valuable things taken by soldiers in war were divided among the whole army, each man getting his share according to rank. Such things were called spoils.

When the next time came for dividing spoils, Clovis asked that he might have the vase over and above his regular share, his intention being to return it to the bishop. But one of the soldiers objected, saying that the king should have no more than his fair share, and at the same time shattered the vase with his ax. Clovis was very angry, but at the time said nothing. Soon afterwards, however, there was the usual examination of the arms of the soldiers to see that they were in proper condition for active service. Clovis himself took part in the examination, and when he came to the soldier who had broken the vase, he found fault with the condition of his weapons and with one blow of his battle-ax struck the man dead.

The next war that Clovis engaged in was with some tribes of the Goths who occupied the country called Aquitaine lying south of the River Loire. He defeated them and added Aquitaine to the kingdom of the Franks.

Clovis afterwards made war upon other people of Gaul and defeated them. At last all the provinces from the lower Rhine to the Pyrenees Mountains were compelled to acknowledge him as king. He then went to reside at the city of Paris, which he made the capital of his kingdom. He died there AD. 511.

The dynasty or family of kings to which he belonged is known in history as the Merovingian dynasty. It was so called from Merovæus (Me-ro-væ'-us), the father of Childeric and grandfather of Clovis.

Written Summation

When Clovis stepped out in front of his own army, accompanied by some of his savage warriors, Syagrius also came forward. But the moment he saw the king of the Franks, he laughed loudly and exclaimed, "A boy! A boy has come to fight me! The Franks with a boy to lead them have come to fight the Romans."

Model Practice 1

Model Practice 2

Model Practice 3

Justinian the Great

from Famous Men of the Middle Ages
by John H. Haaren, LL.D. and A. B. Poland, Ph.D.
527 - 565 AD

In the time of Clovis, the country now called Bulgaria was inhabited by Goths. One day a poor shepherd boy, about sixteen years of age, left his mountain home in that country to go to the city of Constantinople, which was many miles away. The boy had no money to pay the expenses of the journey, but he was determined to go, even though he had to walk every step of the road and live on fruits that he could gather by the way. He was a bright, clever boy who had spent his life hitherto in a village, but was now eager to go out into the world to seek his fortune.

Some years before, this boy's uncle, who was named Justin, had gone to Constantinople and joined the Roman army. He was so brave and so good a soldier that he soon came to be commander of the imperial guard which attended the emperor.

The poor shepherd boy had heard of the success of his uncle, and this was the reason why he resolved to set off for the big city. So he started down the mountain and trudged along the valley in high hope, feeling certain that he would reach the end of his journey in safety. It was a difficult and dangerous journey, and it took him several weeks, for he had to go through dark forests and to cross rivers and high hills; but at last one afternoon in midsummer, he walked through the main gate of Constantinople, proud and happy that he had accomplished his purpose.

He had no trouble in finding his Uncle Justin; for everybody in Constantinople knew the commander of the emperor's guards. And when the boy appeared at the great man's house and told who he was, his uncle received him with much kindness. He took him into his own family and gave him the best education that could be had in the city.

As the boy was very talented and eager for knowledge, he soon became an excellent scholar. He grew up a tall, good-looking man with black eyes and curly hair, and he was always richly dressed. He was well liked at the emperor's court, and was respected by everybody on account of his learning.

One day a great change came for both uncle and nephew. The emperor died, and the people chose Justin to succeed him. He took the title of Justinus I (Jus-ti'-nus), and so the young scholar, who had once been a poor shepherd boy, was now nephew of an emperor.

After some years Justinus was advised by his nobles to take the young man, who had adopted the name of Justinian, to help him in ruling the empire. Justinus agreed to this proposal, for he was now old and in feeble health, and not able himself to attend to the important affairs of government. He therefore called the great lords of his court together and in their presence he placed a crown on the head of his nephew, who thus became joint emperor with his uncle. The uncle died only a few months after, and then Justinian was declared emperor. This was in the year 527. Justinian reigned for nearly forty years and did so many important things that he was afterwards called Justinian the Great.

He had many wars during his reign, but he himself did not take part in them. He was not experienced as a soldier, for he had spent most of his time in study. He was fortunate enough, however, to have two great generals to lead his armies. One of them was named Belisarius and the other Narses.

Belisarius was one of the greatest soldiers that ever lived. He gained wonderful victories for Justinian and conquered some of the old Roman provinces that had been lost for many years.

The victories of these two generals largely helped to make the reign of Justinian remarkable in history. Many years before he ascended the throne, the Vandals, as you have read, conquered the northern part of Africa and established a kingdom there with Carthage as its capital. The Vandal king in the time of Justinian was named Gelimer (Gel'-i-mer), and he lived in Carthage.

Justinian resolved to make war on this king in order to recover Northern Africa and make it again a part of the Empire. So Belisarius was sent to Africa with an army of thirty-five thousand men and five thousand horses that were carried on a fleet of six hundred ships. It took this fleet three months to make the voyage from Constantinople to Africa. (The same voyage may now be made in a very few days. But in the time of Belisarius there were no steamships, and nothing was known of the power of steam for moving machinery.) The ships or galleys were sailing vessels; and when there was no wind, they could make no progress, except by rowing.

When Belisarius reached Africa, he left five men as a guard in each vessel, and with the body of his army, he marched for some days along the coast. The people received him in a friendly way, for they had grown tired of the rule of the Vandals and preferred to be under the government of the Romans.

About ten miles from Carthage, he met a large army led by the brother of Gelimer. A battle immediately took place, and the Vandals were utterly defeated. Gelimer's brother was killed, and the king himself, who had followed with another army and joined the fight, was also defeated and fled from the field. Belisarius then proceeded to Carthage and took possession of the city.

Soon afterwards, Gelimer collected another army and fought the Romans in another battle, twenty miles from Carthage; but Belisarius again defeated him, and the Vandal king again fled. This was the end of the Vandal king in Africa. In a short time, Gelimer gave himself up to Belisarius, who took him to Constantinople. Justinian set apart an estate for him to live upon, and the conquered king passed the rest of his life in peaceful retirement.

After conquering the Vandals, Justinian resolved to conquer Italy, which was then held by the Ostrogoths. A large army was put together and placed under the command of Belisarius and Narses. They immediately set out for Italy. When they arrived there, they marched straight to Rome, and after some fighting took possession of the city. But in a few months, Vitiges (vit'-i-ges), king of the Goths, appeared with an army before the gates and challenged Belisarius and Narses to come out and fight.

The Roman generals, however, were not ready to fight, and so the Ostrogoth king laid siege to the city, thinking that he would compel the Romans to surrender.

But instead of having any thought of surrender, Belisarius was preparing his men to fight, and when they were ready, he attacked Vitiges and defeated him. Vitiges retired to Ravenna, and Belisarius quickly followed, and made such an assault on the city that it was compelled to surrender. The Ostrogoth army was captured, and Vitiges was taken to Constantinople a prisoner.

Belisarius and Narses then went to Northern Italy and, after a long war, conquered all the tribes there. Thus the power of Justinian was established throughout the whole country, and the city of Rome was again under the dominion of a Roman emperor.

While his brave generals were winning these victories for the Empire, Justinian himself was busy in making improvements of various kinds at the capital. He erected great public buildings, which were not only useful but ornamental to the city. The most remarkable of them was the very magnificent cathedral of St. Sophia (So-phi'-a), for a long time the grandest church structure in the world. The great temple still exists in all its beauty and grandeur, but is now used as an Islamic mosque.

But the most important thing that Justinian did—the work for which he is most celebrated—was the improving and collecting of the laws. He made many excellent new laws and reformed many of the old laws, so that he became famous as one of the greatest of the world's legislators. For a long time, the Roman laws had been difficult to understand. There was a vast number of them, and different writers differed widely as to what the laws really were and what they meant.

Justinian employed a great lawyer named Tribonian (trib-o'-ni-an) to collect and simplify the principal laws. The collection which he made was called the CODE OF JUSTINIAN. It still exists, and is the model according to which most of the countries of Europe have made their laws.

Justinian also did a great deal of good by establishing a number of industries in Constantinople. It was he who first brought silkworms into Europe.

To the last year of his life, Justinian was strong and active and a hard worker. He often worked or studied all day and all night without eating or sleeping. He died in 565 at the age of eighty-three years.

Written Summation

He had many wars during his reign, but he himself did not take part in them. He was not experienced as a soldier, for he had spent most of his time in study. He was fortunate enough, however, to have two great generals to lead his armies. One of them was named Belisarius and the other Narses.

Model Practice 1

Model Practice 2

Model Practice 3

Mohammed

from Famous Men of the Middle Ages
by John H. Haaren, LL.D. and A. B. Poland, Ph.D.
570 - 632 AD

A great number of people in Asia and Africa and much of those in Turkey in Europe profess the Muslim religion. The proper name for their religion is "Islam," which means obedience, or submission.

The founder of this religion was a man named Mohammed (Mo-ham'-med). He was born in the year 570, in Mecca, a city of Arabia. His parents were poor people, though, it is said, they were descended from Arabian princes. They died when Mohammed was a child, and his uncle, a kind-hearted man named Abu Talib (A'-bu-Ta-lĭb'), took him home and brought him up.

When the boy grew old, enough he took care of his uncle's sheep and camels. Sometimes he went on journeys with his uncle to different parts of Arabia, to help him in his business as a trader. On these journeys, Mohammed used to ride on a camel, and he soon became a skillful camel driver.

Mohammed was very faithful and honest in all his work. He always spoke the truth and never broke a promise. "I have given my promise," he would say, "and I must keep it." He became so well known in Mecca for being truthful and trustworthy that people gave him the name of El Amin, which means "The Truthful."

At this time, he was only sixteen years of age; but the rich traders had so much confidence in him that they gave him important business to attend to, and trusted him with large sums of money. He often went with caravans to a port on the shore of the Red Sea, sixty-five miles from Mecca, and sold there the goods carried by the camels. Then he guided the long line of camels back to Mecca, and faithfully paid to the owners of the goods the money he had received.

Mohammed had no school education. He could neither read nor write. But he was not ignorant. He knew well how to do the work intrusted to him, and was a first-rate man of business.

One day, when Mohammed was about twenty-five years old, he was walking through the bazaar or market-place, of Mecca when he met the chief camel-driver of a wealthy woman named Khadijah (Kha-dī'-jah). This woman was a widow, who was carrying on the business left to her by her husband. As soon as the camel driver saw Mohammed, he stopped him and said, "My mistress wishes to see you before noon. I think she intends to engage you to take charge of her caravans."

Mohammed waited to hear no more. As quickly as possible, he went to the house of Khadijah; for he was well pleased at the thought of being employed in so important a service. The widow received him in a very friendly way. She said, "I have heard much of you among the traders. They say that though you are young you are a good caravan manager and can be trusted. Are you willing to take charge of my caravans and give your whole time and service to me?"

Mohammed was delighted.

"I accept your offer," said he, "and I shall do all I can to serve and please you."

Khadijah then engaged him as the manager of her business, and he served her well and faithfully. She thought a great deal of him, and he was much attracted to her, and soon they came to love one another and were married.

As he was now the husband of a rich woman, he did not need to work very hard. He still continued to attend to his wife's business, but he did not make as many journeys as before. He spent much of his time thinking about religion. He learned all that he could about Judaism and Christianity, but he was not satisfied with either of them.

At that time, most of the people of Arabia worshiped idols. Very few of them were Christians.

Mohammed was very earnest and serious. In a cave on Mount Hira, near Mecca, he spent several weeks every year in prayer and religious meditation. He declared that, while praying in his cave, he often had visions of God and heaven. He said that many times the angel Gabriel appeared to him and revealed to him the religion which he afterwards taught his followers. As he himself could not write, he committed to memory all that the angel told him, and had it written in a book. This book is called the "Qur'an."

When Mohammed returned home after the angel had first spoken to him, he told his wife of what he had seen and heard. She at once believed and became a convert to the new religion. She fell upon her knees at the feet of her husband and cried out, "There is but one God. Mohammed is God's prophet."

Mohammed then told the story to other members of his family. Some of them believed and became his first followers. Soon afterwards, he began to preach to the people. He spoke in the market and other public places. Most of those who heard him laughed at what he told them, but some poor people and a few slaves believed him and adopted the new religion. Others said he was a dreamer and a fool.

Mohammed, however, paid no heed to the insults he received. He went on telling about the appearance of Gabriel and preaching the doctrines which he said the angel had ordered him to teach the people.

Often while speaking in public, Mohammed had what he called a "vision of heavenly things." At such times, his face grew pale as death, his eyes became red and staring, he spoke in a loud voice, and his body trembled violently. Then he would tell what he had seen in his vision.

After a time, the number of his followers began to increase. People came from distant parts of Arabia and from neighboring countries to hear him. One day, six of the chief men of Medina (Me-dī'-na), one of the largest cities of Arabia, listened earnestly to his preaching and were converted. When they returned home, they talked of the new religion to their fellow citizens, and a great many of them became believers.

But the people of Mecca, Mohammed's own home, were nearly all opposed to him. They would not believe what he preached, and they called him an impostor. The people of the tribe to which he himself belonged were the most bitter against him. They even threatened to put him to death as an enemy of the gods.

About this time, Mohammed's uncle and wife died. He then had hardly any friends in Mecca. He therefore resolved to leave that city and go to Medina. Numbers of the people there believed his doctrines and wished him to come and live among them. So he secretly left his native town and fled from his enemies. With a few faithful companions, he made his escape to Medina.

It was in the year of our Lord 622 that Mohammed fled from Mecca. This event is very important in Muslim history. It is called "the flight of the prophet," or "the Hijra," a word which means FLIGHT. The Hijra is the beginning of the Muslim era; and so in all countries where the rulers and people are Muslims, the years are counted from the Hijra instead of from the birth of Christ.

On his arrival in Medina, the people received Mohammed with great rejoicing. He lived there the remainder of his life. A splendid church was built for him in Medina. It was called a mosque, and all Islamic places of worship are called by this name. It means a place for prostration or prayer.

Mohammed thought that it was right to spread his religion by force, and to make war on "unbelievers", as he called all people who did not accept his teaching. He therefore put together an army and fought against unbelievers. He gained many victories. He marched against Mecca with an army of ten thousand men, and the city surrendered with little resistance. The people then joined his religion and destroyed their idols. Before long, all the inhabitants of Arabia and many of the people of the neighboring countries became Muslims.

Mohammed died in Medina in the year of our Lord 632, or year 11 of the Hijra. He was buried in the mosque in which he had held religious services for so many years; and Medina has been honored ever since, because it contains the tomb of the Prophet. It is believed by his followers that the body still lies in the coffin in the same state as when it was first buried. There is also a story that the coffin of Mohammed rests somewhere between heaven and earth, suspended in the air. But this fable was invented by enemies to bring ridicule on the prophet and his religion.

The tomb of Mohammed is visited every year by people from all Muslim countries. Mecca, the birthplace of the prophet, is also visited by vast numbers of pilgrims. Every Muslim is bound by his religion to make a visit or pilgrimage to Mecca at least once in his life. Whenever a Muslim prays, no matter in what part of the world he may be, he turns his face towards Mecca.

Muslims pray five times every day, and there is a church officer called a mu-ez'zin, who gives them notice of the hour for prayer. This he does by going on the platform of the tower of the mosque and chanting in a loud voice, "Come to prayer, come to prayer. There is no god, but God. He giveth life, and he dieth not. I praise his perfection. God is great."

After Mohammed died, a person was appointed to be his successor as head of the Muslim church. He was called the caliph, a word which means successor.

Written Summation

When Mohammed returned home after the angel had first spoken to him, he told his wife of what he had seen and heard. She at once believed and became a convert to the new religion. She fell upon her knees at the feet of her husband and cried out, "There is but one God. Mohammed is God's prophet."

Model Practice 1

Model Practice 2

Model Practice 3

Charles Martel and Pepin

from Famous Men of the Middle Ages
by John H. Haaren, LL.D. and A. B. Poland, Ph.D.
714 - 741 AD

After the death of Mohammed, the Saracens became great warriors. They conquered many countries and established the Muslim religion in them. In 711, the Saracens invaded and conquered a great part of Spain and founded a powerful kingdom there, which lasted about seven hundred years.

They intended to conquer the land of the Franks next, and then all Europe.

They thought it would be easy to conquer the Franks, because the Frankish king at that time was a very weak man. He was one of a number of kings who were called the "Do-Nothings." They reigned from about 638 to 751. They spent all their time in amusements and pleasures, leaving the affairs of the government to be managed by persons called Mayors of the Palace.

The Mayors of the Palace were officers who at first managed the king's household. Afterwards, they were made guardians of kings who came to the throne when very young. So long as the king was under age, the Mayor of the Palace acted as chief officer of the government in his name. And as several of the young kings, even when they were old enough to rule, gave less attention to business than to pleasure, the mayors continued to do all the business, until at last they did everything that the king ought to have done. They made war, led armies in battle, raised money and spent it, and carried on the government as they pleased, without consulting the king.

The "Do-nothings" had the title of king, but nothing more. In fact, they did not desire to have any business to do. The things they cared for were dogs, horses, and sport.

One of the most famous of the mayors was a man named Pepin (Pep'-in). Once a year, Pepin had the king dressed in his finest clothes and paraded through the city of Paris where the court was held. A splendid throng of nobles and courtiers accompanied the king, and did him honor as he went along the streets in a gilded chariot drawn by a long line of beautiful horses. The king was cheered by the people, and he acknowledged their greetings most graciously.

After the parade, the king was escorted to the great hall of the palace, which was filled with nobles. Seated on a magnificent throne, he saluted the assemblage and made a short speech. The speech was prepared beforehand by Pepin and committed to memory by the king. At the close of the ceremony, the royal "nobody" retired to his country house and was not heard of again for a year.

Pepin died in 714 AD., and his son Charles, who was twenty-five years old at that time, succeeded him as mayor of the palace. This Charles is known in history as Charles Martel. He was a brave young man. He had fought in many of his father's battles and had become a skilled soldier. His men were devoted to him.

While he was mayor of the palace, he led armies in several wars against the enemies of the Franks. The most important of his wars was one with the Saracens, who came across the Pyrenees from Spain and invaded the land of the Franks, intending to establish Islam there. Their army was led by Abd-er-Rahman (Abd-er-Rah'-man), the Saracen governor of Spain.

On his march through the southern districts of the land of the Franks, Abd-er-Rahman destroyed many towns and villages, killed a number of the people, and seized all the property he could carry off. He plundered the city of Bordeaux (bor-do'), and, it is said, obtained so many valuable things that every soldier "was loaded with golden vases and cups and emeralds and other precious stones."

But meanwhile Charles Martel was not idle. As quickly as he could, he put together a great army of Franks and Germans and marched against the Saracens. The two armies met between the cities of Tours and Poitiers (pwaw-te-ay) in October, 732. For six days, there was nothing but an occasional skirmish between small parties from both sides; but on the seventh day a great battle took place.

Both Christians and Muslims fought with terrible earnestness. The fight went on all day, and the field was covered with the bodies of the slain. But towards evening, during a resolute charge made by the Franks, Abd-er-Rahman was killed. Then the Saracens gradually retired to their camp. It was not yet known, however, which side had won; and the Franks expected that the fight would be renewed in the morning.

When Charles Martel, with his Christian warriors, appeared on the field at sunrise, there was no enemy to fight. The Muslims had fled in the silence and darkness of the night and had left behind all their valuable spoils. There was now no doubt which side had won.

The Battle of Tours, or Poitiers, as it should be called, is regarded as one of the decisive battles of the world. It decided that Christians, and not Muslims, should be the ruling power in Europe.

Charles Martel is especially celebrated as the hero of this battle. It is said that the name MARTEL was given to him because of his bravery during the fight. Marteau (mar-to') is the French word for hammer, and one of the old French historians says that as a hammer breaks and crushes iron and steel, so Charles broke and crushed the power of his enemies in the Battle of Tours.

But though the Saracens fled from the battlefield of Tours, they did not leave the land of the Franks; and Charles had to fight other battles with them before they were finally defeated. At last, however, he drove them across the Pyrenees, and they never again attempted to invade Frankland.

After his defeat of the Saracens, Charles Martel was looked upon as the great champion of Christianity; and to the day of his death, in 741, he was in reality, though not in name, the king of the Franks.

Charles Martel had two sons, Pepin and Carloman. For a time they ruled together, but Carloman wished to lead a religious life, so he went to a monastery and became a monk. Pepin became the sole ruler.

Pepin was quite low in stature, and therefore was called Pepin the Short. But he had great strength and courage. A story is told of him, which shows how fearless he was.

One day he went with a few of his nobles to a circus to see a fight between a lion and a bull. Soon after the fight began, it looked as though the bull was getting the worst of it. Pepin cried out to his companions, "Will one of you separate the beasts?"

But there was no answer. None of them had the courage to make the attempt. Then Pepin jumped from his seat, rushed into the arena, and with a thrust of his sword killed the lion.

In the early years of Pepin's rule as mayor of the palace, the throne was occupied by a king named Childeric (Chil'-der-ic) III. Like his father and the other "do-nothing" kings, Childeric cared more for pleasures and amusements than for affairs of government. Pepin was the real ruler, and after a while he began to think that he ought to have the title of king, as he had all the power and did all the work of governing and defending the kingdom.

So he sent some friends to Rome to consult the Pope. They said to His Holiness, "Holy father, who ought to be the king of France—the man who has the title, or the man who has the power and does all the duties of king?"

"Certainly," replied the Pope, "the man who has the power and does the duties."

"Then, surely," said they, "Pepin ought to be the king of the Franks; for he has all the power."

The Pope gave his consent, and Pepin was crowned king of the Franks; and thus the reign of Childeric ended and that of Pepin began.

During nearly his whole reign, Pepin was engaged in war. Several times, he went to Italy to defend the Pope against the Lombards. These people occupied certain parts of Italy, including the province still called Lombardy.

Pepin conquered them and gave as a present to the Pope that part of their possessions which extended for some distance around Rome. This was called "Pepin's Donation." It was the beginning of what is known as the "temporal power" of the Popes, that is, their power as rulers of part of Italy.

Pepin died in 768.

Written Summation

After the parade, the king was escorted to the great hall of the palace, which was filled with nobles. Seated on a magnificent throne, he saluted the assemblage and made a short speech. The speech was prepared beforehand by Pepin and committed to memory by the king. At the close of the ceremony, the royal nobody retired to his country house and was not heard of again for a year.

Model Practice 1

Model Practice 2

Model Practice 3

Charlemagne

from Famous Men of the Middle Ages
by John H. Haaren, LL.D. and A. B. Poland, Ph.D.
768 - 814 AD

Pepin had two sons Charles and Carloman. After the death of their father, they ruled together, but in a few years Carloman died, and Charles became sole king.

This Charles was the most famous of the kings of the Franks. He did so many great and wonderful things that he is called Charlemagne (shar-le-main'), which means Charles the Great.

He was a great soldier. For thirty years, he carried on a war against the Saxons. Finally, he conquered them, and their great chief, Wittekind, submitted to him. The Saxons were a people of Germany, who lived near the land of the Franks. They spoke the same language and were of the same race as the Franks, but had not been civilized by contact with the Romans.

They were still pagans, just as the Franks had been before Clovis became a Christian. They actually offered human sacrifices.

After Charlemagne conquered them, he made their lands part of his kingdom. A great number of them, among whom was Wittekind, then became Christians and were baptized. Soon they had churches and schools in many parts of their country.

Another of Charlemagne's wars was against the Lombards.

Pepin, as you have read, had defeated the Lombards and given to the Pope part of the country held by them. The Lombard king now invaded the Pope's lands and threatened Rome itself; so the Pope requested help from Charlemagne.

Charlemagne quickly marched across the Alps and attacked the Lombards. He drove them out of the Pope's lands and took possession of their country.

After he had conquered the Lombards, he carried on war, in 778, in Spain. A large portion of Spain was then held by the Moorish Saracens. But a Muslim leader from Damascus had invaded their country, and the Moors invited Charlemagne to help them. He therefore led an army across the Pyrenees. He succeeded in putting his Moorish friends in possession of their lands in Spain and then set out for his own country

On the march, his army was divided into two parts. Charlemagne himself led the main body, and a famous warrior named Roland commanded the rear guard. While marching through the narrow pass of Roncesvalles (ron-thes-val'-yes), among the Pyrenees, Roland's division was attacked by a tribe called the Basques (basks), who lived on the mountain slopes of the neighboring region.

High cliffs walled in the pass on either side. From the tops of these cliffs, the Basques hurled down rocks and trunks of trees upon the Franks, and crushed many of them to death. Besides this, the wild mountaineers descended into the pass and attacked them with weapons. Roland fought bravely; but at last he was overpowered, and he and all his men were killed.

Roland had a friend and companion named Oliver, who was as brave as himself. Many stories and songs have been written telling of the wonderful adventures they were said to have had and of their wonderful deeds in war.

The work of Charlemagne in Spain was quickly undone; for Abd-er-Rahman, the leader of the Muslims who had come from Damascus, soon conquered almost all the territory south of the Pyrenees.

For more than forty years, Charlemagne was king of the Franks; but a still greater dignity was to come to him. In the year 800, some of the people in Rome rebelled against the Pope, and Charlemagne went with an army to put down the rebellion. He entered the city with great pomp and soon conquered the rebels.

On Christmas day, he went to the church of St. Peter, and as he knelt before the altar, the Pope placed a crown upon his head, saying, "Long live Charles Augustus, Emperor of the Romans."

The people assembled in the church shouted the same words; and so Charlemagne was now emperor of the Western Roman Empire, as well as king of the Franks.

Charlemagne built a splendid palace at Aix-la-Chapelle (aks-la-shap-el'), a town in Germany.

Charlemagne was a tall man, with a long, flowing beard, and a noble appearance. He dressed in a very simple style; but when he went into battle he wore armor, as was the custom for kings and nobles, and often for ordinary soldiers in his day.

Armor was made of leather or iron, or both together. There was a helmet of iron for the head, and a breastplate to cover the breast, or a coat of mail to cover the body. The coat of mail was made of small iron or steel rings linked together, or fastened on to a leather shirt. Coverings for the legs and feet were often attached to the coat.

Charlemagne was a great king in many other ways besides the fighting of battles. He did much for the good of his people. He made many excellent laws and appointed judges to see that the laws were carried out. He established schools and placed good teachers in charge of them. He had a school in his palace for his own children, and he employed as their teacher a very learned Englishman named Alcuin (al'-kwin).

In those times, few people could read or write. There were not many schools anywhere, and in most places, there were none at all. Even the kings had little education. Indeed, few of them could write their own names, and most of them did not care about sending their children to school. They did not think that reading or writing was of much use; but thought that it was far better for boys to learn to be good soldiers, and for girls to learn to spin and weave.

Charlemagne had a very different opinion. He was fond of learning; and whenever he heard of a learned man, living in any foreign country, he tried to get him to come and live in Frankland.

The fame of Charlemagne as a great warrior and a wise emperor spread all over the world. Many kings sent messengers to him to ask his friendship, and bring him presents. Harun-al-Rashid (hah-roon'-al-rash'-eed), the famous caliph, who lived at Bagdad, in Asia, sent him an elephant and a clock which struck the hours.

The Franks were much astonished at the sight of the elephant; for they had never seen one before. They also wondered much at the clock. In those days, there were in Europe no clocks such as we have; however, water clocks and hourglasses were used in some places. The water clock was a vessel into which water trickled. It contained a float that pointed to a scale of hours at the side of the vessel. The float gradually rose as the water trickled in.

The hourglasses measured time by the falling of fine sand from the top to the bottom of a glass vessel made with a narrow neck in the middle for the sand to go through.

Charlemagne died in 814. He was buried in the church which he had built at Aix-la-Chapelle. His body was placed in the tomb, seated upon a grand chair, and dressed in royal robes, with a crown on his head, a sword at his side, and a Bible in his hand.

This famous emperor is known in history as Charlemagne, which is the French word for the German name Karl der Grosse (Charles the Great), the name by which he was called at his own court during his life. The German name would really be a better name for him; for he was a German, and German was the language that he spoke. The common name of his favorite residence, Aix-la-Chapelle, also is French, but he knew the place as Aachen (ä'-chen).

The great empire which Charlemagne built up held together only during the life of his son. Then it was divided among his three grandsons. Louis took the eastern part, Lothaire (Lo-thaire') took the central part, with the title of emperor, and Charles took the western part.

Written Summation

Pepin had two sons Charles and Carolman. After the death of their father, they ruled together, but in a few years Carloman died, and Charles became sole king.

This Charles was the most famous of the kings of the Franks. He did so many great and wonderful things that he is called Charlemagne, which means Charles the Great.

Model Practice 1

Model Practice 2

Model Practice 3

Egbert

from Famous Men of the Middle Ages
by John H. Haaren, LL.D. and A. B. Poland, Ph.D.
802 - 837 AD

Egbert the Saxon lived at the same time as did Harun-al-Rashid and Charlemagne. He was the first king who ruled all England as one kingdom. Long before his birth, the people known to us as Britons lived there, and they gave to the island the name Britain.

But Britain was invaded by the Romans under Julius Cæsar and his successors, and all that which we now call England was added to the Empire of Rome. The Britons were driven into Wales and Cornwall, the western sections of the island.

The Romans kept possession of the island for nearly four hundred years. They did not leave it until 410, the year that Alaric sacked the city of Rome. At this time, the Roman legions withdrew from Britain.

Some years before this, the Saxons, Angles and Jutes—German tribes—had settled near the shores of the North Sea. They learned much about Britain; for trading vessels, even at that early day, crossed the Channel. Among other things, the men from the north learned that Britain was crossed with good Roman roads, and dotted with houses of brick and stone; that walled cities had taken the place of tented camps; and that the country for miles round each city was green every spring with waving wheat, or white with orchard blossoms.

After the Roman legions had left Britain, the Jutes, led by two great captains named Hengist and Horsa, landed upon the southeastern coast and made a settlement.

Britain proved a pleasant place to live in, and soon the Angles and Saxons also left the North Sea shores and invaded the beautiful island.

The new invaders met with brave resistance. The Britons were headed, legend says, by King Arthur, about whom many marvelous stories are told. His court was held at Caerleon (cär'-le-on), in North Wales, where his hundred and fifty knights banqueted at their famous "Round Table."

The British king and his knights fought with desperate heroism. But they could not drive back the Saxons and their companions and were obliged to seek refuge in the western mountainous parts of the island, just as their forefathers had done when the Romans invaded Britain. Thus nearly all England came into the possession of the three invading tribes.

Arthur and his knights were devoted Christians. For the Romans had not only made good roads and built strong walls and forts in Britain, but they had also brought the Christian religion into the island. And at about the time of the Saxon invasion, St. Patrick was founding churches and monasteries in Ireland and was baptizing whole clans of the Irish at a time. It is said that he baptized 12,000 persons with his own hand. Missionaries were sent by the Irish Church to convert the wild Picts of Scotland and, at a later day, the distant barbarians of Germany and Switzerland.

The Saxons, Angles, and Jutes believed in the old Norse gods, and Tiew and Woden and Thor and Frigga were worshiped on the soil of Britain for more than a hundred years.

The Britons tried to convert their conquerors, but the invaders did not care to be taught religion by those whom they had conquered. So the British missionaries found the work unusually hard. Aid came to them in a singular way. Near the year 575 AD., the Saxons quarreled and fought with their friends, the Angles. They took some Angles prisoners and carried them to Rome to sell at the great slave-market there. A monk named Gregory passed one day through the market and saw these captives. He asked the dealer who they were. "Angles," was the answer.

"Oh," said the monk, "they would be ANGELS instead of ANGLES if they were only Christians; for they certainly have the faces of angels."

Years after, when that monk was the Pope of Rome, he remembered this conversation and sent the monk Augustine (Au-gus'-tine) to England to teach the Christian religion to the savage but angel-faced Angles. Augustine and the British missionaries converted the Anglo-Saxons two hundred years before the German Saxons were converted.

Still, though both Angles and Saxons called themselves Christians, they were seldom at peace. For more than two hundred years, they fought frequently. Various chiefs tried to make themselves kings. Eventually, there came to be no less than seven small kingdoms in South Britain.

In 784, Egbert claimed to be heir of the kingdom called Wessex; but the people elected another man and Egbert had to flee for his life. He went to the court of Charlemagne, and was with the great king of the Franks in Rome on Christmas Day, 800, when the Pope placed the crown on Charles' head and proclaimed him emperor.

Soon after this, a welcome message came to Egbert. The mind of the people in Wessex had changed and they had elected him king. So bidding farewell to Charlemagne, he hurried to England.

Egbert had seen how Charlemagne had compelled the different quarreling tribes of Germany to yield allegiance to him and how after uniting his empire he had ruled it well.

Egbert did in England what Charlemagne had done in Germany. He either persuaded the various petty kingdoms of the Angles, the Saxons and the Jutes to recognize him as their ruler, or forced them to do so. Thus under him all England became one united kingdom.

But Egbert did even better than this. He did much to harmonize the different tribes by his wise conciliation. The name "England" is a memorial of this; for though Egbert himself was a Saxon, he advised that to please the Angles the country should be called Anglia (An'-gli-a), that is, Angleland or England, the land of the Angles, instead of Saxonia (Sax-on-i'-a), or Saxonland.

Written Summation

After the Roman legions had left Britain, the Jutes, led by two great captains named Hengist and Horsa, landed upon the southeastern coast and made a settlement.

Britain proved a pleasant place to live in, and soon the Angles and Saxons also left the North Sea shores and invaded the beautiful island.

Model Practice 1

Model Practice 2

Model Practice 3

Alfred the Great

from Famous Men of the Middle Ages
by John H. Haaren, LL.D. and A. B. Poland, Ph.D.
871 - 901 AD

The Danes were neighbors of the Norwegian Vikings, and like them were fond of the sea and piracy. They plundered the English coasts for more than a century; and most of northern and eastern England became, for a time, a Danish country with Danish kings.

What saved the rest of the country to the Saxons was the courage of the great Saxon king, Alfred.

Alfred was the son of Ethelwulf, king of the West Saxons. He had a loving mother who brought him up with great care. Up to the age of twelve, it is said, he was not able to read well, in spite of the efforts of his mother and others to teach him.

When Alfred was a boy, there were no printed books. The wonderful art of printing was not invented until about the year 1440—nearly six hundred years later than Alfred's time. Moreover, the art of making paper had not yet been invented. Consequently the few books in use in Alfred's time were written by skillful penmen, who wrote generally on leaves of parchment, which was sheepskin carefully prepared so that it might retain ink.

One day Alfred's mother showed him and his elder brothers a beautiful volume, which contained a number of the best Saxon ballads. Some of the words in this book were written in brightly colored letters. Moreover, upon many of the leaves were painted pictures of gaily dressed knights and ladies.

"Oh, what a lovely book!" exclaimed the boys.

"Yes, it is lovely," replied the mother. "I will give it to whichever of you children can read it the best in a week."

Alfred began at once to take lessons in reading and studied hard day after day. His brothers passed their time in amusements and made fun of Alfred's efforts. They thought he could not learn to read as well as they could, no matter how hard he should try.

At the end of the week, the boys read the book to their mother, one after the other. Much to the surprise of his brothers, Alfred proved to be the best reader, and his mother gave him the book.

While still very young, Alfred was sent by his father to Rome to be anointed by His Holiness, the Pope. It was a long and tiresome journey, made mostly on horseback.

With imposing, solemn ceremony, the Holy Father anointed him. Afterwards he spent a year in Rome receiving religious instruction.

In the year 871, when Alfred was twenty-two years old, the Danes invaded various parts of England. Some great battles were fought, and Alfred's elder brother Ethelred, king of the West Saxons, was killed. Thus, Alfred became king.

The Danes still continued to fight the Saxons and defeated Alfred in a long and severe struggle. They took for themselves the northern and eastern parts of England.

Moreover, Danes from Denmark continued to cross the sea and ravage the coast of Saxon England. They kept the people in constant alarm. Alfred therefore determined to meet the pirates on their own element—the sea. So he built and equipped the first English navy, and in 875 gained the first naval victory ever won by the English.

A few years after this, however, great numbers of Danes from the northern part of England came pouring into the Saxon lands. Alfred himself was obliged to flee for his life.

For many months, he wandered through forests and over hills to avoid capture by the Danes. He sometimes made his home in caves and in the huts of shepherds and cowherds. Often, he tended the cattle and sheep and was glad to get a part of the farmer's dinner in pay for his services.

Once, when very hungry, he went into the house of a cowherd and asked for something to eat. The cowherd's wife was baking cakes and said she would give him some when they were done.

"Watch the cakes and do not let them burn, while I go across the field to look after the cows," said the woman as she hurried away. Alfred took his seat on the chimney corner to do as he was told. But soon his thoughts turned to his troubles, and he forgot about the cakes.

When the woman came back, she cried out with vexation, for the cakes were burned and spoiled. "You lazy, good-for-nothing man!" she said, "I warrant you can eat cakes fast enough; but you are too lazy to help me bake them."

With that, she drove the poor hungry Alfred out of her house. In his ragged dress, he certainly did not look like a king, and she had no idea that he was anything but a poor beggar.

Eventually, some of Alfred's friends discovered where he was hiding and joined him. In a little time, a body of soldiers came to him and built a strong fort. From this fort, Alfred and his men went out now and then and fought small parties of the Danes. Alfred was successful, and his army grew larger and larger.

One day he disguised himself as a wandering minstrel and went into the camp of the Danes. He strolled here and there, playing on a harp and singing Saxon ballads. At last, Guthrum (Guth'-rum), the commander of the Danes, ordered the minstrel to be brought to his tent.

Alfred went. "Sing to me some of your charming songs," said Guthrum. "I never heard more beautiful music." So the kingly harpists played and sang for the Dane, and went away with handsome presents. But better than that, he had gained information that was of the greatest value.

In a week, he attacked the Danish forces and defeated them in a battle which lasted all day and far into the night. Guthrum was taken prisoner and brought before Alfred.

Taking his harp in his hands, Alfred played and sang one of the ballads with which he had entertained Guthrum in the camp.

The Dane started in amazement and exclaimed, "You, then, King Alfred, were the wandering minstrel?"

"Yes," replied Alfred. "I was the musician whom you received so kindly. Your life is now in my hands; but I will give you your liberty if you will become a Christian and never again make war on my people."

"King Alfred," said Guthrum. "I will become a Christian, and so will all my men if you will grant liberty to them as to me; and henceforth, we will be your friends."

Alfred then released the Danes, and they were baptized as Christians.

An old road running across England from London to Chester was then agreed upon as the boundary between the Danish and Saxon kingdoms; and the Danes settled in East Anglia, as the eastern part of England was called.

Years of peace and prosperity followed for Alfred's kingdom. During these years, the king rebuilt the towns that had been destroyed by the Danes, erected new forts, and greatly strengthened his army and navy.

He also encouraged trade, and he founded a school like the one established by Charlemagne. He himself translated a number of Latin books into Saxon, and probably did more for the cause of education than any other king that ever wore the English crown.

Written Summation

"Oh, what a lovely book!" exclaimed the boys.

"Yes, it is lovely," replied the mother. "I will give it to whichever of you children can read it the best in a week."

Model Practice 1 (adapted from the original)

Model Practice 2

Model Practice 3

Rollo the Viking

from Famous Men of the Middle Ages
by John H. Haaren, LL.D. and A. B. Poland, Ph.D.
Died 931 AD

For more than two hundred years during the Middle Ages, the Christian countries of Europe were attacked on the southwest by the Saracens of Spain, and on the northwest by the Norsemen, or Northmen. The Northmen were so called because they came into Middle Europe from the north. Sometimes they were called Vikings (Vi'-kings), or pirates, because they were adventurous sea-robbers who plundered all countries which they could reach by sea.

Their ships were long and swift. In the center was placed a single mast, which carried one large sail. For the most part, however, the Norsemen depended on rowing, not on the wind, and sometimes there were twenty rowers in one vessel.

The Vikings were a terror to all their neighbors; but the two regions that suffered most from their attacks were the Island of Britain and that part of Charlemagne's empire in which the Franks lived.

Nearly fifty times in two hundred years, the lands of the Franks were invaded. The Vikings sailed up the large rivers into the heart of the region which we now call France and captured and pillaged cities and towns. Some years after Charlemagne's death, they went as far as his capital, Aix (aks), took the place, and stabled their horses in the cathedral which the great emperor had built.

In the year 860, they discovered Iceland and made a settlement upon its shores. A few years later, they sailed as far as Greenland and established settlements which existed for about a century.

These Vikings were the first European discoverers of the North American continent. Ancient books found in Iceland tell the story of the discovery. According to these writings, a Viking ship was driven during a storm to a strange coast, which is now known as Labrador.

When the captain of the ship returned home, he told what he had seen. His tale so excited the curiosity of a young Viking prince, Leif the Lucky, that he sailed to the newly discovered coast.

Going ashore, he found that the country abounded in wild grapes; and so he called it Vinland, or the land of Vines. Vinland is thought to have been a part of what is now Labrador or Newfoundland.

The Vikings were not aware that they had found a great unknown continent. No one in the more civilized parts of Europe knew anything about their discovery; and after a while the story of the Vinland voyages seems to have been forgotten, even among the Vikings themselves.

The Vikings had many able chieftains. One of the most famous was Rollo the Walker, so called because he was such a giant that he could not find a horse strong enough to carry him. Therefore, he always had to walk. However, he did on foot what few could do on horseback.

In 885, seven hundred ships, commanded by Rollo and other Viking chiefs, left the harbors of Norway, sailed to the mouth of the Seine (San), and started up the river to capture the city of Paris.

Rollo and his men stopped on the way at Rouen (rö-on'), which also was on the Seine, but nearer its mouth. The citizens had heard of the giant, and when they saw the river covered by his fleet, they were dismayed. However, the bishop of Rouen told them that Rollo could be as noble and generous as he was fierce. He advised them to open their gates and trust the mercy of the Viking chief. This was done, and Rollo marched into Rouen and took possession of it. The bishop had given good advice, for Rollo treated the people very kindly.

Soon after capturing Rouen, he left the place, sailed up the river to Paris, and joined the other Viking chiefs. And now for six long miles the beautiful Seine was covered with Viking vessels, which carried an army of thirty thousand men.

A noted warrior named Eudes (Ude) was Count of Paris, and he had advised the Parisians to fortify the city. So not long before the arrival of Rollo and his companions, two walls with strong gates had been built around Paris.

It was no easy task for even Vikings to capture a strongly walled city. We are told that Rollo and his men built a high tower and rolled it on wheels up to the walls. At its top was a floor well manned with soldiers.

But the people within the city shot hundreds of arrows at the besiegers, and threw down rocks, or poured boiling oil and pitch upon them.

The Vikings thought to starve the Parisians, and for thirteen months, they encamped round the city. At length food became very scarce, and Count Eudes determined to go for help. He went out through one of the gates on a dark, stormy night, and rode post-haste to the king. He told him that something must be done to save the people of Paris.

So the king gathered an army and marched to the city. But no battle was fought. The Vikings seemed to have been afraid to risk one. They gave up the siege, and Paris was relieved.

Rollo and his men went to the Duchy of Burgundy, where, as now, the finest crops were raised and the best wines were made.

Perhaps after a time Rollo and his Vikings went home; but we do not know what he did for about twenty-five years. We do know that he abandoned his old home in Norway in 911. Then he and his people sailed from the icy shore of Norway and again sailed up the Seine in hundreds of Viking vessels.

Of course, on arriving in the land of the Franks, Rollo at once began to plunder towns and farms.

Charles, then king of the Franks, although his people called him the Simple, or Senseless, had enough sense to see that this must be stopped.

So he sent a message to Rollo and proposed that they should have a talk about peace. Rollo agreed and they met. The king and his troops stood on one side of a little river, and Rollo and his Vikings stood on the other. Messages passed between them. The king asked Rollo what he wanted.

"Let me and my people live in the land of the Franks. Let us make ourselves home here. And my Vikings and I will become your vassals," answered Rollo. He asked for Rouen and the neighboring land. So the king gave him that part of France. And ever since, it has been called Normandy, the land of the Northmen.

When it was decided that the Vikings should settle in France and be subjects of the Frankish king, Rollo was told that he must kiss the foot of Charles in token that he would be the king's vassal. The haughty Viking refused. "Never," said he, "will I bend my knee before any man, and no man's foot will I kiss." After some persuasion, however, he ordered one of his men to perform the act of homage for him. The king was on horseback and the Norseman, standing by the side of the horse, suddenly seized the king's foot and drew it up to his lips. This almost made the king fall from his horse, to the great amusement of the Norsemen.

Becoming a vassal to the king meant that if the king went to war Rollo would be obliged to join his army and bring a certain number of armed men—one thousand or more.

Rollo now granted parts of Normandy to his leading men on condition that they would bring soldiers to his army and fight under him. They became his vassals, as he was the king's vassal.

The lands granted to vassals in this way were called feuds, and this plan of holding lands was called the Feudal System.

It was established in every country of Europe during the Middle Ages.

The poorest people were called serfs. They were almost slaves and were never permitted to leave the estate to which they belonged. They did all the work. They worked chiefly for the landlords, but partly for themselves.

Having been a robber himself, Rollo knew what a shocking thing it was to ravage and plunder, and he determined to change his people's habits. He made strict laws and hanged robbers. His duchy thus became one of the safest parts of Europe.

The Northmen learned the language of the Franks and adopted their religion.

The story of Rollo is especially interesting to us, because Rollo was the forefather of that famous Duke of Normandy who, less than a hundred and fifty years later, conquered England and brought into that country the Norman nobles with their French language and customs.

Written Summation

These Vikings were the first European discoverers of the North American continent. Ancient books found in Iceland tell the story of the discovery. According to these writings, a Viking ship was driven during a storm to a strange coast, which is now known as Labrador. One such book detailing early Viking explorations is titled <u>Book of the Icelanders.</u>

Model Practice 1 (adapted from the original)

Model Practice 2

Model Practice 3

Canute the Great

from Famous Men of the Middle Ages
by John H. Haaren, LL.D. and A. B. Poland, Ph.D.
1014 - 1035 AD

The Danes, you remember, had the eastern and northern parts of England in the time of Alfred. Alfred's successors drove them farther and farther north, and at length the Danish kingdom in England ended for a time.

But the Danes in Denmark did not forget that there had been such a kingdom, and in the year 1013 Sweyn (swane), King of Denmark, invaded England and defeated the Anglo-Saxons. Ethelred, their king, fled to Normandy.

Sweyn now called himself the king of England. But in a short time, he died, and his son Canute succeeded to the throne. Canute was nineteen years old. He had been his father's companion during the war with the Anglo-Saxons, and thus had had a good deal of experience as a soldier.

After the death of Sweyn, some of the Anglo-Saxons recalled King Ethelred and revolted against the Danes.

Canute, however, went to Denmark and raised one of the largest armies of Danes that had ever been assembled. With this powerful force, he sailed to England. When he landed, Northumberland and Wessex acknowledged him as king. Shortly after this Ethelred died.

Canute now thought he would find it easy to get possession of all England. This was a mistake.

Ethelred left a son named Edmund Ironside who was a very brave soldier. He became, by his father's death, the king of Saxon England and at once raised an army to defend his kingdom. A battle raged, and Edmund was victorious. This was the first of five battles fought in one year. In none of them could the Danes do more than gain a slight advantage now and then.

However, the Saxons were at last defeated in a sixth battle through the act of a traitor. Edric, a Saxon noble, took his men out of the fight. His treachery so weakened the Saxon army that Edmund Ironside had to surrender to Canute.

But the young Dane had greatly admired Edmund for the way in which he had fought against heavy odds, so he now treated him most generously. Canute took certain portions of England, and the remainder, he gave to Edmund Ironside.

Thus for a short time, the Anglo-Saxon people had at once a Danish and a Saxon monarch.

Edmund died in 1016, and after his death, Canute became sole ruler.

He ruled wisely. He determined to make his Anglo-Saxon subjects forget that he was a foreign conqueror. To show his confidence in them, he sent back to Denmark the army he had brought over the sea, keeping on a part of his fleet and a small body of soldiers to act as guards at his palace.

He now depended on the support of his Anglo-Saxon subjects, and he won their love.

Although a king—and it is generally believed that kings like flattery—Canute is said to have rebuked his courtiers when they flattered him. On one occasion, when they were talking about his achievements, one of them said to him, "Most noble king, I believe you can do anything."

Canute sternly rebuked the courtier for words and said, "Come with me, gentlemen."

He led them from the palace grounds to the seashore where the tide was rising and had his chair placed at the edge of the water.

"You say I can do anything," he said to the courtiers. "Very well, I who am king and the lord of the ocean now command these rising waters to go back and not dare wet my feet."

But the tide was disobedient and steadily rose and rose, until the feet of the king were in the water.

Turning to his courtiers, Canute said, "Learn how feeble is the power of earthly kings. None is worthy the name of king but He whom heaven and earth and sea obey."

During Canute's reign, England had peace and prosperity, and the English people have held his memory dear.

Written Summation

Canute, however, went to Denmark and raised one of the largest armies of Danes that had ever been assembled. With this powerful force, he sailed to England. When he landed, Northumberland and Wessex acknowledged him as king. Shortly after this Ethelred died.

Model Practice 1

Model Practice 2

Model Practice 3

El Cid

from Famous Men of the Middle Ages
by John H. Haaren, LL.D. and A. B. Poland, Ph.D.
1040 - 1099 AD

Late one sunny afternoon, twenty-one knights were riding along the highway in the northern part of Spain. As they were passing a deep mire, they heard cries for help, and turning, saw a poor leper who was sinking in the mud. One of the knights, a handsome young man, was touched by the cries. He dismounted, rescued the poor fellow, and took him upon his own horse, and thus the two rode to the inn. The other knights wondered at this.

When they reached the inn where they were to stop for the night, they wondered still more, for their companion gave the leper a seat next to himself at the table. After supper, the knight shared his own bed with the leper. If the knight had not done this, the leper would have been driven out of the town, with nothing to eat and no place in which to sleep. At midnight, while the young man was fast asleep, the leper breathed upon his back. This act awakened the knight, who turned quickly in his bed and found that the leper was gone.

The knight called for a light and searched, but in vain. While he was wondering about what had happened, a man in shining garments appeared before him and said, "Rodrigo, are you asleep or awake?"

The knight answered, "I am awake, but who are you that brings such brightness?"

The vision replied, "I am St. Lazarus, the leper to whom you were so kind. Because I have breathed upon you, you shall accomplish whatever you shall undertake in peace or in battle. All shall honor you. Therefore, go on and evermore do good."

With that, the vision vanished.

The promise of St. Lazarus was fulfilled. In time, young Rodrigo became the great hero of Spain. The Spaniards called him Campeador (cam-pe-ä-dor'), or Champion. The Saracens called him "El Cid," or Lord. His real name was Rodrigo Diaz de Bivar, but he is usually spoken of as "El Cid."

The Goths, after the death of Alaric, had taken Spain away from the Romans. The Saracens, or, as they were usually called, the Moors, had crossed the sea from Africa and in turn had taken Spain from the Goths. In the time of Charles Martel, the Goths had lost all Spain except the small mountain district in the northern part. In the time of El Cid, the Goths had driven the Moors down to about the middle of Spain. War went on all the time between the two races, and many men spent their lives in fighting.

El Cid was a subject of Fernando of Castile. Fernando had a dispute with the king of Aragon about a city which each claimed. They agreed to decide the matter by combat. Each was to choose a champion. The champions were to fight, and the king whose champion won was to have the city. Fernando chose El Cid, and though the other champion was called the bravest knight in Spain, the youthful warrior vanquished him.

When Alfonzo, a son of Fernando, succeeded to the throne, he became angry with El Cid without just cause and banished him from Christian Spain.

El Cid was in need of some money, so he filled two chests with sand and sent word to two wealthy money lenders that he wished to borrow six hundred Spanish marks, and would put into their hands his treasures of silver and gold which were packed in two chests. But the money lenders had to solemnly swear not to open the chests until a full year had passed. They gladly agreed. They took the chests and loaned him six hundred marks.

El Cid was ready for his journey. Three hundred of his knights went into banishment with him. They crossed the mountains and entered the land of the Moors. Soon they reached the town of Alcocer, captured it, and lived in it.

Then the Moorish king of Valencia ordered two chiefs to take three thousand horsemen, recapture the town, and bring El Cid to him, alive.

So El Cid and his men were shut up in Alcocer. Famine threatened them, and they determined to cut their way through the army of the Moors. Suddenly and swiftly, they poured from the gate of Alcocer, and a terrible battle ensued. The two Moorish chiefs were captured and thirteen hundred of their men were killed in the battle. El Cid then became a vassal of the Moorish king of Saragossa.

After a while, Alfonzo recalled El Cid from banishment and gave him seven castles and the lands adjoining them. He needed El Cid's help in the greatest of all his plans against the Moors. He was determined to capture Toledo. He attacked it with a large army in which there were soldiers from many foreign lands. El Cid is said to have been the commander. After a long siege, the city fell, and the victorious army marched across the great bridge built by the Moors.

Valencia was one of the largest and richest cities in Moorish Spain. It was strongly fortified, but El Cid determined to attack it.

The plain about the city was irrigated by streams that came down from the neighboring hills. To prevent El Cid's army from coming near the city, the Saracens flooded the plain. But El Cid camped on high ground above the plain and from that point besieged the city. Food became very scarce in Valencia. Wheat, barley and cheese were all so dear that none but the rich could buy them. People ate horses, dogs, cats and mice, until in the whole city only three horses and a mule were left alive.

Then on June 15, 1094, the governor went to the camp of El Cid and delivered to him the keys of the city. El Cid placed his men in all the forts and took the citadel as his own dwelling. His banner floated from the towers. He called himself the Prince of Valencia.

When the king of Morocco heard of this, he raised an army of fifty thousand men. They crossed from Africa to Spain and laid siege to Valencia. But El Cid with his men made a sudden sally, routed them, and pursued them for miles. It is said that fifteen thousand soldiers were drowned in the river Guadalquivir (Gua-dal-qui-vir') when they tried to cross.

El Cid was now at the height of his power and lived in great magnificence. One of the first things he did was to repay the two friends who had lent him the six hundred marks. He was kind and just to the Saracens who had become his subjects. They were allowed to have their mosques and to worship God as they thought right.

In time, El Cid's health began to fail. He could not lead his men into battle anymore. He sent an army against the Moors, but it was so completely routed that only a few of his men came back to tell the tale. It is said by a Moorish writer, "when the runaways reached him, El Cid died of rage" (1099).

There is a legend that shortly before he died he saw a vision of St. Peter, who told him that he should gain a victory over the Saracens after his death.

So El Cid gave orders that his body should be embalmed. It was so well preserved that it seemed alive. It was clothed in a coat of mail, and the sword that had won so many battles was placed in his hand. Then his body was mounted upon El Cid's favorite horse, fastened to the saddle, and at midnight was borne out of the gate of Valencia with a guard of a thousand knights.

Silently, they marched to a spot where the Moorish king, with thirty-six chieftains, lay encamped. At daylight, the knights of El Cid made a sudden attack. The Moorish king awoke. It seemed to him that seventy thousand knights, all dressed in robes as white as snow were coming against him. And before them rode a knight, taller than all the rest, holding in his left hand a snow-white banner and in the other a sword of fire. So afraid were the Moorish chief and his men that they fled to the sea. Twenty thousand of them drowned as they tried to reach their ships.

There is a Latin inscription near the tomb of El Cid which may be translated:

Brave and unconquered, famous in triumphs of war,
Enclosed in this tomb lies Roderick the Great of Bivar.*

Written Summation

The vision replied, "I am St. Lazarus, the leper to whom you were so kind. Because I have breathed upon you, you shall accomplish whatever you shall undertake in peace or in battle. All shall honor you. Therefore, go on and evermore do good."

With that, the vision vanished.

Model Practice 1

Model Practice 2

Model Practice 3

Edward the Confessor

from Famous Men of the Middle Ages
by John H. Haaren, LL.D. and A. B. Poland, Ph.D.
1042 - 1066 AD

The Danish kings who followed Canute were not like him. They were cruel, unjust rulers; and all the people of England hated them. So when in the year 1042 the last of them died, Edward, the son of the Saxon Ethelred, was elected king.

He is known in history as Edward the Confessor. He was a man of holy life and after his death was made a saint by the Church, with the title of "The Confessor." Though born in England, he passed the greater part of his life in Normandy as an exile from his native land. He was thirty-eight years old when he returned from Normandy to become king.

As he had lived so long in Normandy, he always seemed more like a Norman than one of English birth. He generally spoke the French language, and he chose Normans to fill many of the highest offices in his kingdom.

For the first eight years of his reign, there was perfect peace in his kingdom, except in the counties of Kent and Essex, where pirates from the North Sea made occasional attacks.

These pirates were mostly Norwegians, whose leader was a barbarian named Kerdric. They would come sweeping down upon the Kentish coast in many ships, make a landing where there were no soldiers, and fall upon the towns and plunder them. Then, as swiftly and suddenly as they had come, they would sail away homeward before they could be captured.

One day Kerdric's fleet arrived off the coast, and as no opposing force was visible, the pirates landed and started toward the nearest town to plunder it.

By a quick march, a body of English soldiers reached the town before the pirates, and when the latter arrived, they found a strong force ready for battle. A short struggle took place. More than half of the pirates were slain, and the remainder were taken prisoners.

After the prisoners had been secured, the English ships that were stationed on the coast attacked the pirate fleet and destroyed it.

Edward took part in the events upon which Shakespeare, five hundred years later, founded his famous tragedy of Macbeth.

> There lived in Scotland during his reign an ambitious nobleman named Macbeth, who invited Duncan, the King of Scotland, to his castle and murdered him. He tried to make it appear that Duncan's attendants had committed the murder, and he caused the king's son and heir, Prince Malcolm, to flee from the land. He then made himself king of Scotland.
>
> Malcolm hurried to England and appealed to King Edward for help.
>
> When the king learned the number of soldiers Malcolm would probably need, he gave orders for double that number to march into Scotland. Malcolm, with this support, attacked Macbeth, and after several well-fought battles drove the usurper from Scotland and took possession of the throne.

Edward did a great deal during his reign to aid the cause of Christianity. He rebuilt the ancient Westminster Abbey in London and erected churches and monasteries in different parts of England.

For many years, the people believed Edward to be the origin of many just laws. And years after his death, the English people, when suffering from bad government, would exclaim, "Oh, for the good laws and customs of Edward the Confessor!" What he really did was to have the old laws faithfully carried out.

Edward the Confessor died in 1066 and was buried in Westminster Abbey.

Written Summation

These pirates were mostly Norwegians, whose leader was a barbarian named Kerdric. They would come sweeping down upon the Kentish coast in many ships, make a landing where there were no soldiers, and fall upon the towns and plunder them. Then, as swiftly and suddenly as they had come, they would sail away homeward before they could be captured.

Model Practice 1

Model Practice 2

Model Practice 3

Peter the Hermit

from Famous Men of the Middle Ages
by John H. Haaren, LL.D. and A. B. Poland, Ph.D.
1050 - 1115 AD

During the Middle Ages, the Christians of Europe traveled to the Holy Land for the purpose of visiting the tomb of Christ and other sacred places. Those who made such a journey were called "pilgrims."

Every year thousands of pilgrims—kings, nobles, and people of humbler rank—went to the Holy Land.

While Jerusalem was in the hands of the Arabian caliphs who reigned at Bagdad, the Christian pilgrims were generally well treated. After about 1070, when the Turks took possession of the city, outrages became so frequent that it seemed as if it would not be safe for Christians to visit the Savior's tomb at all.

About the year, 1095 there lived at Amiens (ä-me-an') France, a monk named Peter the Hermit.

Peter was present at a council of clergy and people held at Clermont in France when his Holiness, Pope Urban II, made a stirring speech. He begged the people to rescue the Holy Sepulcher and other sacred sites from the Muslims.

The council was so roused by his words that they broke forth into loud cries, "God wills it! God wills it!"

"It is, indeed, His will," said the Pope, "and let these words be your war cry when you meet the enemy."

Peter listened with deep attention. Immediately after the council, he began to preach in favor of a war against the Turks. With head and feet bare, and clothed in a long, coarse robe tied at the waist with a rope, he went through Italy from city to city, riding on a donkey. He preached in churches and on the streets—wherever he could secure an audience.

After Peter had traveled through Italy, he crossed the Alps and preached to the people of France, Germany, and neighboring countries. Everywhere he kindled the zeal of the people, and multitudes enlisted as champions of the cross.

Thus began the first of seven wars known as the "Crusades" or "Wars of the Cross," waged to rescue the Holy Land from the Muslims.

It is said that more than 100,000 men, women, and children went on the first Crusade. Each wore on the right shoulder the emblem of the cross.

Peter was in command of one portion of this great multitude. His followers began their journey with shouts of joy and praise.

But they had no proper supply of provisions. So when passing through Hungary they plundered the towns and compelled the inhabitants to support them. This roused the anger of the Hungarians. They attacked the Crusaders and killed a great many of them.

After long delays, about seven thousand of those who had started on the Crusade reached Constantinople. They were still enthusiastic and sounded their war cry, "God wills it!" with as much fervor as when they first joined Peter's standard.

Leaving Constantinople, they went eastward into the land of the Turks. A powerful army led by the sultan met them. The Crusaders fought heroically all day long, but at length were badly beaten. Only a few escaped and found their way back to Constantinople.

Peter the Hermit had left the Crusaders before the battle and returned to Constantinople. He afterwards joined the army of Godfrey of Bouillon.

Godfrey's army was composed of six divisions, each commanded by a soldier of high rank and distinction. It was a well-organized and disciplined force and numbered about half a million men.

It started only a few weeks after the irregular multitude which followed Peter the Hermit, and was really the first Crusading army, for Peter's undisciplined throng could hardly be called an army.

After a long march, Godfrey reached Antioch and laid siege to it.

It was believed that this Muslim stronghold could be taken in a short time; but the city resisted the attacks of the Christians for seven months before surrendering.

Then something happened that none of the Crusaders had dreamed of. An army of two hundred thousand Persians arrived to help the Muslims. They laid siege to Antioch and shut up the Crusaders within its walls for weeks. However, after a number of engagements in which there was great loss of life, the Turks and Persians were driven away.

The way to Jerusalem was now opened. But out of the half million Crusaders who had marched from Europe less than fifty thousand were left. They had won their way at a fearful cost.

Onward, they pushed with brave hearts, until on a bright summer morning they caught the first glimpse of the Holy City in the distance. For two whole years, they had toiled and suffered in the hope of reaching Jerusalem. Now it lay before them.

But it had yet to be taken. For more than five weeks, the Crusaders carried on the siege. Finally, on the 15th of July, 1099, the Turks surrendered. The Muslim flag was hauled down, and the banner of the cross floated over the Holy City.

A few days after the Christians had occupied Jerusalem, Godfrey of Bouillon was chosen king of the Holy Land.

"I will accept the office," he said, "but no crown must be put on my head, and I must never be called king. I cannot wear a crown of gold where Christ wore one of thorns nor will I be called king in the land where once lived the King of Kings."

Peter the Hermit is said to have preached an eloquent sermon on the Mount of Olives. He did not, however, remain long in Jerusalem, but after the capture of the city returned to Europe. He founded a monastery in France and within its walls passed the rest of his life.

Written Summation

The council was so roused by his words that they broke forth into loud cries, "God wills it! God wills it!"

"It is, indeed, His will," said the Pope, "and let these words be your war cry when you meet the enemy."

Model Practice 1

Model Practice 2

Model Practice 3

William the Conqueror

from Famous Men of the Middle Ages
by John H. Haaren, LL.D. and A. B. Poland, Ph.D.
1066 – 1087 AD

On the death of Edward the Confessor, the throne of England was claimed by William, Duke of Normandy.

When Edward took refuge in Normandy. after the Danes conquered England, he stayed at the palace of William. He was very kindly treated there, and William said that Edward had promised in gratitude that William should succeed him as king of England.

One day in the year 1066, when William was hunting with a party of his courtiers in the woods near Rouen, a noble came riding rapidly toward him shouting, "Your Highness, a messenger has just arrived from England, bearing the news that King Edward is dead and that Harold, the son of Earl Godwin, has been placed on the English throne."

William at once called his nobles together and said to them, "I must have your consent that I enforce my claim to England's throne by arms."

The barons gave their consent. So an army of sixty-thousand men was collected, and a large fleet of ships was built to carry this force across the channel.

During the months of preparation, William sent an embassy to the English court to demand of Harold that he give up the throne. Harold refused.

Soon all England was startled by the news that William had landed on the English coast at the port of Hastings with a large force.

Harold immediately marched as quickly as possible from the north to the southern coast. In a week or so, he arrived at a place called Senlac, nine miles from Hastings in the neighborhood of the town in which the Norman army was encamped. He took his position on a low range of hills and waited for William to attack. His men were tired with their march, but he encouraged them and bade them prepare for battle.

On the morning of October 14, 1066, the two armies met. The Norman foot soldiers opened the battle by charging on the English stockades. They ran over the plain to the low hills, singing a war-song at the top of their voices, but they could not carry the stockades although they tried again and again. They therefore attacked another part of the English forces.

William, clad in complete armor, was in the very front of the fight, urging on his troops. At one time, a cry arose in his army that he was slain, and a panic began. William pulled off his helmet and rode along the lines, shouting, "I live! I live! Fight on! We shall conquer yet!"

The battle raged from morning until night. Harold himself fought on foot at the head of his army and behaved most valiantly. His men, tired as they were from their forced march, bravely struggled on hour after hour.

But at last, William turned their lines and threw them into confusion. As the sun went down, Harold was killed, and his men gave up the fight.

From Hastings, William marched toward London. On the way, he received the surrender of some towns and burned others that would not surrender. London submitted and some of the nobles and citizens came forth and offered the English crown to the Norman duke. On December 25, 1066, the "Conqueror," as he is always called, was crowned in Westminster Abbey by Archbishop Ealdred.

Both English and Norman people were present. When the question was asked by the Archbishop, "Will you have William, Duke of Normandy, for your king?" all present answered, "We will."

At first, William ruled England with moderation. The laws and customs were not changed. A few months after the battle of Hastings, the kingdom was so peaceful that William left it in the charge of his brother and went to Normandy for a visit.

While he was gone, many of the English nobles rebelled against him, and on his return he made very severe laws and did some very harsh things. He laid waste an extensive territory, destroying all the houses upon it and causing thousands of persons to die from lack of food and shelter, because the people there had not sworn allegiance to him.

He made a law that all lights should be put out and fires covered with ashes at eight o'clock every evening, so that the people would have to go to bed then. A bell was rung in all cities and towns throughout England to warn the people of the hour. The bell was called the "curfew," from the French words "couvre feu," meaning "to cover fire."

To find out about the lands of England and their owners, so that everybody might be made to pay taxes, he appointed officers in all the towns to report what estates there were, who owned them, and what they were worth. The reports were copied into two volumes, called the "Domesday Book." This book showed that England at that time had a population of a little more than a million.

William made war on Scotland, and conquered it. During a war with the king of France, the city of Mantes (mont) was burned by William's soldiers. As William rode over the ruins, his horse stumbled and the king was thrown to the ground and injured. He was borne to Rouen, where he lay ill for six weeks. His sons and even his attendants abandoned him in his last hours. It is said that in his death struggle, he fell from his bed to the floor, where his body was found by his servants.

Written Summation

On the morning of October 14, 1066, the two armies met. The Norman foot soldiers opened the battle by charging on the English stockades. They ran over the plain to the low hills, singing a war song at the top of their voices, but they could not carry the stockades although they tried again and again. They therefore attacked another part of the English forces.

Model Practice 1 (adapted from the original)

Model Practice 2

Model Practice 3

Frederick Barbarossa

from Famous Men of the Middle Ages
by John H. Haaren, LL.D. and A. B. Poland, Ph.D.
1152 - 1190 AD

Frederick I was one of the most famous of German emperors. He was a tall, stalwart man of majestic appearance. He had a long red beard, so the people called him Barbarossa, or RedBeard. He came to the throne in 1152.

At that time, the province of Lombardy in northern Italy was a part of the German empire.

In 1158 Milan (mï-lan'), the chief city of Lombardy, revolted. Frederick, at their head, led an army of a hundred thousand German soldiers over the Alps to stomp out the revolt. After a long siege, the city surrendered.

But soon it revolted again. The emperor besieged it once more, and once more it surrendered. But this time, the cities' fortifications were destroyed and many of its buildings ruined.

But even then, the spirit of the Lombards was not broken. Milan and the other cities of Lombardy united in a league and defied the emperor. He called upon the German dukes to bring their men to his aid. All responded, except Henry the Lion, duke of Saxony, Frederick's cousin, whom he had made duke of Bavaria also. Frederick is said to have knelt and implored Henry to do his duty, but in vain.

In his campaign against the Lombards, Frederick was unsuccessful. His army was completely defeated, and he was compelled to grant freedom to the cities of Lombardy. Everybody blamed Henry the Lion. The other dukes charged him with treason, and he was summoned to appear before a meeting of the nobles. He failed to come, and the nobles thereupon declared him guilty and took from him everything that he had, except the lands he had inherited from his father.

Frederick now devoted himself to making Germany a united nation. Two of his nobles had been quarreling for a long time. And as a punishment for their conduct, each was condemned, with ten of his counts and barons, to carry dogs on his shoulders from one country to another.

Frederick finally succeeded in keeping the nobles in the different provinces of Germany at peace with one another. He persuaded them to work together for the good of the whole empire. He had no more trouble with them. And for many years, his reign was peaceful and prosperous.

After the Christians had held Jerusalem for eighty-eight years, it was recaptured by the Muslims under the lead of the famous Saladin (Sal'-a-din), in the year 1187. There was much excitement in Christendom, and the Pope proclaimed another Crusade.

Frederick immediately raised an army of Crusaders in the German Empire and, with one hundred and fifty thousand men, started for Palestine.

He marched into Asia Minor, attacked the Muslim forces, and defeated them in two great battles.

But before the brave old warrior reached the Holy Land, his career was suddenly brought to an end. One day his army was crossing a small bridge over a river in Asia Minor. At a moment when the bridge was crowded with troops, Frederick rode up rapidly.

He was impatient to join his son, who was leading the advance guard. And when he found that he could not cross immediately by the bridge, he plunged into the river to swim his horse across.

Both horse and rider were swept away by the current. Barbarossa's heavy armor made him helpless, and he drowned. His body was recovered and buried at Antioch.

Barbarossa was so much loved by his people that it was said, "Germany and Frederick Barbarossa are one in the hearts of the Germans." His death caused the greatest grief among the German Crusaders. They now had little heart to fight the enemy, and most of them at once returned to Germany.

In the Empire, the dead hero was long mourned and for many years, the peasants believed that Frederick was not really dead, but was asleep in a cave in the mountains of Germany, with his gallant knights around him. He was supposed to be sitting in his chair of state, with the crown upon his head, his eyes half-closed in slumber, his beard as white as snow and so long that it reached the ground.

"When the ravens cease to fly round the mountain," said the legend, "Barbarossa shall awake and restore Germany to its ancient greatness."

Written Summation

Frederick now devoted himself to making Germany a united nation. Two of his nobles had been quarreling for a long time. And as a punishment for their conduct, each was condemned, with ten of his counts and barons, to carry dogs on his shoulders from one country to another.

Model Practice 1

Model Practice 2

Model Practice 3

Henry the Second

from Famous Men of the Middle Ages
by John H. Haaren, LL.D. and A. B. Poland, Ph.D.
1154 - 1189 AD

In 1154, while Barbarossa was reigning in Germany, Henry II, one of England's greatest monarchs, came to the throne.

Henry was the son of Geoffrey Plantagenet (Plan-tag'-e-net), Count of Anjou in France, and Matilda, daughter of King Henry I, and granddaughter of William the Conqueror. Count Geoffrey used to wear in his hat a sprig of the broom plant, which is called in Latin "planta genista." From this, he adopted the name Plantagenet, and the kings who descended from him and ruled England for more than three hundred years are called the Plantagenets.

Henry II inherited a vast domain in France and managing this, in addition to England, kept him very busy. One who knew him well said, "He never sits down; he is on his feet from morning till night."

His chief assistant in the management of public affairs was Thomas Becket, whom he made chancellor of the kingdom. Becket was fond of pomp and luxury, and lived in a more magnificent manner than even the king himself.

At this time, the clergy had become almost independent of the king. To bring them under his authority, Henry made Becket Archbishop of Canterbury, thus putting him at the head of the Church in England. The king expected that Becket would carry out all his wishes.

Becket, however, refused to do that which the king most desired, and a quarrel arose between them. At last, to escape the king's anger, Becket fled to France and remained there for six years.

At the end of this time, Henry invited him to come back to England. Not long after, however, the old quarrel began again. One day, while Henry was sojourning in France, he cried out in a moment of passion, while surrounded by a group of knights, "Is there no one who will rid me of this turbulent priest?"

Four knights who heard him understood from this angry speech that he desired the death of Becket, and they went to England to murder the Archbishop. When they met Becket, they first demanded that he should do as the king wished, but he firmly refused. At dusk that same day, they entered Canterbury Cathedral, seeking him again. "Where is the traitor, Thomas Becket?" one of them cried.

Becket boldly answered, "Here am I—no traitor, but a priest of god."

As he finished speaking, the knights rushed upon him and killed him.

The people of England were horrified by this brutal murder. Becket was called a martyr, and his tomb became a place of pious pilgrimage. The Pope canonized him, and for years, he was the most venerated of English saints.

King Henry was in Normandy when the murder occurred. He declared that he had had nothing whatever to do with it, and he punished the murderers.

But from this time on, Henry had many troubles. His own sons rebelled against him, his barons were unfriendly, and conspiracies were formed. Henry thought that God was punishing him for the murder of Becket and so determined to do penance at the tomb of the saint.

For some distance, before he reached Canterbury Cathedral where Becket was buried, he walked over the road with bare head and feet. After his arrival, he fasted and prayed a day and a night. The next day he put scourges into the hands of the cathedral monks and said, "Scourge me as I kneel at the tomb of the saint." The monks did as he bade them, and he patiently bore the pain.

Henry finally triumphed over his enemies and had some years of peace, which he devoted to the good of England.

In the last year of his life, however, he had trouble again. The king of France and Henry's son Richard took up arms against him. Henry was defeated and was forced to grant what they wished. When he saw a list of the barons who had joined the French king, he found among them the name of his favorite son John, and his heart was broken. He died a few days later.

Henry's eldest surviving son, Richard, was crowned at Westminster Abbey in 1190. He took the title of Richard I but is better known as "Cœur de Lion" ("the Lionheart"), a name given to him for his bravery. He had wonderful strength, and his brave deeds were talked about all over the land.

With such a man for their king, the English people became devoted to chivalry, and on every field of battle, brave men vied with another in brave deeds. Knighthood was often the reward of valor. Then, as now, knighthood was usually conferred upon a man by his king or queen. A part of the ceremony involved the sovereign touching the kneeling subject's soldier with the flat of a sword, saying, "Arise, Sir Knight." This was called "the accolade."

Richard did not stay long in England after his coronation. In 1191, he went with Philip of France on a Crusade.

The French and English Crusaders together numbered more than one hundred thousand men. They sailed to the Holy Land and joined an army of Christian soldiers encamped before the city of Acre. The besiegers had despaired of taking the city, but when reinforced, they gained fresh courage.

Richard the Lionheart now performed deeds of valor, which gave him fame throughout Europe. He was the terror of the Saracens. In every attack on Acre, he led the Christians, and when the city was captured, he planted his banner in triumph on its walls.

Every night when the Crusaders encamped, the heralds blew their trumpets, and cried three times, "Save the Holy Sepulcher!" And the Crusaders knelt and said, "Amen!"

The great leader of the Saracens was Saladin. He was a model of heroism and the two leaders, one the champion of the Christians and the other the champion of the Muslims, vied with each other in knightly deeds.

Just before one battle, Richard rode down the Saracen line and boldly called for any one to step forth and fight him alone. No one responded to the challenge, for the most valiant of the Saracens did not dare to meet the Lionheart king.

After the capture of Acre, Richard took Ascalon (As'-ca-lon). Then he made a truce with Saladin, by which the Christians acquired the right for three years to visit the Holy City without paying for the privilege.

Richard now set out on his voyage home. His ship was wrecked, however, on the Adriatic Sea near Trieste. To get to England, he was obliged to go through the lands of Leopold, duke of Austria, one of his bitterest enemies. So he disguised himself as a poor pilgrim returning from the Holy Land.

But he was recognized by a costly ring that he wore and was taken prisoner at Vienna by Duke Leopold. His people in England anxiously awaited his return, and when after a long time he did not appear, they were sadly distressed. There is a legend that a faithful squire named Blondel went in search of him, as a wandering minstrel over central Europe, vainly seeking for news of his master.

At last one day, while singing one of Richard's favorite songs near the walls of the castle where the king was confined, he heard the song repeated from a window. He recognized the voice of Richard. From the window, Richard told him to let the English people and the people of Europe know where he was confined, and the minstrel immediately went upon his mission.

Soon Europe was astounded to learn that brave Richard of England, the great champion of Christendom, was imprisoned. The story of Blondel is probably not true, but it is true that England offered to ransom Richard; that the Pope interceded for him; and that it was finally agreed that he should be returned in exchange of a very large sum of money. The English people quickly paid the ransom and Richard was freed.

The king of France had little love for Richard, and Richard's own brother John had less. Both were sorry that Richard the Lionheart was at liberty.

John had taken charge of the kingdom during his brother's absence, and hoped that Richard might pass the rest of his days in the prison castle of Leopold.

As soon as Richard was released, the French king sent word to John, "The devil is loose again." And a very disappointed man was John when all England rang with rejoicing at Richard's return.

Upon the death of Richard, in 1199, Arthur, the son of his elder brother Geoffrey, was the rightful heir to the throne. John, however, seized the throne himself and cast Arthur into prison. There is a legend that he ordered Arthur's eyes to be put out with red-hot irons. The jailor, however, was touched by the boy's prayer for mercy and spared him. But Arthur was not to escape his uncle long. It is said that one night the king took him out upon the Seine in a little boat, murdered him, and cast his body into the river.

Besides being a king of England, John was duke of Normandy, and Philip, king of France, now summoned him to France to answer for the crime of murdering Arthur. John would not answer the summons and this gave the king of France an excuse for taking possession of Normandy. He did so, and thus this great province was lost forever to England. Nothing in France was left to John except Aquitaine (A-qui-taine'), which had come to him through his mother.

John's government was unjust and tyrannical, and the bishops and barons determined to preserve their rights and the rights of the people. They met on a plain called Runnymede, and there forced John to sign the famous "Magna Carta" ("Great Charter").

The Magna Carta is the most valuable charter ever granted by any sovereign to his people. In it, King John names all the rights which belong to the citizens under a just government, and he promises that not one of these rights shall ever be taken away from any subjects of the English king.

Later in history, for violating this promise, one English king lost his life, and another lost the American colonies.

The Magna Carta was signed in 1215. A year after he signed it, the king died. His son, Henry III, succeeded him.

Written Summation

His chief assistant in the management of public affairs was Thomas Becket, whom he made chancellor of the kingdom. Becket was fond of pomp and luxury, and lived in a more magnificent manner than even the king himself.

Model Practice 1 (adapted from the original)

Model Practice 2

Model Practice 3

Marco Polo

from Famous Men of the Middle Ages
by John H. Haaren, LL.D. and A. B. Poland, Ph.D.
1254 - 1324 AD

Some years before St. Louis led his last Crusade, a boy named Marco Polo was born in Venice. His father was a wealthy merchant who often went on trading journeys to distant lands.

In 1271, when Marco was seventeen years old, he accompanied his father and uncle on a journey through the Holy Land, Persia and Tartary, and at length to the Empire of China—then called Cathay (Ca-thay'). It took the travelers three years to reach Cathay.

The emperor of Cathay was a monarch named Kublai Khan (koo' bli-kän'), who lived in Peking.

Marco's father and uncle had been in Cathay once before and had entertained Kublai Khan by telling him about the manners and customs of Europe.

So when the two Venetian merchants again appeared in Peking, Kublai Khan was glad to see them. He was also greatly pleased with the young Marco, and invited him to the palace.

Important positions at the Chinese court were given to Marco's father and uncle, and so they and Marco lived in the country for some years. Marco studied the Chinese language, and it was not very long before he could speak it.

When he was about twenty-one, Kublai Khan sent him on very important business to a distant part of China. He did the work well and from that time was often employed as an envoy of the Chinese monarch. His travels were sometimes in lands never before visited by Europeans, and he had many strange adventures among the almost unknown tribes of Asia. Step by step, he was promoted. For several years, he was governor of a great Chinese city.

Finally, he, his father, and uncle desired to return to Venice. They had all served Kublai Khan faithfully, and he had appreciated it and given them rich rewards; but he did not wish to let them go.

While the matter was discussed, an embassy arrived in Peking from the king of Persia. This monarch desired to marry the daughter of Kublai Khan, the Princess Cocachin. He had sent to ask her father for her hand. Consent was given, and Kublai Khan fitted out a fleet of fourteen ships to carry the wedding party to Persia.

The Princess Cocachin was a great friend of Marco Polo, and urged her father to allow him to go with the party. Kublai Khan gave his consent. Marco's father and uncle were also allowed to go, and the three Venetians left China.

The fleet with the wedding party on board sailed southward on the China Sea. It was a long and perilous voyage. Stops were made at Borneo, Sumatra, Ceylon and other places, until the ships entered the Persian Gulf and the princess landed safely. After they reached the capital of Persia, the party, including the three Venetians, was entertained by the Persians for weeks in a magnificent manner and costly presents were given to all.

At last, the Venetians left their friends, went to the Black Sea, and took ship for Venice.

They had been away so long and their appearances had changed so much that none of their relations and old friends knew them when they arrived in Venice. Because they were dressed in Tatar costume and sometimes spoke the Chinese language to one another, they found it hard to convince people that they were members of the Polo family.

At length, on order to show that they were the men that they declared themselves to be, they gave a dinner to all their relations and old friends. When the guests arrived, they were greeted by the travelers, arrayed in gorgeous Chinese robes of crimson satin. After the first course, they appeared in crimson damask; after the second, they changed their costumes to crimson velvet; while at the end of the dinner they appeared in the usual garb of wealthy Venetians.

"Now, my friends," said Marco, "I will show you something that will please you." He then brought into the room the rough Tatar coats that he and his father and uncle had worn when they reached Venice. Cutting open the seams, he took from inside the lining packets filled with rubies, emeralds and diamonds. It was the finest collection of jewels ever seen in Venice.

The guests finally believed that their hosts were indeed who they claimed to be.

Eight hundred years before Marco Polo's birth, some of the people of North Italy had fled before Attila to the muddy islands of the Adriatic and founded Venice upon them. Since then the little settlement had become the most wealthy and powerful city of Europe. Venice was the queen of the Adriatic and her merchants were princes. They had vessels to bring the costly wares of the East to their wharves. They had warships to protect their rich cargoes from the pirates of the Mediterranean. And when necessary, they carried on wars. At the time when Marco Polo returned from Cathay, they were at war with Genoa (Gen'-o-a).

The two cities were fighting for the trade of the world. In a great naval battle, the Venetians were completely defeated. Marco Polo was in the battle and with many of his countrymen was captured by the enemy. For a year, he was confined in a Genoese prison.

One of his fellow-prisoners was a skillful penman and Marco dictated to him an account of his experiences in China, Japan, and other Eastern countries. This account was carefully written out. Copies of the manuscript exist to this day. One of these is in a library in Paris. It was carried into France in the year 1307. Another copy is preserved in the city of Berne. It is said that the book was translated into many languages, so that people in all parts of Europe learned about Marco's adventures.

About a hundred and seventy-five years after the book was written, the famous Genoese, Christopher Columbus, planned his voyage across the Atlantic. It is believed that he had read Marco's description of Java, Sumatra and other East India Islands. And when he had reached Haiti (Hai'-ti) and Cuba, he believed he had found the places described by Marco Polo. So Marco Polo may have inspired Christopher Columbus' famous voyages.

Written Summation

Eight hundred years before Marco Polo's birth, some of the people of North Italy had fled before Attila to the muddy islands of the Adriatic and founded Venice upon them. Since then the little settlement had become the most wealthy and powerful city of Europe. Venice was the queen of the Adriatic and her merchants were princes.

Model Practice 1

Model Practice 2

Model Practice 3

William Tell and Arnold von Winkelried

from Famous Men of the Middle Ages
by John H. Haaren, LL.D. and A. B. Poland, Ph.D.
14th century

Far up among the Alps, in the very heart of Switzerland, are three districts, or cantons, as they are called, which are known as the Forest Cantons and are famous in the world's history. About two thousand years ago, the Romans found in these cantons a hardy race of mountaineers, who, although poor, were free men, proud of their independence. They became the friends and allies of Rome, and the cantons were for many years a part of the Roman Empire, but the people always had the right to elect their own officers and to govern themselves.

When Goths and the Vandals and the Huns from beyond the Rhine and the Danube overran the Roman Empire, these three cantons were not disturbed. The land was too poor and rocky to attract men who were fighting for possession of the rich plains and valleys of Europe. So it happened that for century after century, the mountaineers of these cantons lived on in their old, simple way, undisturbed by the rest of the world.

In a canton in the valley of the Rhine lived the Hapsburg family, whose leaders in time grew to be very rich and powerful. They became dukes of Austria, and some of them were elected emperors. One of the Hapsburgs, Albert I, claimed that the land of the Forest Cantons belonged to him. He sent a governor and a band of soldiers to those cantons and made the people submit to his authority.

At this time, a famous mountaineer named William Tell lived in one of the Forest Cantons. He was tall and strong. In all Switzerland, no man had a foot as sure as his on the mountains or a hand as skilled in the use of a bow. He was determined to resist the Austrians.

Secret meetings of the mountaineers were held and all took a solemn oath to stand by each other and fight for their freedom; but they had no arms and were simple shepherds who had never been trained as soldiers. The first thing to be done was to get arms without attracting the attention of the Austrians. It took nearly a year to secure spears, swords, and battle-axes and distribute them among the mountains. Finally, this was done, and everything was ready. All were waiting for a signal to rise.

The story tells us that just at this time Gessler, the Austrian governor, who was a cruel tyrant, hung a cap on a high pole in the market place in the village of Altorf, and forced everyone who passed to bow before it. Tell accompanied by his little son, happened to pass through the market-place. He refused to bow before the cap and was arrested. Gessler offered to release him if he would shoot an apple from the head of his son. The governor hated Tell and made this offer hoping that the mountaineer's hand would tremble and that he would kill his own son. It is said that Tell shot the apple from his son's head but that Gessler still refused to release him. That night as Tell was being carried across the lake to prison a storm came up. In the midst of the storm, he sprang from the boat to an over-hanging rock and made his escape. It is said that he killed the tyrant. Some people do not believe this story, but the Swiss do. And if you go to Lake Lucerne some day, they will show you the very rock upon which Tell stepped when he sprang from the boat.

That night the signal fires were lit on every mountain and by the dawn of day the village of Altorf was filled with hardy mountaineers, armed and ready to fight for their liberty. A battle followed and the Austrians were defeated and driven from Altorf. This victory was followed by others.

A few years later, the duke himself came with a large army, determined to conquer the mountaineers. He had to march through a narrow pass, with mountains rising abruptly on either side. The Swiss were expecting him and hid along the heights above the pass. As soon as the Austrians appeared in the pass, the mountaineers hurled rocks and trunks of trees down upon them. Many Austrians were killed and wounded. Their army was defeated, and the duke was forced to recognize the independence of the Forest Cantons.

This was the beginning of the Republic of Switzerland. In time, five other cantons joined them in a compact for liberty.

About seventy years later the Austrians made another attempt to conquer the patriots. They collected a splendid army and marched into the mountains. The Swiss at once armed themselves and met the Austrians at a place called Sempach. In those times, powder had not been invented, and men fought with spears, swords, and battle-axes. The Austrian soldiers stood shoulder to shoulder, each holding a long spear whose point projected far in front of him. The Swiss were armed with short swords and spears and it was impossible for them to get to the Austrians. For a while, their cause looked hopeless, but among the ranks of the Swiss was a brave man from one of the Forest Cantons. His name was Arnold von Winkelried (Win'-kel-ried). As he looked upon the bristling points of the Austrian spears, he saw that his comrades had no chance to win unless an opening could be made in that line. He determined to make such an opening even at the cost of his life. Extending his arms as far as he could, he rushed toward the Austrian line and gathered within his arms as many spears as he could grasp.

"Make way for liberty!" he cried—
Then ran, with arms extended wide,
As if his dearest friend to clasp;
Ten spears he swept within his grasp.
"Make way for liberty!" he cried—
Their keen points met from side to side.
He bowed among them like a tree,
And thus made way for liberty.

Pierced through and through, Winkelried fell dead, but he had made a gap in the Austrian line, and into this gap rushed the Swiss patriots. Victory was theirs and the Cantons were free.

Written Summation

At this time, a famous mountaineer named William Tell lived in one of the Forest Cantons. He was tall and strong. In all Switzerland, no man had a foot as sure as his on the mountains or a hand as skilled in the use of a bow. He was determined to resist the Austrians.

Model Practice 1

Model Practice 2

Model Practice 3

King Robert Bruce

from Famous Men of the Middle Ages
by John H. Haaren, LL.D. and A. B. Poland, Ph.D.
1306—1329 AD

The most famous king that Scotland ever had was Robert Bruce. He lived in the days when Edward I, Edward II, and Edward III were kings of England.

During the reign of Edward I, the king of Scotland died and thirteen men claimed the throne. Instead of fighting to decide which of them should be king, they asked Edward to settle the question. When he met the Scottish nobles and the rivals, each of whom thought that he would be wearing the crown, Edward told them that he would himself be their king. Just then, an English army marched up. What could the nobles do but kneel at the feet of Edward and promise to be his vassals? This they did; and so Scotland became a part of Edward's kingdom and Baliol (Ba'-li-ol), one of the rivals who claimed the Scottish throne, was made the vassal king.

Some time after this Edward ordered Baliol to raise an army and help him fight the French. Baliol refused to do this, so Edward marched with an army into Scotland and took him prisoner. He was determined that the Scotch should have no more kings of their own. So he carried away the sacred stone of Scone (scoon), on which all kings of Scotland had to sit when they were crowned, and put it in Westminster Abbey in London. (It remained there until 1996, when it was returned to Scotland. When it is not in use during coronation ceremonies, the stone is kept in Edinburgh Castle). It is said to have been the very stone that Jacob used for a pillow on the night that he saw, in his dream, angels ascending and descending on the ladder that reached from earth to heaven.

Edward now supposed, because he had this sacred stone and had put King Baliol in prison, that he had conquered Scotland.

But the men whom he appointed to govern the Scotch ruled unwisely and nearly all the people were discontent. Suddenly, an army of Scots was raised. It was led by Sir William Wallace, a knight who was almost a giant in size. Wallace's men drove the English out of the country and Wallace was made the "Guardian of the Realm."

Edward then led a great army against him. The Scottish soldiers were nearly all on foot. Wallace arranged them in hollow squares—spearmen on the outside, bowmen within. The English horsemen dashed vainly against thc walls of spear-points. But King Edward then brought his archers to the front. Thousands of arrows flew from their bows and thousands of Wallace's men fell dead. The spears were broken and the Scotch were defeated. Wallace barely escaped with his life. He was afterwards betrayed to Edward, who cruelly put him to death.

But the Scotch had learned what they could do and they still went on fighting for freedom, under two leaders named Robert Bruce and John Comyn. In response, Edward marched against them with another large army. Again, he won a great victory, and the nobles once more swore to obey him.

But in spite of this oath, Bruce meant to free Scotland if he could, and win the crown. He was privately crowned king of Scotland in the Abbey of Scone in 1306.

Bruce said to his wife, "Henceforth you are the queen, and I am the king of our country."

"I fear," said his wife, "that we are only playing at being king and queen, like children in their games."

"Nay, I shall be king in earnest," said Bruce.

The news that Bruce had been crowned roused all Scotland, and the people took up arms to fight under him against the English. But again King Edward defeated the Scotch and Bruce himself fled to the Grampian Hills.

For two months, he was closely pursued by the English who used bloodhounds to track him. He and his followers had many narrow escapes. Once he had to scramble barefoot up steep rocks, and another time all the party would have been captured had not Bruce awakened just in time to hear the approach of the enemy. He and his men lived by hunting and fishing.

However, many brave patriots joined them, until after a while Bruce had a small army. Five times, he attacked the English, and five times, he was beaten. After his last defeat, he fled from Scotland and took refuge in a wretched hut on an island off the north coast of Ireland. Here he stayed all alone during one winter.

It is said that one day, while he was very downhearted, he saw a spider trying to spin a web between two beams of his hut. The little creature tried to throw a thread from one beam to another, but failed. Not discouraged, it tried four times more without success.

"Five times has the spider failed," said Bruce. "That is just the number of times the English have defeated me. If the spider has courage to try again, I also will try to free Scotland!"

He watched the spider. It rested for a while as if to gain strength, and then threw its slender thread toward the beam. This time it succeeded.

"I thank God!" exclaimed Bruce. "The spider has taught me a lesson. No more will I be discouraged."

About this time, Edward I died and his son, Edward II, succeeded to the throne of England. For about two years, the new king paid little attention to Scotland.

Meantime Bruce captured nearly all the Scotch castles that were held by the English, and the nobles and chiefs throughout the country acknowledged him as their king.

At last, Edward II marched into Scotland at the head of a hundred thousand men. Bruce met him at Bannockburn on June 24, 1314, with thirty thousand soldiers.

Before the battle began, Bruce rode along the front of his army to encourage his men. Suddenly an English knight, Henry de Bohun, galloped across the field and tried to strike him down with a spear. Bruce saw his danger in time and with a quick stroke of his battle-axe cleft the knight's skull.

The Scotch army shouted again and again at this feat of their commander, and they went into the battle feeling sure that the victory would be theirs. They rushed upon the English with fury and although outnumbered three to one, completely defeated them. Thousands of the English died and a great number captured.

In spite of this terrible blow, Edward never gave up his claim to the Scottish crown. But his son Edward III, in 1328, recognized Scotland's independence and acknowledged Bruce as her king.

Written Summation

Bruce said to his wife, "Henceforth you are the queen, and I am the king of our country."

"I fear," said his wife, "that we are only playing at being king and queen, like children in their games."

"Nay, I shall be king in earnest," said Bruce.

Model Practice 1

Model Practice 2

Model Practice 3

Edward the Black Prince

from Famous Men of the Middle Ages
by John H. Haaren, LL.D. and A. B. Poland, Ph.D.
1330 – 1376 AD

One of the most famous warriors of the Middle Ages was Edward the Black Prince. He was so called because he wore black armor in battle.

The Black Prince was the son of Edward III who reigned over England from 1327 to 1377. He won his fame as a soldier in the wars which his father carried on against France.

You remember that the early kings of England, from the time of William the Conqueror, had possessions in France. Henry II, William's grandson, was the duke of Normandy and lord of Brittany and other provinces, and when he married Eleanor of Aquitaine, she brought him that province also.

Henry's son John lost all the French possessions of the English crown except a part of Aquitaine, and Edward III inherited this. So when Philip of Valois (val-wah') became king of France, about a year after Edward had become king of England, Edward had to do homage to Philip.

To be king of England and yet to do homage to the king of France—to bend the knee before Philip and kiss his foot—was something Edward did not like. He thought it was quite beneath his dignity, as his ancestor Rollo had thought when told that he must kiss the foot of King Charles.

So Edward tried to persuade the nobles of France that he himself ought by right to be the king of France instead of being only a vassal. Philip of Valois was only a cousin of the late French King Charles IV. Edward was the son of his sister. But there was a curious old law in France, called the Salic Law, which forbade that daughters should inherit lands. This law barred the claim of Edward, because his claim came through his mother. Still he determined to win the French throne by force of arms.

A chance came to quarrel with Philip. Another of Philip's vassals rebelled against him, and Edward helped the rebel. He hoped by doing so to weaken Philip and more easily overpower him.

Philip at once declared that Edward's possessions in France were forfeited. Then Edward raised an army of thirty thousand men, and with it invaded France.

The Black Prince was now only about sixteen years of age, but he had already shown himself brave in battle, and his father put him in command of one of the divisions of the army.

Thousands of French troops led by King Philip hurried from Paris to meet the advance of the English; and on the 26th of August, 1346, the two armies fought a hard battle at the village of Crécy.

During the battle, the division of the English army commanded by the Black Prince had to bear the attack of the whole French force.

The prince fought so bravely and managed his men so well that King Edward, who was overlooking the field of battle from a windmill on the top of a hill, sent him words of praise for his gallant work.

Again and again, the prince's men drove back the French in splendid style. But at last they seemed about to give way before a fierce charge, and the earl of Warwick hastened to Edward to advise him to send the prince aid.

"Is my son dead or unhorsed or so wounded that he cannot help himself?" asked the king.

"No, Sire," was the reply; "but he is hard pressed."

"Return to your post, and come not to me again for aid so long as my son lives," said the king. "Let the boy prove himself a true knight and win his spurs."

The earl went to the prince and told him what his father had said. "I will prove myself a true knight," exclaimed the prince. "My father is right. I need no aid. My men will hold their post as long as they have strength to stand."

Then he rode where the battle was still furiously raging, and encouraged his men. The king of France led his force a number of times against the prince's line, but could not break it and was at last compelled to retire.

The battle now went steadily against the French, although they far outnumbered the English. Finally, forty thousand of Philip's soldiers lay dead upon the field and nearly all the remainder of his army was captured. Philip gave up the struggle and fled. Among those who fought on the side of the French at Crécy was the blind king of Bohemia, who always wore three white feathers in his helmet. When the battle was at its height, the blind king had his followers lead him into the thick of the fight, and he dealt heavy blows upon his unseen foes until he fell mortally wounded. The three white feathers were taken from his helmet by the Black Prince, who forever after wore them himself.

As soon as he could, King Edward rode over the field to meet his son. "Prince," he said, as he greeted him, "you are the conqueror of the French." Turning to the soldiers, who had gathered around him, the king shouted, "Cheer, cheer for the Black Prince! Cheer for the hero of Crécy!"

What cheering then rose on the battlefield! The air rang with the name of the Black Prince.

Soon after the battle of Crécy, King Edward laid siege to Calais; but the city resisted his attack for twelve months. During the siege, the Black Prince aided his father greatly.

After the capture of Calais, it was agreed to stop fighting for seven years, and Edward's army embarked for England.

In 1355, Edward again declared war against the French. The Black Prince invaded France with an army of sixty thousand men. He captured rich towns and gathered a great deal of booty. While he was preparing to move on Paris, the king of France raised a great army and marched against him.

The Black Prince had lost so many men by sickness that he had only about ten thousand when he reached the city of Poitiers. Suddenly, near the city, he was met by the French force of about fifty-five thousand, splendidly armed and commanded by the king himself.

"God help us!" exclaimed the prince, as he looked at the long lines of the French marching on the plain before him.

Early on the morning of September 14, 1356, the battle began. The English were few in number, but they were determined to contest every inch of ground and not surrender while a hundred of them remained to fight. For hours, they withstood the onset of the French. At last a body of English horsemen charged furiously on one part of the French line, while the Black Prince attacked another part.

This sudden movement caused confusion among the French. Many of them fled from the field. When the Black Prince saw this, he shouted to his men, "Advance, English banners, in the name of God and St. George!" His army rushed forward and the French were defeated. Thousands of prisoners were taken, including the king of France and many of his nobles.

The king was sent to England, where he was treated with the greatest kindness. When, some time afterwards there was a splendid procession in London to celebrate the victory of Poitiers, he was allowed to ride in the procession on a beautiful white horse, while the Black Prince rode on a pony at his side.

The Black Prince died in 1376. He was sincerely mourned by the English people. They felt that they had lost a prince who would have made a great and good king.

Written Summation

"Is my son dead or unhorsed or so wounded that he cannot help himself?" asked the king.

"No, Sire," was the reply; "but he is hard pressed."

"Return to your post, and come not to me again for aid so long as my son lives," said the king. "Let the boy prove himself a true knight and win his spurs."

Model Practice 1 (adapted from the original)

Model Practice 2

Model Practice 3

Henry V

from Famous Men of the Middle Ages
by John H. Haaren, LL.D. and A. B. Poland, Ph.D.
1413 – 1422 AD

Of all the kings that England ever had, Henry V was perhaps the greatest favorite among the people. They liked him because he was handsome and brave and, above all, because he conquered France.

In his youth, Prince Hal, as the people called him, had a number of merry companions who sometimes got themselves into trouble by their pranks. Once one of them was arrested and brought before the chief justice of the kingdom.

Prince Hal was displeased because sentence was given against his companion and he drew his sword, threatening the judge. Upon this, the judge bravely ordered the prince to be arrested and put into prison.

Prince Hal submitted to his punishment with good grace and his father is reported to have said, "Happy is the monarch who has so just a judge, and a son so willing to obey the law."

One of Prince Hal's companions was a fat old knight named Sir John Falstaff. Once Falstaff was boasting that he and three men had beaten and almost killed two men in buckram suits who had attacked and tried to rob them. The prince led him on and gave him a chance to brag as much as he wanted to, until finally Falstaff swore that there were at least a hundred robbers and that he himself fought with fifty. Then Prince Hal told their companions that only two men had attacked Falstaff and his friends, and that he and another man who was present were those two. And he said that Falstaff, instead of fighting, had run as fast as his legs could carry him.

There was real goodness as well as merriment in Prince Hal. And so the people found; for when he became king on the death of his father, he told his wild companions that the days of his wildness were over. And he advised them to lead better lives in future.

As Henry V, Prince Hal became famous in English history because of his war with France.

Normandy, you remember, had belonged to Henry's ancestor, William the Conqueror. It had been taken from King John of England by the French king, Philip Augustus, in 1203.

Soon after his coronation, Henry sent a demand to the French king that Normandy should be restored, and he made the claim which his great-grandfather, Edward III, had made that he was by right the king of France.

Of course, the king of France would not acknowledge this. Henry therefore raised an army of thirty thousand men and invaded France.

Before he began to attack the French, he gave strict orders to his men that they were to harm no one who was not a soldier and to take nothing from the houses or farms of any persons who were not fighting.

Sickness broke out among Henry's troops after they landed, so that their number was reduced to about fifteen thousand. Fifty or sixty thousand Frenchmen were encamped on the field of Agincourt (äzh-an-koor') to oppose this little army.

The odds were greatly against Henry. The night before the battle one of his officers said he wished that the many thousand brave soldiers who were quietly sleeping in their beds in England were with the king.

"I would not have a single man more," said Henry. "If god give us victory, it will be plain we owe it to His grace. If not, the fewer we are the less loss for England."

The men drew courage from their king. The English archers poured arrows into the ranks of their opponents; and although the French fought bravely, they were completely routed. Eleven thousand Frenchmen fell. Among the slain were more than a hundred of the nobles of the land.

Agincourt was not the last of Henry's victories. He brought a second army of forty thousand men over to France. Town after town was captured, and at last, Henry and his victorious troops laid siege to Rouen, which was then the largest and richest city in France.

The fortifications were so strong that Henry could not storm them, so he determined to take the place by starving the garrison. He said, "War has three handmaidens—fire, blood, and famine. I have chosen the meekest of the three."

He had trenches dug round the town and placed soldiers in them to prevent citizens from going out of the city for supplies, and to prevent the country people from taking provisions in.

A great number of the country people had left their homes when they heard that the English army was marching towards Rouen, and had taken refuge within the city walls. After the siege had gone on for six months there was so little food left in the place that the commander of the garrison ordered these poor people to go back to their homes.

Twelve thousand were put outside the gates, but Henry would not allow them to pass through his lines; so they starved to death between the walls of the French and the trenches of the English.

As winter came on the suffering of the citizens was terrible. At last, they determined to set fire to the city, open their gates, and make a last desperate attack on the English.

Henry wished to preserve the city and offered such generous terms of surrender that the people accepted them. Not only Rouen but the whole of Normandy, which the French had held for two hundred years, was now forced to submit to Henry.

The war continued for about two years more, and the English gained possession of such a large part of France that at Christmas Henry entered Paris itself in triumph.

Strangely, the king against whom he had been fighting and over whom he was triumphing sat by his side as he rode through the streets. What did this mean? It meant that the French were so terrified by the many victories of Henry that all—king and people—were willing to give him whatever he asked.

A treaty was made that as the king was feeble Henry should be regent of the kingdom and that when the king died Henry should succeed him as king of France.

In the treaty, the French king also agreed to give to Henry his daughter, the Princess Katherine, in marriage. She became the mother of the English King, Henry VI.

The arrangement that an English sovereign should be king of France was never put into effect. In less than two years after the treaty was signed, the reign of the great conqueror came to an end. Henry died.

In the reign of his son, all his work in gaining French territory was undone. By the time that Henry VI was twenty years old, England, as you will read in the story of Joan of Arc, had nothing left of all that had been won by so many years of war except the single town of Calais.

Written Summation

"I would not have a single man more," said Henry. "If god give us victory, it will be plain we owe it to His grace. If not, the fewer we are the less loss for England."

The men drew courage from their king. The English archers poured arrows into the ranks of their opponents; and although the French fought bravely, they were completely routed. Eleven thousand Frenchmen fell.

Model Practice 1

Model Practice 2

Model Practice 3

Joan of Arc

from Famous Men of the Middle Ages
by John H. Haaren, LL.D. and A. B. Poland, Ph.D.
1412 – 1431 AD

In the long wars between the French and English, not even the Black Prince or King Henry V gained as much fame as a young French peasant girl, Joan of Arc.

She was born in the little village of Domrémy (dom-re-me'). Her father had often told her about the sad condition of France—how the country was largely in the possession of England, and how the French king did not dare to be crowned.

And so the thought came to her mind, "How I pity my country!" She brooded over the matter very much. Eventually, she claimed to have visions of angels and heard strange voices, which said to her, "Joan, you can deliver the land from the English. Go to the relief of King Charles." These strange visions and voices made the young girl believe that she had a mission from God, and she determined to try to save France.

When she told her father and mother of her purpose, they attempted to persuade her that the visions of angels and the voices telling her of the divine mission were but dreams.

"I tell thee, Joan," said her father, "it is thy fancy. Thou hadst better have a kind husband to take care of thee, and do some work to employ thy mind."

"Father, I must do what God has willed, for this is no work of my choosing," she replied. "Mother, I would far rather sit and spin by your side than take part in war. My mission is no dream. I know that I have been chosen by the Lord to fulfill His purpose and nothing can prevent me from going where He purposes to send me."

The village priest, her young companions, even the governor of the town, all tried to stop her, but it was in vain.

To the governor she said, "I must do the work my Lord has laid out for me."

Little by little, people began to believe in her mission. At last, all stopped trying to discourage her and some who were wealthy helped her make the journey to the town of Chinon (she-non'), where the French king, Charles the Seventh, was living.

When Joan arrived at Chinon, a force of French soldiers was preparing to go to the south of France to relieve the city of Orleans, which the English were besieging.

King Charles received Joan kindly and listened to what she had to say with deep attention. The girl spoke modestly, but with a calm belief that she was right.

"Gracious King," she said, "my name is Joan. God has sent me to deliver France from her enemies. You shall shortly be crowned in the cathedral of Rheims (remz). I am to lead the soldiers you are about to send for the relief of Orleans. So God has directed, and under my guidance, victory will be theirs."

The king and his nobles talked the matter over and finally decided to allow Joan to lead an army of about five thousand men against the English at Orleans.

When she left Chinon at the head of her soldiers, in April, 1429, she was in her eighteenth year. Mounted on a fine war-horse and clad in white armor from head to foot, she rode along past the cheering multitude, "seeming rather," it has been said, "of heaven than earth." In one hand, she carried an ancient sword that she had found near the tomb of a saint, and in the other, a white banner embroidered with lilies.

The rough soldiers who were near her discontinued their oaths and coarse manners, and carefully guarded her. She inspired the whole army with courage and faith as she talked about her visions.

When she arrived at the besieged city of Orleans, she fearlessly rode round its walls, while the English soldiers looked on in astonishment. She was able to enter Orleans, despite the efforts of the besiegers to prevent her.

She aroused the city by her cheerful, confident words and then led her soldiers forth to give battle to the English. Their success was amazing. One after another, the English forts were taken.

When only the strongest remained and Joan was leading the attacking force, she received a slight wound and was carried out of the battle to be attended by a surgeon. Her soldiers began to retreat.

"Wait," she commanded, "eat and drink and rest; for as soon as I recover I will touch the walls with my banner and you shall enter the fort."

In a few minutes, she mounted her horse again and riding rapidly up to the fort, touched it with her banner. Her soldier almost instantly carried it. The next day, the enemy's troops were forced to withdraw from before the city and the siege was at end.

The French soldiers were jubilant at the victory and called Joan the "Maid of Orleans." By this name, she is known in history. Her fame spread everywhere, and the English as well as the French thought she had more than human power.

She led the French in several other battles, and repeatedly her troops were victorious.

At last, the English were driven far to the north of France. Then Charles, urged by Joan, went to Rheims with twelve thousand soldiers, and there, with splendid ceremonies, was crowned king. Joan holding her white banner, stood near Charles during the coronation.

When the ceremony was finished, she knelt at his feet and said, "O King, the will of God is done and my mission is over! Let me now go home to my parents."

But the king urged her to stay a while longer, as France was not entirely freed from the English. Joan consented, but she said, "I hear the heavenly voices no more and I am afraid."

However, she took part in an attack upon the army of the Duke of Burgundy, but was taken prisoner by him. For a large sum of money, the duke delivered her into the hands of the English, who put her in prison in Rouen. She lay in prison for a year, and finally was charged with sorcery and brought to trial. It was said that she was under the influence of the Evil One. She declared to her judges her innocence of the charge and said, "God has always been my guide in all that I have done. The devil has never had power over me."

Her trial was long and tiresome. At its close, she was doomed to be burned at the stake.

So in the market-place at Rouen, the English soldiers fastened her to a stake surrounded by a great pile of bundled twigs and branches.

A soldier put into her hands a rough cross, which he had made from a stick that he held. She thanked him and pressed it to her bosom. Then a good priest, standing near the stake, read to her the prayers for the dying, and another mounted the bundles branches and held towards her a crucifix, which she clasped with both hands and kissed. When the cruel flames burst out around her, the noble girl uttered the word "Jesus," and expired. A statue of her now stands on the spot where she suffered.

Written Summation

"Father, I must do what God has willed, for this is no work of my choosing," she replied. "Mother, I would far rather sit and spin by your side than take part in war. My mission is no dream. I know that I have been chosen by the Lord to fulfill His purpose and nothing can prevent me from going where He purposes to send me."

Model Practice 1

Model Practice 2

Model Practice 3

Gutenberg

from Famous Men of the Middle Ages
by John H. Haaren, LL.D. and A. B. Poland, Ph.D.
1400 – 1468 AD

While Joan of Arc was busy rescuing France from the English, another wonderful worker was busy in Germany. This was John Gutenberg, who was born in Mainz.

The Germans—and most other people—think that he was the inventor of the art of printing with movable types. So in the cities of Dresden and Mainz, his countrymen have put up statues in his memory.

Gutenberg's father was from a good family. Very likely, he learned to read as a boy. But the books he learned from were not like ours; they were written by hand. A better name for them than books is "manuscripts," which means "hand-writings."

While Gutenberg was growing up, a new way of making books was developed, one that was a great deal better than copying by hand. It is called block-printing. The printer first cut a block of hard wood the size of the page that he was going to print. Then he cut out every word of the written page upon the smooth face of his block. This had to be done very carefully. When it was finished, the printer had to cut away the wood from the sides of every letter. This left the letters raised, as the letters are in books now printed for the blind.

The block was now ready to be used. The letters were inked and paper was laid upon them and pressed down.

With blocks, the printer could make copies of a book a great deal faster than a man could write them by hand. But the making of the blocks took a long time, and each block would print only one page.

Gutenberg enjoyed reading the manuscripts and block books that his parents and their wealthy friends owned. He often said it was a pity that only rich people could own books. Finally, he contrived an easier and quicker way of printing.

He did a great deal of his work in secret, for he thought it was much better that his neighbors did not know what he was doing.

So he looked for a workshop where no one would be able to find him. He was now living in Strasburg, where there was an old abandoned building once inhabited by a number of monks. There was one room of the building that only needed minor repairs to make it usable. So Gutenberg acquired the rights to repair that room and use it as his workshop.

All his neighbors wondered what became of him when he left his home in the early morning, and where he had been when they saw him coming back late in the twilight. Some felt sure that he must be a wizard, and that he had meetings somewhere with the devil, and that the devil was helping him to do some strange business.

Gutenberg did not care what people had to say, and in his quiet room he patiently tried one experiment after another, often feeling very sad and discouraged day after day because his experiments did not succeed.

At last, the time came when he had no money left. He went back to his old home, Mainz, and there met a rich goldsmith named Fust (or Faust).

Gutenberg told him how hard he had tried in Strasburg to find a way to produce books cheaply, and how he had no more money to continue his experiments. Fust became deeply interested and gave Gutenberg the money he needed. But as the experiments did not at first succeed Fust lost patience. He quarreled with Gutenberg and said that he was doing nothing but spending money. Eventually, he sued him in court, and the judge decided in favor of Fust. So everything in the world that Gutenberg had, even the tools with which he worked, came into Fust's possession.

But though he had lost his tools, Gutenberg had not lost his courage. And he had not lost all his friends. One of them had money, and he bought Gutenberg a new set of tools and rented a workshop for him. Now at last Gutenberg's hopes were fulfilled.

First, it is thought that he made types of hard wood. Each type was a little block with a single letter at one end. Such types were a great deal better than block letters. The block letters were fixed and could not be taken out of the words which they composed. The new types were movable so they could be set up to print one page, then taken apart and set up again and again to print any number of pages.

But type made of wood did not always print the letters clearly and distinctly, so Gutenberg gave up wood types and tried metal types. Soon a Latin Bible was printed. It was in two volumes, each of which had three hundred pages, while each of the pages had forty-two lines. The letters were sharp and clear. They had been printed from movable types of metal.

The Dutch claim that Lorenz Coster, a native of Harlem, in the Netherlands, was the first person who printed with movable type. They say that one day Coster was taking a walk in a beech forest not far from Harlem, and that he cut bark from one of the trees and shaped it into letters with his knife.

Not long after this, the Dutch say Coster had made movable types and was printing and selling books in Harlem.

The news that books were being printed in Mainz by Gutenberg went all over Europe, and before he died, printing-presses like his were at work making books in all the great cities of the continent.

About twenty years after his death, when Venice was the richest of European cities, a man named Aldus (Al'-dus) Manutius (Ma-nu'-tius) established the most famous printing house of that time. He was at work printing books two years before Columbus sailed on his first voyage. The descendents of Aldus continued the business after his death for about one hundred years. The books published by them were called "Aldine," from Aldus. They were the most beautiful that had ever come from the press. They are admired and valued to this day.

Written Summation

While Joan of Arc was busy rescuing France from the English, another wonderful worker was busy in Germany. This was John Gutenberg, who was born in Mainz.

The Germans—and most other people—think that he was the inventor of the art of printing with movable types. So in the cities of Dresden and Mainz, his countrymen have put up statues in his memory.

Model Practice 1

Model Practice 2

Model Practice 3

Warwick the Kingmaker

from Famous Men of the Middle Ages
by John H. Haaren, LL.D. and A. B. Poland, Ph.D.
1428 – 1471 AD

The earl of Warwick, known as the "kingmaker," was the most famous man in England for many years after the death of Henry V. He lived in a great castle with two towers higher than most church spires. It is one of the handsomest dwellings in the world and is visited every year by thousands of people. The kingmaker had a guard of six hundred men. At his house in London, meals were served to so many people that six fat oxen were eaten at breakfast alone. He had a hundred and ten estates in different parts of England and no less than 30,000 persons were fed daily at his expense. He owned the whole city of Worcester, and three islands besides this, Jersey, Guernsey and Alderney, so famed in our time for their cattle, also belonged to him.

He had a cousin of whom he was as fond of as if he were a brother. This was Richard, duke of York, who was also own cousin to King Henry VI, the son of Henry V.

One evening as the sun was setting, and the warders were going to close the gates of the city of York for the night, a loud blast of a horn was heard. It was made by the sentry on the wall near the southern gate. An armed troop was approaching. When they drew near the gate, their scarlet coats embroidered with the figure of a boar proved them to be the men of the earl of Warwick. The earl himself was behind them. The gate was opened.

Passing through it and on to the castle, the earl and his company were soon within its strong stone walls.

"Cousin," said the earl of Warwick to the duke of York as they sat talking before a huge log fire in the great room of the castle, "England will not long endure the misrule of a king who is half the time out of his mind."

The earl spoke the truth. Every now and then Henry VI lost his reason, and the duke of York, or some other nobleman, had to govern the kingdom for him.

The earl of Warwick added, "You are the rightful heir to the throne. The claim of Henry VI comes through Lancaster, the fourth son of Edward III—yours through Lionel, the second. His claim comes through his father only—yours through both your father and mother. It is a better claim and it is a double claim."

"That is true, my cousin of Warwick," replied the duke of York, "but we must not plunge England into war."

"Surely not if we can help it," replied the earl. "Let us first ask for reform. If the king heeds our petition, well and good. If not, I am determined, cousin of York, that you shall sit on the throne of England instead of our insane sovereign."

Soon, a petition was drawn up, signed, and presented to Henry, asking that Henry do something to make the people content.

The king paid no attention to it. Then a war began. It was the longest and most terrible that ever took place in England. It lasted for thirty years.

Those who fought on the king's side were called Lancastrians, because Henry's ancestor, John of Gaunt, was the duke of Lancaster. The friends of Richard were called Yorkists, because he was duke of York. The Lancastrians took a red rose for their badge; the Yorkists a white one. For this reason, the long struggle was called the "War of the Roses."

In the first great battle, the Red Rose party was defeated and the king himself was taken prisoner.

The victors now thought that the duke of York ought to be made king at once. However, a parliament was called to decide the question, and it was agreed that Henry should be king as long as he lived, but that at his death the crown should pass to the duke of York.

Most people though this was a wise arrangement; but Queen Margaret, Henry's wife, did not like it at all, because it took from her son the right to reign after his father's death. So she went to Scotland and the North of England, where she had many friends, and raised an army.

She was a brave woman and led her men in a battle in which she gained the victory. The duke of York was killed, and the queen ordered some of her men to cut off his head, put upon it a paper crown in mockery, and fix it over one of the gates of the city of York.

Warwick attacked the queen as soon as he could; but again she was victorious and captured from Warwick her husband, the king, whom the earl had held prisoner for some time past.

This was a great triumph for Margaret, for Henry became king once more.

But the people were still discontent. The York party was determined that Edward, the son of the old duke of York, should be made king. So thousands flocked to the White Rose standard and Warwick marched to London at their head.

The queen saw that her only safety was in flight. She left London and the kingmaker entered the city in triumph.

The citizens had been very fond of the old duke of York, and when his party proclaimed his handsome young son King Edward IV, the city resounded with the cry "God save King Edward."

Brave Queen Margaret was completey defeated in another battle. The story is told that after this she fled into a forest with her young son. A robber met them, but Margaret, with wonderful courage, said to him, "I am your queen and this is your prince. I entrust him to your care."

The man was pleased with the confidence that she showed. He took her and the young prince to a safe hiding place, and helped them to escape from England in a sailing vessel.

Edward IV now seemed to be seated securely upon the throne. But trouble was near. Warwick wished him to follow his advice. Edward thought he could manage without any advice. Then the king and the kingmaker quarreled, and at last became open enemies and fought one another on the field of battle. The end of it was that Warwick was defeated, and driven out of the country. He sailed across the channel and sought refuge in France.

There whom should he meet but his old enemy, Queen Margaret. She had beaten him in battle, and had beheaded his cousin Richard, duke of York; he had beaten her and driven her from her kingdom; and twice he had made her husband prisoner and taken from him his crown. In spite of all this the two became fast friends, and the kingmaker agreed to make war upon Edward and restore Henry to the throne.

He asked assistance from Louis XI, King of France, who supplied him with men and money. So with an army of Frenchmen, the kingmaker landed on the shores of England. Thousands of Englishmen who were tired of Edward flocked to Warwick's standard. And when he reached London, he had an army of sixty thousand men.

Edward fled without waiting for a battle and escaped to the Netherlands in a sailing-vessel. The kingmaker had now no one to resist him. The gates of London were opened to him, and the citizens heartily welcomed him. Marching to the Tower, he brought out the old king and placed him once more upon the throne.

But though Edward had fled, he was not discouraged. He followed the example of the kingmaker and asked aid from foreign friends. The duke of Burgundy supplied him with money and soldiers, and he was soon back in England.

His army grew larger and larger every day. People had been very dissatisfied with Edward and had rejoiced when Henry replaced him as king, because if Henry was not clever he was good. But in a short time, they learned that England needed a king who was not only good but capable.

So when Edward and his French soldiers landed, most people in England welcomed them. The kingmaker was now on the wrong side.

Edward met him in battle at a place called Barnet, and completely defeated him. Warwick was killed, and Henry once more became prisoner.

In another battle, both Margaret and her son were made prisoners. The son was brutally murdered in the presence of King Edward. Margaret was placed in the Tower, and King Henry, who died soon after the battle of Tewksbury, was probably poisoned by order of Edward.

In 1438, after a reign of twenty-two years, Edward died, leaving two sons. Both were boys, so Edward's brother, Richard, duke of Gloucester, was made regent until young Edward V, the older of the two, should come of age.

But Richard was determined to make himself king. So he put both the young princes in the Tower. He than hired ruffians to murder them. One night, when the little princes were asleep, the murderers smothered them with pillows and buried their bodies at the foot of a stairway in the Tower, and there, after many years, their bones were found.

After Richard had murdered his two nephews, he was crowned king, as Richard III, was very pleased that his plans had succeeded so well. He thought that now no one could lay claim to the throne. But he was mistaken. One person did claim it. This was Henry Tudor, earl of Richmond.

Henry's father, Edmund Tudor, was only a Welsh gentleman, but was the half-brother of Henry VI through their mother Queen Katherine. Henry's mother was descended from John of Gaunt, fourth son of Edward III, and thus through his mother he was of royal blood and a Lancastrian.

When Richard III by his wickedness and cruelty had made all England hate him, the Red Rose party gathered about Henry Tudor, raised an army, and fought against the king in the battle of Bosworth.

Richard was a bad man, but he was brave, and he fought like a lion. However, it was all in vain. He was defeated and killed. His body was thrown on the back of a horse, carried to a church near the field of battle and buried.

The battered crown which Richard had worn was picked up and placed on Henry's head and the whole Lancastrian army shouted, "Long live King Henry!"

Parliament voted that Henry Tudor and his heirs should be kings of England. Not long afterwards, Henry married the heiress of the house of York. Thus, both the Red Roses and the White were satisfied, as the king was a Lancastrian and the queen a Yorkist. So the long and terrible Wars of the Roses came to an end.

Written Summation

Most people thought this was a wise arrangement; but Queen Margaret, Henry's wife, did not like it at all, because it took from her son the right to reign after his father's death. So she went to Scotland and the North of England, where she had many friends, and raised an army.

Model Practice 1

Model Practice 2

Model Practice 3

Christopher Columbus

from Famous men of Modern times
by John H. Haaren, LL.D. and A. B. Poland, Ph.D.
1435 – 1506 AD

One day in the autumn of 1486 a stranger knocked at the gate of a convent called "La Rabida," not far from the little Spanish seaport of Palos. He held by the hand a little boy, and when the monk who opened the door asked what was wanted he answered, "My child and I are tired and hungry. Will you give us a morsel of bread and let us rest here awhile?"

They were invited to enter, and food was set before them. During the meal the stranger began to talk about the Western Ocean and what must be on the other side of it. "Most men," he said, "think that beyond the Azores there is nothing but a sea of darkness; but I believe that beyond those islands there is another and a larger land."

The prior of the convent, and the physician of Palos who happened to be present, were greatly interested in what their visitor had to say, and asked him to tell them his name and something of his history.

"I am called Christopher Columbus," he said. "I was born in Genoa, and there my boyhood was spent. I loved as a child to watch the sailors haul up the anchor and let loose the sails when a ship began her voyage. My play was to learn the names of the ropes and find out what each was for.

"My father sent me to the University of Pavia; and there I learned about the stars that guide the seaman on his way. I also learned to draw maps and charts. While drawing those maps, I used to wonder whether there was not some land beyond the Canaries and the Azores.

"At fifteen I became a sailor. I went on voyages to England and Ireland, to Greece and elsewhere. On one of my voyages our ship was wrecked on the rocky coast of Portugal, but I got to land by the help of a plank. I stayed awhile in Portugal, and there I married the daughter of a sea captain who was the governor of Porto Santo, one of the Madeira Islands.

"I afterwards visited Porto Santo, and there I met many men whose lives were spent in sailing the sea. They told me some wonderful tales. One said that a Portuguese pilot named Martin Vincente had picked up at sea, twelve hundred miles west of Portugal, a piece of strange wood that had been carved by the hand of man. My brother-in-law said that he had seen at Porto Santo great pieces of jointed canes; and that a friend had told him about two human bodies which had been washed up at Flores, very broad-faced and not at all like Christians.

"All these things made me believe more firmly in the idea of a land to the westward; and at length I determined to find that land.

"But I was poor. I could not buy a ship nor pay a crew. I went to my native Genoa, where the masts in the harbor rise as close as the trees in a wood. I explained my plans to the rich merchants there, and begged them to help me. But my countrymen were afraid to send any vessel of theirs beyond the Azores. They thought that west of those islands, there was nothing but the 'Sea of Darkness.'

"I went to Lisbon and asked the Portuguese king for help. Again I was disappointed; but I was not discouraged.

"I then came to Spain, and at last the good Queen Isabella heard my story. A council of learned men was called to consider my plan. They said it was wild, and advised her Majesty to give me no aid.

"Thus, I am again disappointed. The little money that I had is spent, and I am a beggar. It seems as if the world is against me. Yet I am sure that there is a land beyond the sea."

The prior, the physician, and the monks who had gathered about Columbus were much interested. Father Perez, one of the monks, had been confessor to Queen Isabella, and he wrote a letter to her begging that she would see Columbus again. She consented, and Columbus went from the convent to the palace to see her.

The queen again refused his request, and Columbus set out for France hoping that the king of that country might help him. But one of the officers of Isabella's court persuaded her to change her mind, and a messenger was sent to bring Columbus back into the royal presence.

King Ferdinand and Queen Isabella were in camp at Santa Fe near Granada, which they had but lately captured from the Moors; and there they signed an agreement to supply Columbus with two ships, and to pay the crews.

It was easy for the sovereigns to promise crews and to pay them; but it was very hard to find men who were willing to sail on such a voyage. Even the criminals, who were promised pardon if they would go, refused. To sail into the "Sea of Darkness" seemed certain death to them.

At last, however, all difficulties were overcome.

Two wealthy gentlemen added a third ship to the two supplied by the king and queen; and the wonderful voyage began. The Santa Maria with a crew of fifty men was commanded by Columbus himself; the Pinta with thirty men was in the charge of Martin Pinzon; and the Nina or "Baby" with twenty-four men was commanded by Martin's brother, Vincente Pinzon.

At eight o'clock on the morning of August 3, 1492, the sails were hoisted, and the little expedition left the harbor of Palos.

On the third day out, the Pinta lost her rudder. Fortunately they were then not far from the Canary Islands. They therefore steered for Teneriffe where they had the vessel repaired.

When they had sailed about six weeks, they were astonished to find that the magnetic needle varied from its usual direction. Soon after observing this, they reached a part of the ocean where a great field of seaweed lay all around them. This was what is called the " Sargasso Sea," and the ships of Columbus were the first that ever sailed across it.

They observed another strange thing. The wind in this part of the ocean blew steadily, night and day, to the westward. It was the northeast trade wind, which was unknown to sailors along the coast and in the inland seas.

They had excellent weather; but the men began to be fearful lest they could never beat back against the trade wind; and it was hard to keep them in good spirits.

Happily, soon afterward, they saw some birds, and that made them sure that land was not far off. Then the Pinta fished up a fragment of sugar cane and a log of wood; and the Nina sighted a green branch covered with dog-rose flowers.

At ten o'clock one night, Columbus saw a light ahead; and the next morning they landed on one of the Bahama Islands. Which island this was we are not quite sure; but it was probably the one which the natives called Guanahani. Columbus named it San Salvador.

When Columbus stepped from his boat, he carried with him the royal banner of Spain. Kneeling upon the shore with his companions, he kissed the ground, gave thanks to God, and took possession of the land in the name of Ferdinand and Isabella.

The expedition afterwards discovered the islands of Cuba, Haiti and others of the West India group.

On the shore of Haiti, the Santa Maria went ashore and became a wreck. With the two remaining vessels, Columbus soon afterwards set sail for Spain, and on the 15th of March, 1493, he dropped anchor in the port of Palos.

Ferdinand and Isabella were then at Barcelona, and they received him with great honor. He showed them curious plants and gayly-colored parrots, and, more interesting than these, nine natives whom he had brought from the newly discovered islands.

There was now no doubt that Columbus was right, and that the "Sea of Darkness" beyond the Azores was only a dream.

It was determined that Columbus should make another expedition. In six months seventeen vessels and fifteen hundred men were ready to sail, and the second great voyage was begun. It was on this voyage that Jamaica, Porto Rico, and several smaller islands were discovered.

Most of the fifteen hundred men, however, went with Columbus, not in the hope of discovering new lands, but for the purpose of colonizing the island of Haiti. Columbus had learned on his first voyage that on that island there were deposits of gold; so now a mining town was founded in the gold region of Haiti, and the work of digging was begun. But the Spaniards were not fond of work. They therefore made slaves of the natives and forced them to dig in the mines; and a large quantity of gold was secured.

Some of the greedy colonists thought of another and easier way of making money. They captured a number of the natives and sent them to Spain to be sold as slaves; and, strange to say, Columbus permitted this.

When Queen Isabella heard of it, she was very angry with Columbus, and asked him who had given him the right to make slaves of her subjects. She commanded that every one of the Indians should be made free and sent home.

This enslaving of the Indians was the beginning of the downfall of Columbus. Isabella never afterwards felt toward him as she had before.

However, when he returned to Spain he related a pitiful tale about the sufferings of the colonists in Haiti; and the queen furnished him with supplies for them, and provided a fleet of six vessels with which he set sail on May 30, 1498.

On this third voyage, a new land was discovered. One day, three hill-tops were seen rising out of the sea, and soon the ships approached a large island. Columbus called it, from its three peaks, Trinidad, and the island is still known by that name.

From Trinidad, they sailed to the southwest until they approached another shore. Columbus had now discovered the southern grand division of the New World, but he did not know this. He supposed that the land was only another island. He was anxious to get back to the colony on the island of Haiti, and so, sailing now to the northward, the ships in due time reached their harbor.

In Haiti, there were men plotting against Columbus. Some of the colonists who had not found so much gold as they had hoped for, returned to Spain and complained to the king that Columbus was managing the colony badly.

Ferdinand and Isabella partly believed what they said. As Columbus had done one wrong thing when he made slaves of the Indians, the king and queen thought he might do wrong in other things.

Accordingly, they sent to Haiti a man named Bobadilla to take charge of the colony; and Bobadilla on his arrival, accused Columbus of cruelty and injustice, and sent him to Spain in chains. The captain of the vessel in which he sailed wished to remove these fetters, but Columbus would not allow him to do so. He wore them to the end of the voyage, and kept them as relics ever afterwards.

As soon as the vessel reached Spain, Columbus wrote a letter to the king and queen telling them what he had done, and what had been done to him. When Isabella read it, she is said to have shed tears. His fetters were at once removed, and Ferdinand and Isabella refused to listen to the charges which Bobadilla had made against him.

Columbus never so much as imagined that he had discovered a new continent. He supposed that Cuba, Jamaica, and the other islands which he visited were some of what are called the "Indies", or islands near India. For a long time everybody else supposed so too; and hence it is that Cuba and the neighboring islands have always been called the West Indies.

About this time, the Pope divided between Spain and Portugal all the newly-discovered lands, and all that might afterwards be discovered. The dividing line was a meridian passing three hundred leagues west of the Azores. Spain's share was all that lay west of this meridian, and Portugal's all that lay east of it.

Spain was jealous of Portugal, and anxious to secure a part of that kingdom's share. Columbus suggested a way to do this. He assured Ferdinand and Isabella that by sailing still farther to the westward, beyond the West Indies, it would be possible to reach some of the islands which might be claimed by Portugal; and of course he was correct in this view.

He asked the sovereigns for a fleet with which to make the attempt; and in 1502, with four ships and a hundred and fifty men, he set sail from Cadiz. On the voyage he landed at Jamaica and other islands; but although he was absent more than two years, he accomplished nothing of importance.

He returned to Spain in 1504, and died two years later.

His body was buried at Valladolid (val ya do leed'), but was afterwards carried across the ocean and interred in the cathedral of Santo Domingo on the island of Haiti. When that island was ceded by the Spaniards to France, the remains of the great navigator were removed to Havana; and there they rested until after the war between the United States and Spain, when they were taken back to Spain.

Written Summation

Two wealthy gentlemen added a third ship to the two supplied by the king and queen, and the wonderful voyage began. The *Santa Maria* with a crew of fifty men was commanded by Columbus himself; the *Pinta* with thirty men was in the charge of Martin Pinzon; and the *Nina* or "Baby" with twenty-four men was commanded by Martin's brother, Vincente Pinzon.

Model Practice 1

Model Practice 2

Model Practice 3

Vasco da Gama

from Famous men of Modern times
by John H. Haaren, LL.D. and A. B. Poland, Ph.D.
1469 - 1524 AD

One day in the year 1497, King Manuel of Portugal was at work in his study. It was five years since Columbus had brought the news to Ferdinand of Aragon that a way to the Indies had been discovered by sailing westward; for Columbus, as we have learned, supposed that the islands on which he had landed were some of the East India islands. Manuel was busy planning an expedition which he hoped might discover a passage to the Indies by sailing eastward.

A nobleman entered the room where he was sitting. "Vasco da Gama," said the king when he saw him, "I make you captain of my expedition. Take any one of the ships you please, and let your brother command another. If it please God, you will discover India."

Three ships, not larger than the schooners which sail up and down our rivers, were lying at anchor in the harbor of Lisbon. They were named Michael, Gabriel, and Raphael after the three archangels. They were laden with everything which the king and Vasco thought might be useful on a voyage of discovery, and among the men who were to sail in them were carpenters, blacksmiths, rope makers, and such other skilled workmen as were likely to be of service.

When the vessels were ready to start, a solemn service was held in the great cathedral of Lisbon. All who were going on the expedition were there. The king and queen were also present; and when the bishop had pronounced the blessing, the king presented to Vasco da Gama the royal standard. "Let it fly," he said, "at the masthead of your ship."

From the cathedral, Vasco and his men marched to the harbor. The ships were decorated with flags, and the king's standard was run up at the masthead of the one which Vasco was to command. Guns were fired, the anchors were heaved, the sails were loosed, and the little fleet floated down to the mouth of the river.

There in the port of Belem they waited three days for a fair wind, and then the voyage began. A Portuguese writer says, "So many tears were shed when they were sailing away that the shore may well be named the shore of tears." And Camoens, the great poet of Portugal wrote, "Uncounted as the grains of golden sand, the tears of thousands fell on Belem's strand."

The ships were so long sailing down the coast of Africa that the sailors became discouraged. They insisted that the land must extend entirely across the sea, and that it had no end.

Vasco da Gama knew that it had an end; for another great navigator, named Bartholomew Diaz, had already found the end and called it the "Cape of Storms," because of the very bad weather he had encountered there.

Near this cape Vasco also met with storms, and his men wished to turn back. But, like Columbus, Vasco was determined to go on. Some of the men formed a conspiracy to kill him, and he was obliged to put the mutineers in irons. At length, they doubled the cape, sailed to the northeastward, and left the storms behind them.

The ships had been greatly damaged by the winds and waves. They were leaking badly, and the sailors had to work at the pumps night and day. Wearied and disheartened they again requested that the voyage might be given up, and that they might be allowed to return to their homes.

Vasco saw that the ships must be repaired, and, besides this, all were in need of water. He therefore steered toward the land and kept a sharp lookout for a safe harbor.

If you look at the map of Africa, you will see that part of the southeast coast is called Natal, (na tal'). This is the Portuguese name for Christmas Day. Vasco named this part of the coast Natal because he sailed past it on that day.

Farther on, the voyagers were delighted to see the mouth of a river. Steering into it, and sailing some distance up the stream, they found a place where they could land. There they stayed some time and repaired their ships. One, however, was so battered and broken that she could not be made seaworthy; they therefore took her to pieces and used the wood to repair the other two.

Vasco named this stream the "River of Mercy."

One day some of the natives came to visit them. The sailors offered them slices of bread with marmalade; but their visitors did not taste a morsel until they saw the Portuguese eating. When they had once tasted, it seemed as though they would never have enough.

Da Gama showed them a looking glass, a thing they had never seen before. They were greatly amused, and laughed loudly when they saw their faces reflected in it.

Sailing from the River of Mercy, Vasco steered northward, keeping always in sight of land. After some days he saw a ship at anchor and at once sent a boat to find out where he was. But the native sailors were afraid, and jumping into a canoe paddled away as fast as they could.

The Portuguese boat soon overtook them, and then all but one of the natives threw themselves into the sea and swam to shore. The one man remaining in the canoe could not swim, and so the Portuguese took him on board one of their ships. He proved to be a Moor, and as he was able to act as an interpreter, he became very useful to them.

Not long after this another vessel was seen. She was under full sail, but Vasco's ship soon came up with her. Two negroes on board the strange vessel spoke a language that some of the negroes on the ships of the Portuguese understood; and from them they learned that she was on her way to a harbor of India called Cambay. This was good news to da Gama, and they followed her into an African harbor called Mozambique (mo zam beek').

It was now nearly a year since they had sailed from Lisbon; and all were delighted to enter a port where they could see houses and people.

Soon after they came to anchor, the sheik or governor of the city of Mozambique paid them a visit. He came upon two canoes lashed together, poles and planks being placed upon them to make a floor, above which was stretched a large piece of matting. Under the matting sat the sheik and ten companions. The sheik wore a jacket of velvet; a blue cloth embroidered with threads of gold was wrapped round his body; and a silken sash was tied round his waist. A dagger was stuck in his sash, and he carried a sword in his hand.

When he reached the ships, trumpets were sounded, and Vasco and his officers greeted him with the heartiest welcome. The Moor interpreted everything that they said, or that the Portuguese said to them.

The sheik asked the Portuguese of what merchandise they were in search. Thereupon they showed him some pepper, cinnamon, and ginger. He then promised to send pilots who would steer their vessels to India; and after he left the ships two men came on board who said they had been sent for that purpose.

Before the Portuguese were ready to resume their voyage, the sheik invited Vasco to dine with him, and advised that all the sick men should be sent on shore.

Vasco learned from the Moor with him that this was a trick to get them into the sheik's power, and so he declined the invitation.

A boat was sent to get fresh water, and one of the sheik's pilots went to show the Portuguese where the spring was. He said that midnight was the only time at which they could row to the spring because of the tide. But from midnight until morning he kept them rowing about from place to place, and no water was found.

Seeing at length that the Portuguese were growing angry, he jumped overboard and swam a long distance under water, not rising till he was far away from the boat. In this way he escaped.

Vasco now sailed away, but he put the other pilot in irons. He could not trust him; for the Moor had found out that the sheik had ordered both the pilots to steer the ships upon the shoals and wreck them.

The next harbor Vasco reached was Mombasa (Mom bas' a). The sheik of Mozambique had sent word to the king, who was a friend of his, that two ships would soon arrive at Mombasa whose captains were great robbers—that they meant to bring a large fleet and take possession of Mombasa and Mozambique; and that the wisest thing to do was to make prisoners of the strangers and put them to death.

As soon as the king of Mombasa learned that the two ships had actually arrived outside the harbor he sent a kind message to Vasco, inviting him to land and make a treaty. He sent two pilots to take the vessels into the harbor because there were dangerous shoals at its entrance. He also sent a large boat loaded with sheep, sugar cane, citrons, lemons and oranges, as a present.

The sick men were delighted with the fruit. Vasco sent two men on shore to buy some other things that were needed; but the king said they might have whatever they wished without paying.

A guide was given to them who took them all over the city, and particularly to a part where, he said, Christians lived. The people there pretended to be Christians but were not. They treated the Portuguese kindly, and begged them to stop all night at their houses.

This kindness was only pretended. The truth was that the king had given orders to the pilots to run Vasco's vessels on the shoals of the harbor, and they tried to do it. Vasco's ship, however, did not obey the helm when they were turning to enter the harbor; but it went so close to the shoal, that the officer in command ordered the sailors to let go the anchor and haul down the sails. In a moment this was done, and the other ship did the same. The two pilots, thinking their plans were discovered, jumped into the water and swam to a boat and escaped.

Vasco determined to leave these treacherous people at once, but his anchor had become fixed so firmly in the rocks of the shoal that the crew could not raise it. They labored at this all night, and the cable parting in the morning, they had to leave the anchor and sail away without it.

The next port that they reached was Melinda. Here they were treated with real kindness; for a soothsayer, whom the king trusted, told him that the Portuguese would some day be lords of India, and that he had better make a treaty with them.

The king therefore invited Vasco and his brother to land and settle upon the terms of a treaty. The Portuguese, however, were distrustful. They proposed that the king and they should have their talk sitting in boats near the shore, and to this the king agreed. Vasco and his brother dressed themselves in their handsomest suits and went in their boats seated on chairs that were covered with crimson velvet. Each of the boats carried two small guns which were fired as a salute, and then the crews rowed toward the shore.

The king now came on board one of the boats, and sat on a seat prepared for him. He said.that he wished to be always friendly with the king of Portugal. Vasco da Gama and his brother knelt to kiss the king's hand, but he made them rise. Then the trumpets sounded and the ships fired all their guns.

Vasco presented to the king a splendid sword in a case of gold, saying, "Sire, we give you this sword in the name of our king and promise to maintain peace and friendship with you forever." The king answered "I promise and swear by my religion to keep peace and frendship forever with my new brother the king of Portugal." Thousands of the king's people were gathered on the shore and witnessed all this.

After the treaty had been made, Vasco wished at once to sail to India. But he had to cross the great Indian Ocean, and favorable winds would not blow until August, and it was now only May. So for three months the Portuguese remained at Melinda.

Just before they sailed Vasco erected, on a hill near the city, a white marble column on which was inscribed the name of King Manuel.

As a parting gift the king of Melinda sent to the Portuguese a large boatload of rice, butter, sugar, cocoanuts, sheep, fowls and vegetables.

Sailing eastward now for about twenty days Vasco at length sighted land. It was the shore of Calicut, a city in India. The vessels were soon anchored in the harbor.

Thus, the great sea route to the land of silks and spices had been discovered. A factory, or trading house, was established at Calicut, and for the next hundred years little Portugal was the sovereign of the eastern seas, and the greatest commercial nation of Europe.

Da Gama died in 1524. The Portuguese honor him as we honor Columbus; and Camoens made him the hero of his "Lusiad," the greatest poem in the Portuguese language.

Written Summation

Three ships, not larger than the schooners which sail up and down our rivers, were lying at anchor in the harbor of Lisbon. They were named Michael, Gabriel, and Raphael after the three archangels. They were laden with everything which the king and Vasco thought might be useful on a voyage of discovery.

Model Practice 1 (adapted from the original)

Model Practice 2

Model Practice 3

Sir Walter Raleigh

from Famous Men of Modern Times
by John H. Haaren, LL.D. and A. B. Poland, Ph.D.
1552 - 1618 AD

Another famous Englishman who lived in the days of Queen Elizabeth was Sir Walter Raleigh. He was a soldier and statesman, a poet and historian, but the most interesting fact about him is that he was the first Englishman who attempted to plant colonies in the region now known as the United States.

He was born in Devonshire, England, in 1552. At about the time that he was growing up, great sympathy was felt in England for the Huguenots, as the French protestants were called, and Raleigh enlisted as a volunteer in the Huguenot army. He was in France at the time of the massacre of St. Bartholomew, in 1572, but we do not know how long he remained there.

In 1580 he went to Ireland as captain of a company of a hundred men, to aid in putting down a rebellion there.

Returning to England at the age of thirty, he became one of Queen Elizabeth's courtiers. He constantly sought to please her. A story is told that one day when Elizabeth was out walking at Greenwich, she came to a muddy place. Raleigh was in attendance upon her, and quickly took off his costly coat and spread it over the mud so that it formed a carpet for the queen to walk on. This gallant act is said to have gained him high favor from Elizabeth.

Whether the story is true or not it is certain that for some years he was the greatest favorite at the court.

In Queen Elizabeth's reign, the English began to take great interest in the new country of North America. Raleigh and his half-brother, Sir Humphrey Gilbert, obtained from Queen Elizabeth permission to colonize any land in North America which was not already claimed by a Christian nation.

Five ships were fitted out and sailed from England, in 1583, under the command of Gilbert. Raleigh was unable to go, but he bore a large part of the expense of the expedition.

Hardly had the voyage begun when one of the ships, owing to sickness among the crew, was obliged to return to England. Gilbert, with the other ships, kept on his course across the Atlantic, and at last reached Newfoundland, where he went on shore and took possession of the island in the name of Queen Elizabeth.

Gilbert now sailed onward with the fleet.

Near Cape Breton Island, the largest vessel stuck in the mud, and was broken to pieces by the force of the waves; all but fourteen, out of nearly a hundred men on board, lost their lives. Gilbert thought that now it would be impossible to carry out the colonization plan, so with his three remaining ships he started back to England.

A terrible storm came on, but the vessels kept together for a time. When last seen, Gilbert was sitting in the stern of his ship, reading a book. He shouted to those on board the other ships, "We are as near to heaven by sea as by land." During the night his ship disappeared, and not one on board was saved, but the other vessels succeeded in reaching England.

Raleigh was not discouraged by this failure. In the following year he sent to America another expedition.

In due time his vessels reached the coast of what is now known as North Carolina. Everybody was charmed with the beauty of the country. But after exploring the coast for some distance, and taking possession of the region in the name of Elizabeth, the expedition for some reason returned to England without making a settlement.

The description which the explorers gave of the country which they had visited interested Queen Elizabeth. As she was called the "Virgin Queen," Raleigh suggested that she should give the name "Virginia" to the newly discovered territory. She did this, and the state of Virginia, which formed part of the territory thus discovered, obtained its name in that way.

Raleigh soon organized a third expedition which sailed in 1585 with about a hundred colonists. Seven vessels carried them. The fleet was commanded by Sir Richard Grenville while the colonists were in charge of a noted soldier named Ralph Lane.

After a long voyage they reached Roanoke Island, on the coast of North Carolina. Grenville returned to England with the fleet, while Lane was left on Roanoke Island to establish a settlement.

The colonists probably quarreled with the Indians. Their provisions failed, and they could get none from the red men. No ship from England came with supplies, and the colonists were thoroughly discouraged.

The next year a fleet under command of Sir Francis Drake called there by chance, and all the colonists returned home.

One of them, named Thomas Hariot, in an account of the colony, spoke of a herb "called by the natives yppomoc," and told how it was smoked by them in pipes. This herb was tobacco. Hariot and his companions had learned to like it, and they carried a quantity home with them.

This was the first Virginia tobacco imported into England. Some of it was given to Raleigh who smoked it in silver pipes. Queen Elizabeth also learned the art, and she made smoking fashionable among people of high rank in England.

In 1587 Raleigh sent out to Virginia a fourth expedition. It consisted of three ships carrying one hundred and fifty colonists under Captain White.

After landing his passengers, White returned to England for supplies. When he got back to America, three years later, he found that the colonists had disappeared, and it was never learned what became of them. Thus failed Raleigh's last attempt to colonize Virginia.

So confident was he that the new world would be colonized, that he wrote of Virginia, "I shall yet live to see it an English nation." And this he did, for he lived until 1618, and Jamestown had then been founded ten years.

In return for his services in quelling the Irish rebellion, the queen gave him a large grant of land in Ireland. The most interesting fact about this Irish property is that Raleigh raised there the first potatoes grown in Europe.

You have read how Philip II of Spain attempted, in 1588, to invade England with his famous Armada, and how that great fleet was destroyed. There was in England a great hatred of the Spaniards and a great desire to injure them.

At that time Spain claimed most of the new world so far as it had been explored, and her ships were all the time coming home laden with the products of her possessions, and particularly with silver from her mines.

Raleigh fitted out privateers to capture such vessels, and a large Spanish ship was taken.

She was the most valuable prize which, up to that time, had ever been brought into an English port. The queen herself had an interest in the expedition and was greatly pleased with her share of the plunder.

Raleigh had still a great desire to plant colonies, and he now turned his attention to South America. He placed a vessel in command of a certain Captain Whiddon, and sent him, in 1594, to explore the region now known as Guiana.

Fabulous stories had been told of the amount of gold in this province. It was said that the king, when he was going to make an offering to his gods, covered his body all over with gold dust, and from this the Spaniards called him "El Dorado," that is, "the gilded man."

In 1595, Raleigh himself set sail with five ships for the land of "the Gilded King." He entered the mouth of the Orinoco and sailed up the great river for a distance of about four hundred miles. But the river rose so high that navigation was imperilled; and Raleigh therefore returned to the coast and soon afterward sailed back to England.

War with Spain still continued; and, in 1597, an English expedition under Howard and Essex was fitted out to attack Cadiz, a seaport on the Spanish coast. Raleigh was in one of the ships and rendered important service. The English destroyed or captured the ships of a large Spanish fleet in the harbor, and the city itself was surrendered.

This exploit was one of the most brilliant ever achieved by the English navy. After it, the Spaniards never regained their power upon the sea.

All through the reign of Elizabeth, Raleigh was highly esteemed by the queen and by the people. Up to the date of her death he was a member of Parliament. But, in 1603, James I succeeded Elizabeth. He disliked Raleigh, and therefore stripped him of all his offices and accused him of entering into a plot against the king.

Raleigh was arrested and brought to trial. One who was present wrote that when the trial began, he would have gone a hundred miles to see him hanged; but that before it closed, he would have gone two hundred to save his life.

Although nothing was proved against him, Raleigh was condemned to death. Only when he stood on the scaffold was his sentence changed to imprisonment for life.

For thirteen years he was confined in the Tower of London; and there he wrote his great work The History of the World. It is reported that the Prince of Wales often visited him in the Tower, and said, "No man but my father would keep such a bird in such a cage." In 1616 Raleigh was released so that he might go on another expedition to the golden land of Guiana and capture Spanish merchant vessels. But disease broke out among his crews, and Raleigh himself was stricken down with fever before they reached the Orinoco. His son was killed in a fight with the Spaniards; and, in 1618, the poor father returned to England brokenhearted.

Shortly after his arrival, he was arrested and condemned to die the very next morning under the sentence of death which had been passed upon him fifteen years before.

Even then his courage did not leave him. On the scaffold he asked to see the axe. "This gives me no fear," he said. "It is a sharp medicine to cure me of all diseases." To someone who told him to lay his head toward the north, he replied, "What matter how the head lies, so the heart be right."

Raleigh's attempts at colonization were the beginnings of the great movement which led to the establishment of the Thirteen Colonies; and those colonies formed the basis for the United States of America.

Written Summation

Returning to England at the age of thirty, he became one of Queen Elizabeth's courtiers. He constantly sought to please her. A story is told that one day when Elizabeth was out walking at Greenwich, she came to a muddy place. Raleigh was in attendance upon her, and quickly took off his costly coat and spread it over the mud so that it formed a carpet for the queen to walk on.

Model Practice 1

Model Practice 2

Model Practice 3

Galileo

from Famous Men of Modern Times
by John H. Haaren, LL.D. and A. B. Poland, Ph.D.
1564 - 1642 AD

Sometime in the year 1583, repairs were going on in the cathedral of an old Italian city called Pisa; and, accidentally, a workman had set swinging a great lamp which was suspended from the high roof of the building. People came into the church and knelt for a few minutes to say their prayers and then went out without noticing that the lamp kept on swinging to and fro.

A young man about eighteen years of age came into the church. He noticed the swinging lamp; and he also thought that it took just the same time to make each of its swings.

With his right hand, he clasped his left wrist. He knew that the times between pulse beats are practically equal. So, feeling his pulse and watching the swinging lamp, he was trying to measure the one by the other.

The young man who watched the swinging lamp was Galileo; and he found that its motions were equal in duration.

Before his time no pendulum had ever swung in a clock. No clock with a pendulum had been thought of. But after Galileo published his great discovery that pendulums made their swings in equal periods of time, a man named Huygens (Hi' genz) made a pendulum clock.

It was found that pendulums about a yard long make each swing in a second; and so, at first, clocks' were made with pendulums which beat seconds.

From Galileo's watching the swinging lamp, all our clocks may fairly be said to have been invented.

The father of Galileo hoped that his son would become a physician; but the young man liked to study mathematics, and his father permitted him to follow the bent of his genie.

Not long after graduating at the university, and when not quite twenty-five, Galileo was made professor of physics. He taught his classes about pumps and machinery, why smoke rises in the air, why birds' wings enable them to fly. and why fishes' fins send them through the water.

Nobody in Europe at that time knew much about such matters. There were no steam engines; no railroad trains were in existence; no steamers were crossing the seas.

People knew very little about such simple things as the falling of stones and feathers, and pieces of iron and lead. Even learned men thought that two pounds of lead would fall twice as fast as one pound, one hundred pounds one hundred times as fast, and so on.

One day Galileo asked some of his friends to climb with him the leaning tower of Pisa. This tower is one of the famous buildings of Europe. The odd thing about it is that it does not stand up straight like the tower or spire of a church, but leans over, as some of our trees do.

Some of Galileo's friends stayed at the foot of the tower; some went to the top. Heavy and light things were carried up and dropped from the summit of the tower; and one pound of iron reached the ground at the same instant as did a piece that weighed ten pounds.

While Galileo was professor at Pisa, the people of Europe who watched the heavens saw a new star in the sky.

"Have you seen the new star? What do you think it is?" were questions that everybody was asking. Some thought it was only a meteor; but Galileo said, "No! It must be a star, because a meteor would surely be moving, and that star seems still." He gave three lectures upon it and people went by hundreds to hear him.

Galileo, like everybody else, could look at the star only with the naked eye. He tried to contrive something that would show both it and the other stars more plainly. He had seen spectacles. His grandfather wore a pair. He had also read somewhere that if two eyeglasses are placed one above the other, things seen through them would appear nearer and larger.

Some bright man in Holland fixed an eyeglass at one end of a tube and another like it at the other end; and so made the first telescope.

Galileo had heard about this. He bought a piece of lead pipe and fixed a glass at either end. His telescope magnified only three times; but it made things look nearer and larger.

He was as pleased with it as a child with a new toy. Wealthy and noble Venetians looked through it with wonder; just as when you look through a microscope at the point of a needle you are surprised to see how blunt it is.

Then Galileo used stronger lenses. His second telescope magnified eight times; and a third was made which magnified thirty times.

He looked at the moon; and he saw what no human being had ever seen before. There are mountains on the moon. He saw their bright tops and the shadows which they threw.

Then he looked at the planet Venus. . She no longer looked like the other stars; but sometimes she seemed to be round like the full moon, sometimes horned, like the old and new moons.

With his naked eye, Galileo counted only six stars in the Pleiades. People years before had seen seven; and it was believed that one had been lost. Galileo looked one bright night and his telescope showed him forty. He looked at the Milky Way and found that its whiteness is the dim light of millions of stars so far away that they seem as small as the finest dust.

He then made a fourth and larger telescope, and turned it upon the farthest away of the known planets. Jupiter, like Venus, seemed no more a star. It was round like the moon at the full.

But another and greater wonder appeared. Close to the edge of Jupiter's disk were three tiny stars. Two were seen on the east side of the planet and one on the west. They were Jupiter's moons.

Galileo watched on another night and found that instead of three there were four. We now know that there are sixty-three.

He told the other professors in the university what he had seen, and the news quickly spread. The newly-found moons were called planets, just as our own moon was; and so it seemed that Galileo had made the number of planets eleven, instead of seven.

One of the professors was so angry that he would not even look through the telescope. Another man said," The head has only seven openings—two eyes, two ears, two nostrils and one mouth, and how can there be more than seven planets? "

Galileo had an old friend called Kepler, who was the greatest astronomer then living. Galileo wrote to him, "Oh, my dear Kepler, how I wish we could have one good laugh together. Why are you not here? What shouts of laughter we should have at their glorious folly!"

About sixty years before this, Copernicus had printed a book in which he said that the earth was not still, as people thought, but that it was all the time moving round the sun.

Galileo did not at first believe this, and said in one of his letters that it was "folly." Then he saw that it was probably true; and when he looked through his telescope at the planets, he became certain of it.

When people said that the system of Copernicus was contrary to the teaching of the Scriptures, Galileo tried to explain the sense in which the passages in the Bible are to be taken. He was then accused of teaching what would do harm to religion, and was summoned to Rome. His trial took place in 1616, and he promised to give up his opinions concerning the Copernican system.

But his enemies still pursued him, and in 1633 Galileo was again accused of heresy and of breaking the promise he had made in 1616. The main part of the charge was that Galileo had denied that God is a personal being and that miracles are not miracles at all. As to breaking the promise he had made in 1616, Galileo admitted that he had felt proud of his arguments in favor of the Copernican system, and in one of his books he had made out rather a strong case for it. He denied, however, having expressly taught the Copernican system. Unfortunately, Galileo did not tell the truth in thus denying what he had taught, and he was sentenced to an indefinite term of imprisonment.

The imprisonment was not severe, although Galileo complained of it. He was to remain with an old friend and disciple; but at the end of six months, he was permitted to return to his home near Florence.

His friends were allowed to visit him; but he was not allowed to go outside the gate to visit them. This was sad for him; but sadder still was the loss of his sight; for his eyes had seen more of the glory of the heavens than all the millions of eyes that had ever looked at the stars since the world began.

He died in 1642, and his body was interred in the Cathedral of Santa Croce.

Written Summation

Galileo, like everybody else, could look at the star only with the naked eye. He tried to contrive something that would show both it and the other stars more plainly. He had seen spectacles. His grandfather wore a pair. He had also read somewhere that if two eyeglasses are placed one above the other, things seen through them would appear nearer and larger.

Model Practice 1

Model Practice 2

Model Practice 3

CHAPTER
II

Text Excerpts
from
Primary Source Documents

Lines for written summations have not been included in this section. These selections are somewhat complicated, detailed, and advanced for written summations by students at this stage. These selections are best used for oral narrations as an introduction to ideas from the time period studied.

They also serve as a great introduction to primary source material, introducing children to the idea that they are capable of evaluating history for themselves. Copywork and dictation from primary source documents are excellent selections of living literature (aka living books).

The Confessions of Saint Augustine (excerpt)

354 – 430 AD

Theft is punished by Thy law, O Lord, and the law written in the hearts of men, which iniquity itself effaces not. For what thief will abide a thief? Not even a rich thief, one stealing through want. Yet I lusted to thieve, and did it, compelled by no hunger, nor poverty, but through a cloyedness of well doing, and a pamperedness of iniquity. For I stole that, of which I had enough, and much better. Nor cared I to enjoy what I stole, but joyed in the theft and sin itself. A pear tree there was near our vineyard, laden with fruit, tempting neither for color nor taste. To shake and rob this, some lewd young fellows of us went, late one night (having according to our pestilent custom prolonged our sports in the streets till then), and took huge loads, not for our eating, but to fling to the very hogs, having only tasted them. And this, but to do what we liked only, because it was misliked. Behold my heart, O God, behold my heart, which Thou hadst pity upon in the bottom of the bottomless pit. Now, behold, let my heart tell Thee what it sought there, that I should be gratuitously evil, having no temptation to ill, but the ill itself. It was foul, and I loved it. I loved to perish. I loved mine own fault, not that for which I was faulty, but my fault itself. Foul soul, falling from Thy firmament to utter destruction; not seeking aught through the shame, but the shame itself!

For there is an attractiveness in beautiful bodies, in gold and silver, and all things; and in bodily touch, sympathy hath much influence, and each other sense hath his proper object answerably tempered. Wordly honor hath also its grace, and the power of overcoming, and of mastery; whence springs also the thirst of revenge. But yet, to obtain all these, we may not depart from Thee, O Lord, nor decline from Thy law. The life also which here we live hath its own enchantment, through a certain proportion of its own, and a correspondence with all things beautiful here below. Human friendship also is endeared with a sweet tie, by reason of the unity formed of many souls. Upon occasion of all these, and the like, is sin committed, while through an immoderate inclination towards these goods of the lowest order, the better and higher are forsaken,- Thou, our Lord God, Thy truth, and Thy law. For these lower things have their delights, but not like my God, who made all things; for in Him doth the righteous delight, and He is the joy of the upright in heart.

When, then, we ask why a crime was done, we believe it not, unless it appear that there might have been some desire of obtaining some of those which we called lower goods, or a fear of losing them. For they are beautiful and comely; although compared with those higher and beatific goods, they be abject and low. A man hath murdered another; why? He loved his wife or his estate; or would rob for his own livelihood; or feared to lose some such things by him; or, wronged, was on fire to be revenged. Would any commit murder upon no cause, delighted simply in murdering? Who would believe it? For as for that furious and savage man, of whom it is said that he was gratuitously evil and cruel, yet is the cause assigned; "lest" (saith he) "through idleness hand or heart should grow inactive." And to what end? That, through that practice of guilt, he might, having taken the city, attain to honors, empire, riches, and be freed from fear of the laws, and his embarrassments from domestic needs, and consciousness of villainies. So then, not even Catiline himself loved his own villainies, but something else, for whose sake he did them.

What then did wretched I so love in thee, thou theft of mine, thou deed of darkness, in that sixteenth year of my age? Lovely thou wert not, because thou wert theft. But art thou any thing, that thus I speak to thee? Fair were the pears we stole, because they were Thy creation, Thou fairest of all, Creator of all, Thou good God; God, the sovereign good and my true good. Fair were those pears, but not them did my wretched soul desire; for I had store of better, and those I gathered, only that I might steal. For, when gathered, I flung them away, my only feast therein being my own sin, which I was pleased to enjoy. For if aught of those pears came within my mouth, what sweetened it was the sin. And now, O Lord my God, I enquire what in that theft delighted me; and behold it hath no loveliness; I mean not such loveliness as in justice and wisdom; nor such as is in the mind and memory, and senses, and animal life of man; nor yet as the stars are glorious and beautiful in their orbs; or the earth, or sea, full of embryo life, replacing by its birth that which decayeth; nay, nor even that false and shadowy beauty which belongeth to deceiving vices.

For so doth pride imitate exaltedness; whereas Thou alone art God exalted over all. Ambition, what seeks it, but honors and glory? Whereas Thou alone art to be honored above all, and glorious for evermore. The cruelty of the great would fain be feared; but who is to be feared but God alone, out of whose power what can be wrested or withdrawn? When, or where, or whither, or by whom? The tendernesses of the wanton would fain be counted love: yet is nothing more tender than Thy charity; nor is aught loved more healthfully than that Thy truth, bright and beautiful above all. Curiosity makes semblance of a desire of knowledge; whereas Thou supremely knowest all. Yea, ignorance and foolishness itself is cloaked under the name of simplicity and uninjuriousness; because nothing is found more single than Thee: and what less injurious, since they are his own works which injure the sinner? Yea, sloth would fain be at rest; but what stable rest besides the Lord? Luxury affects to be called plenty and abundance; but Thou art the fullness and never failing plenteousness of incorruptible pleasures. Prodigality presents a shadow of liberality: but Thou art the most overflowing Giver of all good. Covetousness would possess many things; and Thou possessest all things. Envy disputes for excellency: what more excellent than Thou? Anger seeks revenge: who revenges more justly than Thou? Fear startles at things unwonted and sudden, which endangers things beloved, and takes forethought for their safety; but to Thee what unwonted or sudden, or who separateth from Thee what Thou lovest? Or where but with Thee is unshaken safety? Grief pines away for things lost, the delight of its desires; because it would have nothing taken from it, as nothing can from Thee.

Now, behold, let my heart tell Thee what it sought there, that I should be gratuitously evil, having no temptation to ill, but the ill itself. It was foul, and I loved it. I loved to perish. I loved mine own fault, not that for which I was faulty, but my fault itself.

Model Practice 1

Model Practice 2

Model Practice 3

Of The Greatest Good (excerpt)

from Consolations of Philosophy
from Library Of The World's Best Literature, Ancient And Modern, Vol. 5
by Boëtius
475-525

Boëtius was a thorough student of Greek philosophy, and formed the plan of translating all of Plato and Aristotle and reconciling their philosophies. This work he never completed. He wrote a treatise on music which was used as a textbook as late as the present century; and he translated the works of Ptolemy on astronomy, of Nicomachus on arithmetic, of Euclid on geometry, and of Archimedes on mechanics. His great work in this line was a translation of Aristotle, which he supplemented by a commentary in thirty books. Among his writings are a number of works on logic and a commentary on the 'Topica' of Cicero. In addition to these, five theological tracts are ascribed to him, the most important being a discussion of the doctrine of the Trinity.

The work which has done most to perpetuate his name is the 'Consolations of Philosophy,' in five books,--written during his imprisonment at Pavia,--which has been called "the last work of Roman literature." It is written in alternate prose and verse, and treats of his efforts to find solace in his misfortune. The first book opens with a vision of a woman, holding a book and sceptre, who comes to him with promises of comfort. She is his lifelong companion, Philosophy. He tells her the story of his troubles. In the second book, Philosophy tells him that Fortune has the right to take away what she has bestowed, and that he still has wife and children, the most precious of her gifts; his ambition to shine as statesman and philosopher is foolish, as no greatness is enduring. The third book takes up the discussion of the Supreme Good, showing that it consists not in riches, power, nor pleasure, but only in God. In the fourth book the problems of the existence of evil in the world and the freedom of the will are examined; and the latter subject continues through the fifth book. During the Middle Ages this work was highly esteemed, and numerous translations appeared. In the ninth century Alfred the Great gave to his subjects an Anglo-Saxon version; and in the fourteenth century Chaucer made an English translation, which was published by Caxton in 1480. Before the sixteenth century it was translated into German, French, Italian, Spanish, and Greek.

It is now perhaps best known for the place it occupies in the spiritual development of Dante. He turned to it for comfort after the death of his Beatrice in 1291. Inspired by its teachings, he gave himself up for a time to the study of philosophy, with the result of his writing the 'Convito,' a book in which he often refers to his favorite author. In his 'Divine Comedy' he places Boëtius in the Heaven of the Sun, together with the Fathers of the Church and the schoolmen.

Every mortal is troubled with many and various anxieties, and yet all desire, through various paths, to arrive at one goal. That is, they strive by different means to attain one happiness—in a word, God. He is the beginning and the end of every good, and He is the highest happiness. Then said the Mind:--This, methinks, must be the highest good, so that men should neither need, nor moreover be solicitous, about any other good besides it; since he possesses that which is the roof of all other good, inasmuch as it includes all other good, and has all other kinds within it. It would not be the highest good if any good were external to it, because it would then have to desire some good which itself had not. Then answered Reason, and said:--It is very evident that this is the highest happiness, for it is both the roof and the floor of all good. What is that then but the best happiness, which gathers the other felicities all within it, and includes and holds them within it; and to it there is a deficiency of none, neither has it need of any, but they come all from it and again all to it, as all waters come from the sea and again all come to the sea? There is none in the little fountain, which does not seek the sea, and again from the sea it returns into the earth, and so it flows gradually through the earth, till it again comes to the same fountain that it before flowed from, and so again to the sea.

Now, this is an example of the true good, which all mortal men desire to obtain, though they by various ways think to arrive at it. For every man has a natural good in himself, because every mind desires to obtain the true good; but it is hindered by the transitory good, because it is more prone thereto. For some men think that it is the best happiness that a man be so rich that he have need of nothing more, and they choose their life accordingly. Some men think that this is the highest good, that he be among his fellows the most honorable of his fellows; and they with all diligence seek this. Some think that the supreme good is in the highest power. These strive either themselves to rule, or else to associate themselves to the friendship of rulers. Some persuade themselves that it is best that a man be illustrious and celebrated and have good fame; they therefore seek this both in peace and in war. Many reckon it for the greatest good and for the greatest happiness that a man be always blithe in this present life, and follow all his lusts. Some indeed who desire these riches are desirous thereof because they would have the greater power that they may the more securely enjoy these worldly lusts, and also the riches. Many there are who desire power because they would gather money; or again, they are desirous to spread their name.

On account of such and other like frail and perishing advantages, the thought of every human mind is troubled with anxiety and with care. It then imagines that it has obtained some exalted good when it has won the flattery of the people; and to me it seems that it has bought a very false greatness. Some with much anxiety seek wives, that thereby they may above all things have children, and also live happily. True friends, then, I say, are the most precious things of all these worldly felicities. They are not indeed to be reckoned as worldly goods, but as divine; for deceitful fortune does not produce them, but God, who naturally formed them as relations. For of every other thing in this world, man is desirous, either that he may through it obtain power, or else some worldly lust; except of the true friend, whom he loves sometimes for affection and for fidelity, though he expect to himself no other rewards. Nature joins and cements friends together with inseparable love. But with these worldly goods, and with this present wealth, men make oftener enemies than friends. From these, and from many such proofs, it may be evident to all men that all the bodily goods are inferior to the faculties of the soul. We indeed think that a man is the stronger, because he is great in his body. The fairness, moreover, and the strength of the body, rejoices and invigorates the man, and health makes him cheerful. In all these bodily felicities men seek one single happiness, as it seems to them. For whatsoever every man chiefly loves above all other things, that, he persuades himself, is best for him, and that is his highest good. When therefore he has acquired that, he imagines that he may be very happy. I do not deny that these goods and this happiness are the highest good of this present life. For every man considers that thing best which he chiefly loves above other things, and therefore he deems himself very happy if he can obtain what he then most desires. Is not now clearly enough shown to thee the form of the false goods; namely, riches, and dignity, and power, and glory, and pleasure? Concerning pleasure, Epicurus the philosopher said, when he inquired concerning all those other goods which we before mentioned: then said he, that pleasure was the highest good, because all the other goods which we before mentioned gratify the mind and delight it, but pleasure chiefly gratifies the body.

But we will still speak concerning the nature of men, and concerning their pursuits. Though, then, their mind and their nature be now obscured, and they are by that descent fallen to evil and inclined thither, yet they are desirous, so far as they can and may, of the highest good. As the drunken man knows that he should go to his house and to his rest, and yet is not able to find the way thither, so is it also with the mind, when it is weighed down by the anxieties of this world. It is sometimes intoxicated and misled by them, so far that it cannot rightly find out good. Nor yet does it appear to those men that they aught mistake who are desirous to obtain this, namely, that they need labor after nothing more. But they think that they are able to collect together all these goods, so that none may be excluded from the number....

Two things may dignity and power do, if they come to the unwise. It may make him honorable and respectable to other unwise persons. But when he quits the power, or the power him, then is he to the unwise neither honorable nor respectable. Has power, then, the custom of exterminating and rooting out vices from the minds of great men and planting therein virtues? I know, however, that earthly power never sows the virtues, but collects and gathers vices; and when it has gathered them, then it nevertheless shows and does not conceal them. For the vices of great men many men see; because many know them and many are with them. Therefore we always lament concerning power, and also despise it, when we see that it comes to the worst, and to those who are to us most unworthy.

Every mortal is troubled with many and various anxieties, and yet all desire, through various paths, to arrive at one goal. That is, they strive by different means to attain one happiness—in a word, God. He is the beginning and the end of every good, and He is the highest happiness.

Model Practice 1

Model Practice 2

Model Practice 3

Institutes of Justinian (excerpt)

by Caesar Flavius Justinian or Justinian the Great
529 - 534 AD

TITLE I. OF JUSTICE AND LAW

Justice is the set and constant purpose which gives to every man his due.

1 Jurisprudence is the knowledge of things divine and human, the science of the just and the unjust.

2 Having laid down these general definitions, and our object being the exposition of the law of the Roman people, we think that the most advantageous plan will be to commence with an easy and simple path, and then to proceed to details with a most careful and scrupulous exactness of interpretation. Otherwise, if we begin by burdening the student's memory, as yet weak and untrained, with a multitude and variety of matters, one of two things will happen: either we shall cause him wholly to desert the study of law, or else we shall bring him at last, after great labor, and often, too, distrustful of his own powers (the commonest cause, among the young, of ill-success), to a point which he might have reached earlier, without such labor and confident in himself, had he been led along a smoother path.

3 The precepts of the law are these: to live honestly, to injure no one, and to give every man his due.

4 The study of law consists of two branches—law public and law private. The former relates to the welfare of the Roman State; the latter to the advantage of the individual citizen. Of private law then we may say that it is of threefold origin, being collected from the precepts of nature, from those of the law of nations, or from those of the civil law of Rome.

TITLE II. OF THE LAW OF NATURE, THE LAW OF NATIONS, AND THE CIVIL LAW

1 The law of nature is that which she has taught all animals; a law not peculiar to the human race, but shared by all living creatures, whether denizens of the air, the dry land, or the sea. Hence comes the union of male and female, which we call marriage; hence the procreation and rearing of children, for this is a law by the knowledge of which we see even the lower animals are distinguished. The civil law of Rome, and the law of all nations, differ from each other thus. The laws of every people governed by statutes and customs are partly peculiar to itself, partly common to all mankind. Those rules which a state enacts for its own members are peculiar to itself, and are called civil law: those rules prescribed by natural reason for all men are observed by all peoples alike, and are called the law of nations. Thus the laws of the Roman people are partly peculiar to itself, partly common to all nations; a distinction of which we shall take notice as occasion offers.

2 Civil law takes its name from the state wherein it binds; for instance, the civil law of Athens, it being quite correct to speak thus of the enactments of Solon or Draco. So too we call the law of the Roman people the civil law of the Romans, or the law of the Quirites; the law, that is to say, which they observe, the Romans being called Quirites after Quirinus. Whenever we speak, however, of civil law, without any qualification, we mean our own; exactly as, when 'the poet' is spoken of, without addition or qualification, the Greeks understand the great Homer, and we understand Vergil. But the law of nations is common to the whole human race; for nations have settled certain things for themselves as occasion and the necessities of human life required. For instance, wars arose, and then followed captivity and slavery, which are contrary to the law of nature; for by the law of nature all men

from the beginning were born free. The law of nations again is the source of almost all contracts; for instance, sale, hire, partnership, deposit, loan for consumption, and very many others.

3 Our law is partly written, partly unwritten, as among the Greeks. The written law consists of statutes, plebiscites, senatusconsults, enactments of the Emperors, edicts of the magistrates, and answers of those learned in the law.

4 A statute is an enactment of the Roman people, which it used to make on the motion of a senatorial magistrate, as for instance a consul. A plebiscite is an enactment of the commonalty, such as was made on the motion of one of their own magistrates, as a tribune. The commonalty differs from the people as a species from its genus; for 'the people' includes the whole aggregate of citizens, among them patricians and senators, while the term 'commonalty' embraces only such citizens as are not patricians or senators. After the passing, however, of the statute called the lex Hortensia, plebiscites acquired for the first time the force of statutes.

5 A senatusconsult is a command and ordinance of the senate, for when the Roman people had been so increased that it was difficult to assemble it together for the purpose of enacting statutes, it seemed right that the senate should be consulted instead of the people.

6 Again, what the Emperor determines has the force of a statute, the people having conferred on him all their authority and power by the 'lex regia,' which was passed concerning his office and authority. Consequently, whatever the Emperor settles by rescript, or decides in his judicial capacity, or ordains by edicts, is clearly a statute: and these are what are called constitutions. Some of these of course are personal, and not to be followed as precedents, since this is not the Emperor's will; for a favor bestowed on individual merit, or a penalty inflicted for individual wrongdoing, or relief given without a precedent, do not go beyond the particular person: though others are general, and bind all beyond a doubt.

7 The edicts of the praetors too have no small legal authority, and these we are used to call the 'ius honorarium,' because those who occupy posts of honor in the state, in other words the magistrates, have given authority to this branch of law. The curule aediles also used to issue an edict relating to certain matters, which forms part of the ius honorarium.

8 The answers of those learned in the law are the opinions and views of persons authorized to determine and expound the law; for it was of old provided that certain persons should publicly interpret the laws, who were called jurisconsults, and whom the Emperor privileged to give formal answers. If they were unanimous the judge was forbidden by imperial constitution to depart from their opinion, so great was its authority.

9 The unwritten law is that which usage has approved: for ancient customs, when approved by consent of those who follow them, are like statute.

10 And this division of the civil law into two kinds seems not inappropriate, for it appears to have originated in the institutions of two states, namely Athens and Lacedaemon; it having been usual in the latter to commit to memory what was observed as law, while the Athenians observed only what they had made permanent in written statutes.

11 But the laws of nature, which are observed by all nations alike, are established, as it were, by divine providence and remain ever fixed and immutable. But the municipal laws of each individual

state are subject to frequent change, either by the tacit consent of the people, or by the subsequent enactment of another statute.

12 The whole of the law, which we observe, relates either to persons, or to things, or to actions. And first let us speak of persons: for it is useless to know the law without knowing the persons for whose sake it was established.

TITLE III. OF THE LAW OF PERSONS

In the law of persons, then, the first division is into free men and slaves.

1 Freedom, from which men are called free, is a man's natural power of doing what he pleases, so far as he is not prevented by force or law:

2 Slavery is an institution of the law of nations, against nature subjecting one man to the dominion of another.

3 The name 'slave' is derived from the practice of generals to order the preservation and sale of captives, instead of killing them; hence they are also called mancipia, because they are taken from the enemy by the strong hand.

4 Slaves are either born so, their mothers being slaves themselves; or they become so, and this either by the law of nations, that is to say by capture in war, or by the civil law, as when a free man, over twenty years of age, collusively allows himself to be sold in order that he may share the purchase money.

5 The condition of all slaves is one and the same: in the conditions of free men there are many distinctions; to begin with, they are either free born, or made free.

4. The study of law consists of two branches—law public and law private. The former relates to the welfare of the Roman State; the latter to the advantage of the individual citizen. Of private law then we may say that it is of threefold origin, being collected from the precepts of nature, from those of the law of nations, or from those of the civil law of Rome.

Model Practice 1 (modified)

Model Practice 2

Model Practice 3

A Letter from Alcuin to Charlemagne

from the Library of the World's Best Literature, Ancient and Modern, Vol. 1, edited by Charles Dudley Warner
796 AD

I, your Flaccus, in accordance with your entreaty and your gracious kindness, am busied under the shelter of St. Martin's, in bestowing upon many of my pupils the honey of the Holy Scriptures. I am eager that others should drink deep of the old wine of ancient learning. I shall presently begin to nourish still others with the fruits of grammatical ingenuity. And some of them I am eager to enlighten with a knowledge of the order of the stars, that seem painted, as it were, on the dome of some mighty palace. I have become all things to all men *(1 Cor. i. 22)* so that I may train up many to the profession of God's Holy Church and to the glory of your imperial realm, lest the grace of Almighty God in me should be fruitless *(1 Cor. xv. 10)* and your munificent bounty of no avail. But your servant lacks the rarer books of scholastic learning, which in my own country I used to have (thanks to the generous and most devoted care of my teacher and to my own humble endeavors), and I mention it to your Majesty so that, perchance, it may please you who are eagerly concerned about the whole body of learning, to have me dispatch some of our young men to procure for us certain necessary works, and bring with them to France the flowers of England; so that a graceful garden may not exist in York alone, but so that at Tours as well there may be found the blossoming of Paradise with its abundant fruits; that the south wind, when it comes, may cause the gardens along the River Loire to burst into bloom, and their perfumed airs to stream forth, and finally, that which follows in the Canticle, whence I have drawn this simile, may be brought to pass... (Canticle v. 1, 2). Or even this exhortation of the prophet Isaiah, which urges us to acquire wisdom:--"All ye who thirst, come to the waters; and you who have not money, hasten, buy and eat: come, without money and without price, and buy wine and milk" (Isaiah iv. 1.)

And this is a thing which your gracious zeal will not overlook: how upon every page of the Holy Scriptures we are urged to the acquisition of wisdom; how nothing is more honorable for insuring a happy life, nothing more pleasing in the observance, nothing more efficient against sin, nothing more praiseworthy in any lofty station, than that men live according to the teachings of the philosophers. Moreover, nothing is more essential to the government of the people, nothing better for the guidance of life into the paths of honorable character, than the grace which wisdom gives, and the glory of training and the power of learning. Therefore it is that in its praise, Solomon, the wisest of all men, exclaims, "Better is wisdom than all precious things, and more to be desired" (Prov. viii. 11 seq). To secure this with every possible effort and to get possession of it by daily endeavor, do you, my lord King, exhort the young men who are in your Majesty's palace, that they strive for this in the flower of their youth, so that they may be deemed worthy to live through an old age of honor, and that by its means they may be able to attain to everlasting happiness. I, myself, according to my disposition, shall not be slothful in sowing the seeds of wisdom among your servants in this land, being mindful of the injunction, "Sow thy seed in the morning, and at eventide let not thy hand cease; since thou knowest not what will spring up, whether these or those, and if both together, still better is it" (Eccles. xi. 6). In the morning of my life and in the fruitful period of my studies I sowed seed in Britain, and now that my blood has grown cool in the evening of life, I still cease not; but sow the seed in France, desiring that both may spring up by the grace of God. And now that my body has grown weak, I find consolation in the saying of St. Jerome, who declares in his letter to Nepotianus, "Almost all the powers of the body are altered in old men, and wisdom alone will increase while the rest decay." And a little further he says, "The old age of those who have adorned their youth with noble accomplishments and have meditated on the law of the Lord both day and night becomes more and more deeply accomplished with its years, more polished from experience, more wise by the lapse of time; and it reaps the sweetest fruit of ancient learning." In this letter in praise of wisdom, one who wishes can read many things of the scientific pursuits of the ancients, and can understand how eager were these ancients to abound in the grace of wisdom. I have noted that your zeal, which is pleasing to God and praiseworthy, is always advancing toward this wisdom and takes pleasure in it. And that you are adorning the magnificence of your worldly rule with still greater intellectual splendor. In this may our Lord Jesus Christ, who is himself the supreme type of divine wisdom, guard you and exalt you, and cause you to attain to the glory of His own blessed and everlasting vision.

I am eager that others should drink deep of the old wine of ancient learning. I shall presently begin to nourish still others with the fruits of grammatical ingenuity. And some of them I am eager to enlighten with a knowledge of the order of the stars, that seem painted, as it were, on the dome of some mighty palace.

Model Practice 1 (grammatically adapted from the original--poetry)

Model Practice 2

Model Practice 3

The Life of King Alfred, (excerpt)

by Asser, Bishop of Sherborne
888 AD

This work is ascribed, on its own internal authority, to Asser, who is said to have been Bishop of St. David's, of Sherborne or of Exeter, in the time of king Alfred. Though most of the public events recorded in this book are to be found in the Saxon Chronicle, yet for many interesting circumstances in the life of our great Saxon king we are indebted to this biography alone. But, as if no part of history is ever to be free from suspicion, or from difficulty, a doubt has been raised concerning the authenticity of this work. (1) There is also another short treatise called the Annals of Asser, or the Chronicle of St. Neot, different from the present: it is published in vol. iii. of Gale and Fell's "Collection of Historians". And it has been suspected by a living writer that both of these works are to be looked upon as compilations of a later date, the arguments upon which this opinion is founded are drawn principally from the abrupt and incoherent character of the work before us. But we have neither time nor space to enter further into this question. As the work has been edited by Petrie, so has it been here translated, and the reader, taking it upon its own merits, will find therein much of interest about our glorious king, concerning whom he will lament with me that all we know is so little, so unsatisfying.

--- J.A. Giles (London, 1847)

In the year of our Lord's incarnation 866, which was the eighteenth of king Alfred, Ethelred, brother of Ethelbert, king of the West Saxons, undertook the government of the kingdom for five years; and the same year a large fleet of pagans came to Britain from the Danube, and wintered in the kingdom of the Eastern-Saxons, which is called in Saxon East-Anglia; and there they became principally an army of cavalry. But, to speak in nautical phrase, I will no longer commit my vessel to the power of the waves and of its sails, or keeping off from land steer my round-about course through so many calamities of wars and series of years, but will return to that which first prompted me to this task; that is to say, I think it right in this place briefly to relate as much as has come to my knowledge about the character of my revered lord Alfred, king of the Anglo-Saxons, during the years that he was an infant and a boy.

He was loved by his father and mother, and even by all the people, above all his brothers, and was educated altogether at the court of the king. As he advanced through the years of infancy and youth, his form appeared more comely than that of his brothers. In look, in speech, and in manners, he was more graceful than they. His noble nature implanted in him from his cradle a love of wisdom above all things. But with shame be it spoken, by the unworthy neglect of his parents and nurses, he remained illiterate even till he was twelve years old or more. He, however, listened with serious attention to the Saxon poems which he often heard recited, and easily retained them in his docile memory. He was a zealous practiser of hunting in all its branches, and hunted with great assiduity and success; for skill and good fortune in this art, as in all others, are among the gifts of God, as we also have often witnessed.

On a certain day, therefore, his mother was showing him and his brother a Saxon book of poetry, which she held in her hand, and said, "Whichever of you shall the soonest learn this volume shall have it for his own." Stimulated by these words, or rather by the Divine inspiration, and allured by the beautifully illuminated letter at the beginning of the volume, he spoke before all his brothers, who, though his seniors in age, were not so in grace, and answered, "Will you really give that book to one of us, that is to say, to him who can first understand and repeat it to yon?" At this his mother smiled with satisfaction, and confirmed what she had before said. Upon which the boy took the book out of her hand, and went to his master to read it, and in due time brought it to his mother and recited it.

After this he learned the daily course, that is, the celebration of the hours, and afterwards certain psalms, and several prayers, contained in a certain book which he kept day and night in his bosom, as we ourselves have seen, and carried about with him to assist his prayers, amid all the bustle and business of this present life. But, sad to say, he could not gratify his most ardent wish to learn the liberal arts, because, as he said, there were no good readers at that time in all the kingdom of the West-Saxons.

This he confessed, with many lamentations and sighs, to have been one of his greatest difficulties and impediments in this life. Namely, that when he was young and had the capacity for learning, he could not find teachers; however, when he was more advanced in life, he was harassed by so many diseases unknown to all the physicians of this island, as well as by the internal and external anxieties of sovereignty, and by continual invasions of the pagans, and had his teachers and writers also so much disturbed, that there was no time for reading. But yet among the impediments of this present life, from infancy up to the present time, and, as I believe, even until his death, he continued to feel the same insatiable desire of knowledge, and still aspires after it.

His noble nature implanted in him from his cradle a love of wisdom above all things. But by the unworthy neglect of his parents and nurses, he remained illiterate even till he was twelve years old or more. He, however, listened with serious attention to the Saxon poems which he often heard recited, and easily retained them in his docile memory.

Model Practice 1

Model Practice 2

Model Practice 3

Pope Urban II Plea for a Crusade 1095 (excerpt)

from The First Crusade: The Accounts of Eyewitnesses and Participants
by August C. Krey
1095 AD

(Parts of the second paragraph were omitted because of the detailed descriptions of torture. Note: This version of the speech was written down several years after it was given. There is some doubt by scholars as to the accuracy of the inflammatory comments.)

THE FIRST CRUSADE

{Robert the Monk.) . . . "Oh, race of Franks, race from across the mountains, race chosen and beloved by God — as shines forth in very many of your works — set apart from all nations by the situation of your country, as well as by your Catholic faith and the honor of the Holy Church! To you our discourse is addressed, and for you our exhortation is intended. We wish you to know what a grievous cause has led us to your country, what peril, threatening you and all the faithful, has brought us.

"From the confines of Jerusalem and the city of Constantinople a horrible tale has gone forth and very frequently has been brought to our ears; namely, that a race from the kingdom of the Persians, an accursed race, a race utterly alienated from God, a generation, forsooth, which has neither directed its heart nor entrusted its spirit to God, has invaded the lands of those Christians and has depopulated them by the sword, pillage, and fire; it has led away a part of the captives into its own country, and a part it has destroyed by cruel tortures; it has either entirely destroyed the churches of God or appropriated them for the rites of its own religion. They destroy the altars, after having defiled them with their uncleanness...

The kingdom of the Greeks is now dismembered by them and deprived of territory so vast in extent that it can not be traversed in a march of two months. On whom, therefore, is the task of avenging these wrongs and of recovering this territory incumbent, if not upon you? You, upon whom above other nations God has conferred remarkable glory in arms, great courage, bodily energy, and the strength to humble the hairy scalp of those who resist you.

"Let the deeds of your ancestors move you and incite your minds to manly achievements; likewise, the glory and greatness of King Charles the Great, and his son Louis, and of your other kings, who have destroyed the kingdoms of the pagans, and have extended in these lands the territory of the Holy Church. Let the Holy Sepulcher of the Lord, our Savior, which is possessed by unclean nations, especially move you, and likewise the holy places, which are now treated with ignominy and irreverently polluted with filthiness. Oh, most valiant soldiers and descendants of invincible ancestors, be not degenerate, but recall the valor of your forefathers!

"However, if you are hindered by love of children, parents, and wives, remember what the Lord says in the Gospel, 'He that loveth father, or mother more than me, is not worthy of me.' 'Everyone that hath forsaken houses, or brethren, or sisters, or father, or mother, or wife, or children, or lands for my name's sake shall receive an hundred-fold and shall inherit everlasting life.' Let none of your possessions detain you, no solicitude for your family affairs, since this land which you inhabit, shut in on all sides by the sea and surrounded by mountain peaks, is too narrow for your large population;

nor does it abound in wealth; and it furnishes scarcely food enough for its cultivators. Hence it is that you murder and devour one another, that you wage war, and that frequently you perish by mutual wounds. Let therefore hatred depart from among you, let your quarrels end, let wars cease, and let all dissensions and controversies slumber. Enter upon the road to the Holy Sepulcher; wrest that land from the wicked race, and subject it to yourselves. That land which, as the Scripture says, 'floweth with milk and honey' was given by God into the possession of the children of Israel.

"Jerusalem is the navel of the world; the land is fruitful above others, like another paradise of delights. This the Redeemer of the human race has made illustrious by His advent, has beautified by His presence, has consecrated by suffering, has redeemed by death, has glorified by burial. This royal city, therefore, situated at the center of the world, is now held captive by His enemies, and is in subjection to those who do not know God, to the worship of the heathen. Therefore, she seeks and desires to be liberated and does not cease to implore you to come to her aid. From you, especially, she asks succor, because, as we have already said, God has conferred upon you, above all nations, great glory in arms. Accordingly, undertake this journey for the remission of your sins, with the assurance of the imperishable glory of the kingdom of heaven."

When Pope Urban had said these and very many similar things in his urbane discourse, he so influenced to one purpose the desires of all who were present that they cried out, "God wills it! God wills it!" When the venerable Roman pontiff heard that, with eyes uplifted to heaven he gave thanks to God and, with his hand commanding silence, said:

"Most beloved brethren, today is manifest in you what the Lord says in the Gospel, 'Where two or three are gathered together in My name there am I in the midst of them.'-° Unless the Lord God had been present in your minds, all of you would not have uttered the same cry. For, although the cry issued from numerous mouths, yet the origin of the cry was one. Therefore I say to you that God, who implanted this in your breasts, has drawn it forth from you. Let this then be your battle cry in combat, because this word is given to you by God. When an armed attack is made upon the enemy, let this one cry be raised by all the soldiers of God: 'God wills it! God wills it!'

"And we do not command or advise that the old or the feeble, or those unfit for bearing arms, undertake this journey. Nor ought women to set out at all without their husbands or brothers or legal guardians. For such are more of a hindrance than aid, more of a burden than an advantage. Let the rich aid the needy; and, according to their means, let them take with them experienced soldiers. The priests and clerks of any order are not to go without the consent of their bishops; for this journey would profit them nothing if they went without such permission. Also, it is not fitting that laymen should enter upon the pilgrimage without the blessing of their priests.

"Whoever, therefore, shall determine upon this holy pilgrimage and shall make his vow to God to that effect and shall offer himself to Him as a living sacrifice, holy, acceptable unto God, shall wear the sign of the cross of the Lord on his forehead, or on his breast. When, having truly fulfilled his vow, he wishes to return, let him place the cross on his back between his shoulders. Such, indeed, by two-fold action will fulfill the precept of the Lord, as He commands in the Gospel, 'He that doth not take his cross and follow after me, is not worthy of me.' "

Hence it is that you murder and devour one another, that you wage war, and that frequently you perish by mutual wounds. Let therefore hatred depart from among you, let your quarrels end, let wars cease, and let all dissensions and controversies slumber. Enter upon the road to the Holy Sepulcher; wrest that land from the wicked race, and subject it to yourselves.

Model Practice 1

Model Practice 2

Model Practice 3

How Can the Absolute Be a Cause? (excerpt)

from Library Of The World's Best Literature, Ancient And Modern, Vol. 2
by Thomas Aquinas
edited by Charles Dudley Warner
1226 - 1274

ON THE VALUE OF OUR CONCEPTS OF THE DEITY

Part I--From the 'Summa Theologica'

It is obvious that terms implying negation or extrinsic relation in no way signify the divine substance, but simply the removal of some attribute from Him, or His relation with other beings, or rather the relation of other beings with Him. As to appellations that are absolute and positive,--such as good, wise, and the like,--various opinions have been entertained. It was held by some that these terms, though used affirmatively, were in reality devised for the purpose of elimination, and not with the intent of positive attribution. Hence, they claimed, when we say that God is a living being, we mean that God's existence is not that of inanimate things; and so on for other predicates. This was the position of Rabbi Moses. According to another view these terms are employed to denote a relation between God and creatures; so that for instance, when we say, God is good, we mean, God is the cause of goodness in all things.

Both interpretations, however, are open to a threefold objection. For, in the first place, neither can offer any explanation of the fact that certain terms are applied to the Deity in preference to others. As He is the source of all good, so He is the cause of all things corporeal. Consequently, if by affirming that God is good, we merely imply that He is the cause of goodness, we might with equal reason assert that He is a corporeal being.

Again, the inference from these positions would be that all terms applied to God have only a secondary import, such, for instance, as we give to the word healthy, as applied to medicine; whereby we signify that it is productive of health in the organism, while the organism itself is said, properly and primarily, to be healthy.

In the third place, these interpretations distort the meaning of those who employ such terms in regard to the Deity. For, when they declare that He is the living God, they certainly mean something else than that He is the cause of our life or that He is different from inanimate bodies.

We are obliged, therefore, to take another view, and to affirm that such terms denote the substantial nature of God, but that, at the same time, their representative force is deficient. They express the knowledge which our intellect has of God; and since this knowledge is gotten from created things, we know Him according to the measure in which creatures represent Him. Now God, absolutely and in all respects perfect, possesses every perfection that is found in His creatures. Each created thing, therefore, inasmuch as it has some perfection, resembles and manifests the Deity. Not as a being of the same species or genus with itself, but as a supereminent source from which are derived its effects. They represent Him, in a word, just as the energy of the terrestrial elements represents the energy of the sun.

Our manner of speech, therefore, denotes the substance of God, yet denotes it imperfectly, because creatures are imperfect manifestations of Him. When we say that God is good, we do not mean that He is the cause of goodness or that He is not evil. Our meaning is this: What we call goodness in creatures preexists in God in a far higher way. Whence it follows, not that God is good because He is the source of good, but rather, because He is good, He imparts goodness to all things else; as St. Augustine says, "Inasmuch as He is good, we are."

HOW CAN THE ABSOLUTE BE A CAUSE?

From the 'Quæstiones Disputatæ'

The relations which are spoken of as existing between God and creatures are not really in Him. A real relation is that which exists between two things. It is mutual or bilateral then, only when its basis in both correlates is the same. Such is the case in all quantitative relations. Quantity being essentially the same in all quanta, gives rise to relations which are real in both terms--in the part, for instance, and in the whole, in the unit of measurement and in that which is measured.

But where a relation originates in causation, as between that which is active and that which is passive, it does not always concern both terms. True, that which is acted upon, or set in motion, or produced, must be related to the source of these modifications, since every effect is dependent upon its cause. And it is equally true that such causes or agencies are in some cases related to their effects, namely, when the production of those effects redounds in some way to the well-being of the cause itself. This is evidently what happens when like begets like, and thereby perpetuates, so far as may be, its own species.... There are cases, nevertheless, in which a thing, without being related, has other things related to it. The cognizing subject is related to that which is the object of cognition--to a thing which is outside the mind. But the thing itself is in no way affected by this cognition, since the mental process is confined to the mind, and therefore does not bring about any change in the object. Hence the relation established by the act of knowing cannot be in that which is known.

The same holds good of sensation. For though the physical object sets up changes in the sense-organ, and is related to it as other physical agencies are related to the things on which they act, still, the sensation implies, over and above the organic change, a subjective activity of which the external activity is altogether devoid. Likewise, we say that a man is at the right of a pillar because, with his power of locomotion, he can take his stand at the right or the left, before or behind, above or below. But obviously these relations, vary them as we will, imply nothing in the stationary pillar, though they are real in the man who holds or changes his position. Once more, a coin has nothing to do with the action that gives it its value, since this action is a human convention; and a man is quite apart from the process which produces his image. Between a man and his portrait there is a relation, but this is real in the portrait only. Between the coin and its current value there is a relation, but this is not real in the coin.

Now for the application. God's action is not to be understood as going out from Him and terminating in that which He creates. His action is Himself; consequently altogether apart from the genus of created being whereby the creature is related to Him. And again, he gains nothing by creating, or, as Avicenna puts it, His creative action is in the highest degree generous. It is also manifest that His action involves no modification of His being--without changing, He causes the changeable. Consequently, though creatures are related to Him, as effects to their cause, He is not really related to them.

Each created thing resembles and manifests the Deity. Not as a being of the same species or genus with itself, but as a supereminent source from which are derived its effects. They represent Him, in a word, just as the energy of the terrestrial elements represents the energy of the sun.

Model Practice 1 (modified)

Model Practice 2

Model Practice 3

The Decameron, (On the Black Death) Volume I (excerpt)

by Giovanni Boccaccio
translated by J.M. Rigg
1350 – 1353 AD

(Warning: The follow describes the effect of the black death in detail. The writing models also deal with death.)

In Florence, despite all that human wisdom and forethought could devise toavert it, as the cleansing of the city from many impurities by officials appointed for the purpose, the refusal of entrance to all sick folk, and the adoption of many precautions for the preservation of health; despite also humble supplications addressed to God, and often repeated both in public procession and otherwise, by the devout; towards the beginning of the spring of the said year the doleful effects of the pestilence began to be horribly apparent by symptoms that showed as if miraculous.

Not such were they as in the East, where an issue of blood from the nose was a manifest sign of inevitable death; but in men and women alike it first betrayed itself by the emergence of certain tumours in the groin or the armpits, some of which grew as large as a common apple, others as an egg, some more, some less, which the common folk called gavoccioli. From the two said parts of the body this deadly gavocciolo soon began to propagate and spread itself in all directions indifferently; after which the form of the malady began to change, black spots or livid making their appearance in many cases on the arm or the thigh or elsewhere, now few and large, now minute and numerous. And as the gavocciolo had been and still was an infallible token of approaching death, such also were these spots on whomsoever they showed themselves. Which maladies seemed to set entirely at naught both the art of the physician and the virtues of physic; indeed, whether it was that the disorder was of a nature to defy such treatment, or that the physicians were at fault—besides the qualified there was now a multitude both of men and of women who practiced without having received the slightest tincture of medical science—and, being in ignorance of its source, failed to apply the proper remedies; in either case, not merely were those that recovered few, but almost all within three days from the appearance of the said symptoms, sooner or later, died, and in most cases without any fever or other attendant malady.

Moreover, the virulence of the pest was the greater by reason that interaction was apt to convey it from the sick to the whole, just as fire devours things dry or greasy when they are brought close to it. Nay, the evil went yet further, for not merely by speech or association with the sick was the malady communicated to the healthy with consequent peril of common death; but any that touched the cloth of the sick, or aught else that had been touched or used by them, seemed thereby to contract the disease.

So marvelous sounds that which I have now to relate, that, had not many, and I among them, observed it with their own eyes, I had hardly dared to credit it, much less to set it down in writing, though I had had it from the lips of a credible witness.

I say, then, that such was the energy of the contagion of the said pestilence, that it was not merely propagated from man to man but, what is much more startling, it was frequently observed, that things which had belonged to one sick or dead of the disease, if touched by some other living creature, not of the human species, were the occasion, not merely of sickening, but of an almost instantaneous death. Whereof my own eyes (as I said a little before) had cognisance, one day among others, by the following experience. The rags of a poor man who had died of the disease being strewn about the open street, two hogs came thither, and after, as is their wont, no little trifling with their snouts, took the rags between their teeth and tossed them to and fro about their chaps; whereupon, almost immediately, they gave a few turns, and fell down dead, as if by poison, upon the rags which in an evil hour they had disturbed.

In which circumstances, not to speak of many others of a similar or even graver complexion, divers apprehensions and imaginations were engendered in the minds of such as were left alive, inclining almost all of them to the same harsh resolution, to wit, to shun and abhor all contact with the sick and all that belonged to them, thinking thereby to make each his own health secure. Among whom there were those who thought that to live temperately and avoid all excess would count for much as a preservative against seizures of this kind. Wherefore they banded together, and, dissociating themselves from all others, formed communities in houses where there were no sick, and lived a separate and secluded life, which they regulated with the utmost care, avoiding every kind of luxury, but eating and drinking very moderately of the most delicate viands and the finest wines, holding converse with none but one another, lest tidings of sickness or death should reach them, and diverting their minds with music and such other delights as they could devise. Others, the bias of whose minds was in the opposite direction, maintained, that to drink freely, frequent places of public resort, and take their pleasure with song and revel, sparing to satisfy no appetite, and to laugh and mock at no event, was the sovereign remedy for so great an evil: and that which they affirmed they also put in practice, so far as they were able, resorting day and night, now to this tavern, now to that, drinking with an entire disregard of rule or measure, and by preference making the houses of others, as it were, their inns, if they but saw in them aught that was particularly to their taste or liking; which they were readily able to do, because the owners, seeing death imminent, had become as reckless of their property as of their lives; so that most of the houses were open to all comers, and no distinction was observed between the stranger who presented himself and the rightful lord. Thus, adhering ever to their inhuman determination to shun the sick, as far as possible, they ordered their life. In this extremity of our city's suffering and tribulation the venerable authority of laws, human and divine, was abased and all but totally dissolved, for lack of those who should have administered and enforced them, most of whom, like the rest of the citizens, were either dead or sick, or so hard bested for servants that they were unable to execute any office; whereby every man was free to do what was right in his own eyes.

Not a few there were who belonged to neither of the two said parties, but kept a middle course between them, neither laying the same restraint upon their diet as the former, nor allowing themselves the same license in drinking and other dissipations as the latter, but living with a degree of freedom sufficient to satisfy their appetites, and not as recluses. They therefore walked abroad, carrying in their hands flowers or fragrant herbs or divers sorts of spices, which they frequently raised to their noses, deeming it an excellent thing thus to comfort the brain with such perfumes, because the air seemed to be everywhere laden and reeking with the stench emitted by the dead and the dying and the odors of drugs.

Some again, the most sound, perhaps, in judgment, as they we also the most harsh in temper, of all, affirmed that there was no medicine for the disease superior or equal in efficacy to flight; following which prescription a multitude of men and women, negligent of all but themselves, deserted their city, their houses, their estate, their kinsfolk, their goods, and went into voluntary exile, or migrated to the country parts, as if God in visiting men with this pestilence in requital of their iniquities would not pursue them with His wrath, wherever they might be, but intended the destruction of such alone as remained within the circuit of the walls of the city; or deeming, perchance, that it was now time for all to flee from it, and that its last hour was come.

Of the adherents of these divers opinions not all died, neither did all escape; but rather there were, of each sort and in every place, many that sickened, and by those who retained their health were treated after the example which they themselves, while whole, had set, being everywhere left to languish in almost total neglect. Tedious were it to recount, how citizen avoided citizen, how among neighbors was scarce found any that shewed fellow-feeling for another, how kinsfolk held aloof, and never met, or but rarely; enough that this sore affliction entered so deep into the minds of men and women, that in the horror thereof brother was forsaken by brother, nephew by uncle, brother by sister, and oftentimes husband by wife; nay, what is more, and scarcely to be believed, fathers and mothers were found to abandon their own children, untended, unvisited, to their fate, as if they had been strangers. Wherefore the sick of both sexes, whose number could not be estimated, were left without resource but in the charity of friends (and few such there were), or the interest of servants, who were hardly to be had at high rates and on unseemly terms, and being, moreover, one and all men and women of gross understanding, and for the most part unused to such offices, concerned themselves no farther than to supply the immediate and expressed wants of the sick, and to watch them die; in which service they themselves not seldom perished with their gains. In consequence of which dearth of servants and dereliction of the sick by neighbors, kinsfolk and friends, it came to pass--a thing, perhaps, never before heard of that no woman, however dainty, fair or well-born she might be, shrank, when stricken with the disease, from the ministrations of a man, no matter whether he were young or no, or scrupled to expose to him every part of her body, with no more shame than if he had been a woman, submitting of necessity to that which her malady required; wherefrom, perchance, there resulted in after time some loss of modesty in such as recovered. Besides which many succumbed, who with proper attendance, would, perhaps, have escaped death; so that, what with the virulence of the plague and the lack of due tendance of the sick, the multitude of the deaths, that daily and nightly took place in the city, was such that those who heard the tale--not to say witnessed the fact--were struck dumb with amazement. Whereby, practices contrary to the former habits of the citizens could hardly fail to grow up among the survivors.

It had been, as today it still is, the custom for the women that were neighbors and of kin to the deceased to gather in his house with the women that were most closely connected with him, to wail with them in common, while on the other hand his male kinsfolk and neighbors, with not a few of the other citizens, and a due proportion of the clergy according to his quality, assembled without, in front of the house, to receive the corpse; and so the dead man was borne on the shoulders of his peers, with funeral pomp of taper and dirge, to the church selected by him before his death. Which rites, as the pestilence waxed in fury, were either in whole or in great part disused, and gave way to others of a novel order. For not only did no crowd of women surround the bed of the dying, but many passed from this life unregarded, and few indeed were they to whom were accorded the lamentations and bitter tears of sorrowing relations; nay, for the most part, their place was taken by the laugh, the jest, the festal gathering; observances which the women, domestic piety in large measure set aside, had adopted with very great advantage to their health. Few also there were whose bodies were attended to the church by more than ten or twelve of their neighbors, and those not the honourable and respected citizens; but a sort of corpse-carriers drawn from the baser ranks who called themselves becchini (1) and performed such offices for hire, would shoulder the bier, and with hurried steps carry it, not to the church of the dead man's choice, but to that which was nearest at hand, with four or six priests in front and a candle or two, or, perhaps, none; nor did the priests distress themselves with too long and solemn an office, but with the aid of the becchini hastily consigned the corpse to the first tomb which they found untenanted. The condition of lower, and, perhaps, in great measure of the middle ranks, of the people shewed even worse and more deplorable; for, deluded by hope or constrained by poverty, they stayed in their quarters, in their houses, where they sickened by thousands a day, and, being without service or help of any kind, were, so to speak, irredeemably devoted to the death which overtook them. Many died daily or nightly in the public streets. Of many others who died at home, the departure was hardly observed by their neighbors, until the stench of their putrefying bodies carried the tidings. And with their corpses and the corpses of others who died on every hand, the whole place was a sepulcher.

It was the common practice of most of the neighbors, moved no less by fear of contamination by the putrefying bodies than by charity towards the deceased, to drag the corpses out of the houses with their own hands, aided, perhaps, by a porter, if a porter was to be had, and to lay them in front of the doors, where any one who made the round might have seen, especially in the morning, more of them than he could count; afterwards they would have biers brought up, or, in default, planks, whereon they laid them. Nor was it once or twice only that one and the same bier carried two or three corpses at once; but quite a considerable number of such cases occurred, one bier sufficing for husband and wife, two or three brothers, father and son, and so forth. And times without number it happened, that, as two priests, bearing the cross, were on their way to perform the last office for some one, three or four biers were brought up by the porters in rear of them, so that, whereas the priests supposed that they had but one corpse to bury, they discovered that there were six or eight, or sometimes more. Nor, for all their number, were their obsequies honoured by either tears or lights or crowds of mourners; rather, it was come to this, that a dead man was then of no more account than a dead goat would be today. From all which it is abundantly manifest, that that lesson of patient resignation, which the sages were never able to learn from the slight and infrequent mishaps which occur in the natural course of events, was now brought home even to the minds of the simple by the magnitude of their disasters, so that they became indifferent to them.

Nay, the evil went yet further. For not merely by speech or association with the sick was the malady communicated to the healthy; but any that touched the cloth of the sick, or aught else that had been touched or used by them, seemed to contract the disease.

Model Practice 1 (modified)

Model Practice 2

Model Practice 3

The Imitation of Christ (excerpt)

by Thomas a Kempis
translated by Rev. William Benham
1418 AD

INTRODUCTORY NOTE

The treatise "Of the Imitation of Christ" appears to have been originally written in Latin early in the fifteenth century. Its exact date and its authorship are still a matter of debate. Manuscripts of the Latin version survive in considerable numbers all over Western Europe, and they, with the vast list of translations and of printed editions, testify to its almost unparalleled popularity. One scribe attributes it to St. Bernard of Clairvaux; but the fact that it contains a quotation from St. Francis of Assisi, who was born thirty years after the death of St. Bernard, disposes of this theory. In England there exist many manuscripts of the first three books, called "Musica Ecclesiastica," frequently ascribed to the English mystic Walter Hilton. But Hilton seems to have died in 1395, and there is no evidence of the existence of the work before 1400. Many manuscripts scattered throughout Europe ascribe the book to Jean le Charlier de Gerson, the great Chancellor of the University of Paris, who was a leading figure in the Church in the earlier part of the fifteenth century. The most probable author, however, especially when the internal evidence is considered, is Thomas Haemmerlein, known also as Thomas a Kempis, from his native town of Kempen, near the Rhine, about forty miles north of Cologne. Haemmerlein, who was born in 1379 or 1380, was a member of the order of the Brothers of Common Life, and spent the last seventy years of his life at Mount St. Agnes, a monastery of Augustinian canons in the diocese of Utrecht. Here he died on July 26, 1471, after an uneventful life spent in copying manuscripts, reading, and composing, and in the peaceful routine of monastic piety.

With the exception of the Bible, no Christian writing has had so wide a vogue or so sustained a popularity as this. And yet, in one sense, it is hardly an original work at all. Its structure it owes largely to the writings of the medieval mystics, and its ideas and phrases are a mosaic from the Bible and the Fathers of the early Church. But these elements are interwoven with such delicate skill and a religious feeling at once so ardent and so sound, that it promises to remain, what it has been for five hundred years, the supreme call and guide to spiritual aspiration.

THE IMITATION OF CHRIST
THE FIRST BOOK
ADMONITIONS PROFITABLE FOR THE SPIRITUAL LIFE

CHAPTER I

Of the imitation of Christ, and of contempt of the world and all its vanities

He that followeth me shall not walk in darkness,(1) saith the Lord. These are the words of Christ; and they teach us how far we must imitate His life and character, if we seek true illumination and deliverance from all blindness of heart. Let it be our most earnest study, therefore, to dwell upon the life of Jesus Christ.

2. His teaching surpasseth all teaching of holy men, and such as have His Spirit find therein the hidden manna.(2) But there are many who, though they frequently hear the Gospel, yet feel but little longing after it, because they have not the mind of Christ. He, therefore, that will fully and with true wisdom understand the words of Christ, let him strive to conform his whole life to that mind of Christ.

3. What doth it profit thee to enter into deep discussion concerning the Holy Trinity, if thou lack humility, and be thus displeasing to the Trinity? For verily, it is not deep words that make a man holy and upright; it is a good life which maketh a man dear to God. I had rather feel contrition than be skilful in the definition thereof. If thou knewest the whole Bible, and the sayings of all the philosophers, what should all this profit thee without the love and grace of God? Vanity of vanities, all is vanity, save to love God, and Him only to serve. That is the highest wisdom, to cast the world behind us, and to reach forward to the heavenly kingdom.

4. It is vanity then to seek after, and to trust in, the riches that shall perish. It is vanity, too, to covet honours, and to lift up ourselves on high. It is vanity to follow the desires of the flesh and be led by them, for this shall bring misery at the last. It is vanity to desire a long life, and to have little care for a good life. It is vanity to take thought only for the life which now is, and not to look forward to the things which shall be hereafter. It is vanity to love that which quickly passeth away, and not to hasten where eternal joy abideth.

5. Be ofttimes mindful of the saying,(3) The eye is not satisfied with seeing, nor the ear with hearing. Strive, therefore, to turn away thy heart from the love of the things that are seen, and to set it upon the things that are not seen. For they who follow after their own fleshly lusts, defile the conscience, and destroy the grace of God.

(1) John viii. 12. (2) Revelations ii. 17. (3) Ecclesiastes i. 8.

CHAPTER II
Of thinking humbly of oneself

There is naturally in every man a desire to know, but what profiteth knowledge without the fear of God? Better of a surety is a lowly peasant who serveth God, than a proud philosopher who watcheth the stars and neglecteth the knowledge of himself. He who knoweth himself well is vile in his own sight; neither regardeth he the praises of men. If I knew all the things that are in the world, and were not in charity, what should it help me before God, who is to judge me according to my deeds?

2. Rest from inordinate desire of knowledge, for therein is found much distraction and deceit. Those who have knowledge desire to appear learned, and to be called wise. Many things there are to know which profiteth little or nothing to the soul. And foolish out of measure is he who attendeth upon other things rather than those which serve to his soul's health. Many words satisfy not the soul, but a good life refresheth the mind, and a pure conscience giveth great confidence towards God.

3. The greater and more complete thy knowledge, the more severely shalt thou be judged, unless thou hast lived holily. Therefore be not lifted up by any skill or knowledge that thou hast; but rather fear concerning the knowledge which is given to thee. If it seemeth to thee that thou knowest many things, and understandest them well, know also that there are many more things which thou knowest not. Be not high-minded, but rather confess thine ignorance. Why desirest thou to lift thyself above another, when there are found many more learned and more skilled in the Scripture than thou? If thou wilt know and learn anything with profit, love to be thyself unknown and to be counted for nothing.

4. That is the highest and most profitable lesson, when a man truly knoweth and judgeth lowly of himself. To account nothing of one's self, and to think always kindly and highly of others, this is great and perfect wisdom. Even shouldest thou see thy neighbor sin openly or grievously, yet thou oughtest not to reckon thyself better than he, for thou knowest not how long thou shalt keep thine integrity. All of us are weak and frail; hold thou no man more frail than thyself.

CHAPTER III
Of the knowledge of truth

Happy is the man whom Truth by itself doth teach, not by figures and transient words, but as it is in itself.(1) Our own judgment and feelings often deceive us, and we discern but little of the truth. What doth it profit to argue about hidden and dark things, concerning which we shall not be even reproved in the judgment, because we knew them not? Oh, grievous folly, to neglect the things which are profitable and necessary, and to give our minds to things which are curious and hurtful! Having eyes, we see not.

2. And what have we to do with talk about genus and species! He to whom the Eternal Word speaketh is free from multiplied questionings. From this One Word are all things, and all things speak of Him; and this is the Beginning which also speaketh unto us.(2) No man without Him understandeth or rightly judgeth. The man to whom all things are one, who bringeth all things to one, who seeth all things in one, he is able to remain steadfast of spirit, and at rest in God. O God, who art the Truth, make me one with Thee in everlasting love. It wearieth me oftentimes to read and listen to many things; in Thee is all that I wish for and desire. Let all the doctors hold their peace; let all creation keep silence before Thee: speak Thou alone to me.

3. The more a man hath unity and simplicity in himself, the more things and the deeper things he understandeth; and that without labour, because he receiveth the light of understanding from above. The spirit which is pure, sincere, and steadfast, is not distracted though it hath many works to do, because it doth all things to the honour of God, and striveth to be free from all thoughts of self-seeking. Who is so full of hindrance and annoyance to thee as thine own undisciplined heart? A man who is good and devout arrangeth beforehand within his own heart the works which he hath to do abroad; and so is not drawn away by the desires of his evil will, but subjecteth everything to the judgment of right reason. Who hath a harder battle to fight than he who striveth for self-mastery? And this should be our endeavour, even to master self, and thus daily to grow stronger than self, and go on unto perfection

4. All perfection hath some imperfection joined to it in this life, and all our power of sight is not without some darkness. A lowly knowledge of thyself is a surer way to God than the deep searching of man's learning. Not that learning is to be blamed, nor the taking account of anything that is good; but a good conscience and a holy life is better than all. And because many seek knowledge rather than good living, therefore they go astray, and bear little or no fruit.

5. O if they would give that diligence to the rooting out of vice and the planting of virtue which they give unto vain questionings: there had not been so many evil doings and stumbling-blocks among the laity, nor such ill living among houses of religion. Of a surety, at the Day of Judgment it will be demanded of us, not what we have read, but what we have done; not how well we have spoken, but how holily we have lived. Tell me, where now are all those masters and teachers, whom thou knewest well, whilst they were yet with you, and flourished in learning? Their stalls are now filled by others,

who perhaps never have one thought concerning them. Whilst they lived they seemed to be somewhat, but now no one speaks of them.

6. Oh how quickly passeth the glory of the world away! Would that their life and knowledge had agreed together! For then would they have read and inquired unto good purpose. How many perish through empty learning in this world, who care little for serving God. And because they love to be great more than to be humble, therefore they "have become vain in their imaginations." He only is truly great, who hath great charity. He is truly great who deemeth himself small, and counteth all height of honour as nothing. He is the truly wise man, who counteth all earthly things as dung that he may win Christ. And he is the truly learned man, who doeth the will of God, and forsaketh his own will.

(1) Psalm xciv. 12; Numbers xii. 8. (2) John viii. 25 (Vulg.).

CHAPTER IV

Of prudence in action

We must not trust every word of others or feeling within ourselves, but cautiously and patiently try the matter, whether it be of God. Unhappily we are so weak that we find it easier to believe and speak evil of others, rather than good. But they that are perfect, do not give ready heed to every newsbearer, for they know man's weakness that it is prone to evil and unstable in words.

2. This is great wisdom, not to be hasty in action, or stubborn in our own opinions. A part of this wisdom also is not to believe every word we hear, nor to tell others all that we hear, even though we believe it. Take counsel with a man who is wise and of a good conscience; and seek to be instructed by one better than thyself, rather than to follow thine own inventions. A good life maketh a man wise toward God, and giveth him experience in many things. The more humble a man is in himself, and the more obedient towards God, the wiser will he be in all things, and the more shall his soul be at peace.

CHAPTER V

Of the reading of Holy Scriptures

It is Truth which we must look for in Holy Writ, not cunning of words. All Scripture ought to be read in the spirit in which it was written. We must rather seek for what is profitable in Scripture, than for what ministereth to subtlety in discourse. Therefore we ought to read books which are devotional and simple, as well as those which are deep and difficult. And let not the weight of the writer be a stumbling-block to thee, whether he be of little or much learning, but let the love of the pure Truth draw thee to read. Ask not, who hath said this or that, but look to what he says.

2. Men pass away, but the truth of the Lord endureth for ever. Without respect of persons God speaketh to us in divers manners. Our own curiosity often hindereth us in the reading of holy writings, when we seek to understand and discuss, where we should pass simply on. If thou wouldst profit by thy reading, read humbly, simply, honestly, and not desiring to win a character for learning. Ask freely, and hear in silence the words of holy men; nor be displeased at the hard sayings of older men than thou, for they are not uttered without cause.

He that followeth me shall not walk in darkness saith the Lord. These are the words of Christ; and they teach us how far we must imitate His life and character, if we seek true illumination and deliverance from all blindness of heart. Let it be our most earnest study, therefore, to dwell upon the life of Jesus Christ.

Model Practice 1(modified)

Model Practice 2

Model Practice 3

Joan of Arc

from Joan of Arc
by Ronald Sutherland Gower
taken from the transcripts of the trials of Joan of Arc
1431

Joan had the following letter despatched to the Duke of Bedford:--

'In the name of Jesus and Mary--You, King of England; and you, Duke of Bedford, who call yourself Regent of France; you, William de la Pole; you, Earl of Suffolk; you, John Lord Talbot; and you, Thomas Lord Scales, who call yourselves Lieutenants of the said Bedford, in the name of the King of Heaven, render the keys of all the good towns which you have taken and violated in France, to the Maid sent hither by the King of Heaven. She is ready to make peace if you will consent to return and to pay for what you have taken. And all of you, soldiers, and archers, and men-at-arms, now before Orleans, return to your country, in God's name. If this is not done, King of England, I, as a leader in war, whenever I shall meet with your people in France, will oblige them to go whether they be willing or not. And if they go not, they will perish; but if they will depart, I will pardon them. I have come from the King of Heaven to drive you out of France. And do not imagine that you will ever permanently hold France, for the true heir, King Charles, shall possess it; for it is God's wish that it should belong to him. And this has been revealed to him by the Maid, who will enter Paris. If you will not obey, we shall make such a stir as hath not happened these thousand years in France. The Maid and her soldiers will have the victory. Therefore the Maid is willing that you, Duke of Bedford, should not destroy yourself.'

And Joan finishes this strange effusion by proposing to Bedford that they should combine in making a holy war for Christianity! This letter, written 'in the name of the Maid,' was dated on a Tuesday in Holy Week. The address ran thus: 'To the Duke of Bedford, so called Regent of the Kingdom of France, or to his Lieutenants, now before the town of Orleans.'

If this is not done, King of England, I, as a leader in war, whenever I shall meet with your people in France, will oblige them to go whether they be willing or not. And if they go not, they will perish; but if they will depart, I will pardon them. I have come from the King of Heaven to drive you out of France.

Model Practice 1

Model Practice 2

Model Practice 3

Dedication of the Revolutions of the Heavenly Bodies (excerpt)

from Prefaces and Prologues to Famous Books
by Nicolaus Copernicus
1543 AD

TO POPE PAUL III:

I can easily conceive, most Holy Father, that as soon as some people learn that in this book which I have written concerning the revolutions of the heavenly bodies, I ascribe certain motions to the Earth, they will cry out at once that I and my theory should be rejected. For I am not so much in love with my conclusions as not to weigh what others will think about them, and although I know that the meditations of a philosopher are far removed from the judgment of the laity, because his endeavor is to seek out the truth in all things, so far as this is permitted by God to the human reason, I still believe that one must avoid theories altogether foreign to orthodoxy. Accordingly, when I considered in my own mind how absurd a performance it must seem to those who know that the judgment of many centuries has approved the view that the Earth remains fixed as center in the midst of the heavens, if I should, on the contrary, assert that the Earth moves. I was for a long time at a loss to know whether I should publish the commentaries which I have written in proof of its motion, or whether it were not better to follow the example of the Pythagoreans and of some others, who were accustomed to transmit the secrets of Philosophy not in writing but orally, and only to their relatives and friends, as the letter from Lysis to Hipparchus bears witness. They did this, it seems to me, not as some think, because of a certain selfish reluctance to give their views to the world, but in order that the noblest truths, worked out by the careful study of great men, should not be despised by those who are vexed at the idea of taking great pains with any forms of literature except such as would be profitable, or by those who, if they are driven to the study of Philosophy for its own sake by the admonitions and the example of others, nevertheless, on account of their stupidity, hold a place among philosophers similar to that of drones among bees. Therefore, when I considered this carefully, the contempt which I had to fear because of the novelty and apparent absurdity of my view, nearly induced me to abandon utterly the work I had begun.

My friends, however, in spite of long delay and even resistance on my part, withheld me from this decision. First among these was Nicolaus Schonberg, Cardinal of Capua, distinguished in all branches of learning. Next to him comes my very dear friend, Tidemann Giese, Bishop of Culm, a most earnest student, as he is, of sacred and, indeed, of all good learning. The latter has often urged me, at times even spurring me on with reproaches, to publish and at last bring to the light the book which had lain in my study not nine years merely, but already going on four times nine. Not a few other very eminent and scholarly men made the same request, urging that I should no longer through fear refuse to give out my work for the common benefit of students of Mathematics. They said I should find that the more absurd most men now thought this theory of mine concerning the motion of the Earth, the more admiration and gratitude it would command after they saw in the publication of my commentaries the mist of absurdity cleared away by most transparent proofs. So, influenced by these advisors and this hope, I have at length allowed my friends to publish the work, as they had long besought me to do.

But perhaps Your Holiness will not so much wonder that I have ventured to publish these studies of mine, after having taken such pains in elaborating them that I have not hesitated to commit to writing my views of the motion of the Earth, as you will be curious to hear how it occurred to me to venture, contrary to the accepted view of mathematicians, and well-nigh contrary to common sense, to form a conception of any terrestrial motion whatsoever. Therefore I would not have it unknown to Your Holiness, that the only thing which induced me to look for another way of reckoning the movements of the heavenly bodies was that I knew that mathematicians by no means agree in their investigations thereof. For, in the first place, they are so much in doubt concerning the motion of the sun and the moon, that they can not even demonstrate and prove by observation the constant length of a complete year; and in the second place, in determining the motions both of these and of the five other planets, they fail to employ consistently one set of first principles and hypotheses, but use methods of proof based only upon the apparent revolutions and motions. For some employ concentric circles only; others, eccentric circles and epicycles; and even by these means they do not completely attain the desired end. For, although those who have depended upon concentric circles have shown that certain diverse motions can be deduced from these, yet they have not succeeded thereby in laying down any sure principle, corresponding indisputably to the phenomena. These, on the other hand, who have devised systems of eccentric circles, although they seem in great part to have solved the apparent movements by calculations which by these eccentrics are made to fit, have nevertheless introduced many things which seem to contradict the first principles of the uniformity of motion. Nor have they been able to discover or calculate from these the main point, which is the shape of the world and the fixed symmetry of its parts; but their procedure has been as if someone were to collect hands, feet, a head, and other members from various places, all very fine in themselves, but not proportionate to one body, and no single one corresponding in its turn to the others, so that a monster rather than a man would be formed from them. Thus in their process of demonstration which they term a "method," they are found to have omitted something essential, or to have included something foreign and not pertaining to the matter in hand. This certainly would never have happened to them if they had followed fixed principles; for if the hypotheses they assumed were not false, all that resulted there from would be verified indubitably. Those things which I am saying now may be obscure, yet they will be made clearer in their proper place.

Therefore, having turned over in my mind for a long time this uncertainty of the traditional mathematical methods of calculating the motions of the celestial bodies, I began to grow disgusted that no more consistent scheme of the movements of the mechanism of the universe, set up for our benefit by that best and most law abiding Architect of all things, was agreed upon by philosophers who otherwise investigate so carefully the most minute details of this world. Wherefore I undertook the task of rereading the books of all the philosophers I could get access to, to see whether any one ever was of the opinion that the motions of the celestial bodies were other than those postulated by the men who taught mathematics in the schools. And I found first, indeed, in Cicero, that Niceta perceived that the Earth moved; and afterward in Plutarch I found that some others were of this opinion, whose words I have seen fit to quote here, that they may be accessible to all:--

"Some maintain that the Earth is stationary, but Philolaus the Pythagorean says that it revolves in a circle about the fire of the ecliptic, like the sun and moon. Heraklides of Pontus and Ekphantus the Pythagorean make the Earth move, not changing its position, however, confined in its falling and rising around its own center in the manner of a wheel."

Taking this as a starting point, I began to consider the mobility of the Earth. And although the idea seemed absurd, yet because I knew that the liberty had been granted to others before me to postulate all sorts of little circles for explaining the phenomena of the stars, I thought I also might easily be permitted to try whether by postulating some motion of the Earth, more reliable conclusions could be reached regarding the revolution of the heavenly bodies, than those of my predecessors.

And so, after postulating movements, which, farther on in the book, I ascribe to the Earth, I have found by many and long observations that if the movements of the other planets are assumed for the circular motion of the Earth and are substituted for the revolution of each star, not only do their phenomena follow logically therefrom, but the relative positions and magnitudes both of the stars and all their orbits, and of the heavens themselves, become so closely related that in none of its parts can anything be changed without causing confusion in the other parts and in the whole universe. Therefore, in the course of the work I have followed this plan: I describe in the first book all the positions of the orbits together with the movements which I ascribe to the Earth, in order that this book might contain, as it were, the general scheme of the universe. Thereafter in the remaining books, I set forth the motions of the other stars and of all their orbits together with the movement of the Earth, in order that one may see from this to what extent the movements and appearances of the other stars and their orbits can be saved, if they are transferred to the movement of the Earth. Nor do I doubt that ingenious and learned mathematicians will sustain me, if they are willing to recognize and weigh, not superficially, but with that thoroughness which Philosophy demands above all things, those matters which have been adduced by me in this work to demonstrate these theories. In order, however, that both the learned and the unlearned equally may see that I do not avoid anyone's judgment, I have preferred to dedicate these lucubrations of mine to Your Holiness rather than to any other, because, even in this remote corner of the world where I live, you are considered to be the most eminent man in dignity of rank and in love of all learning and even of mathematics. So that by your authority and judgment you can easily suppress the bites of slanderers, albeit the proverb hath it that there is no remedy for the bite of a sycophant. If perchance there shall be idle talkers, who, though they are ignorant of all mathematical sciences, nevertheless assume the right to pass judgment on these things, and if they should dare to criticize and attack this theory of mine because of some passage of scripture which they have falsely distorted for their own purpose, I care not at all; I will even despise their judgment as foolish. For it is not unknown that Lactantius, otherwise a famous writer but a poor mathematician, speaks most childishly of the shape of the Earth when he makes fun of those who said that the Earth has the form of a sphere. It should not seem strange then to zealous students, if some such people shall ridicule us also. Mathematics are written for mathematicians, to whom, if my opinion does not deceive me, our labors will seem to contribute something to the ecclesiastical state whose chief office Your Holiness now occupies; for when not so very long ago, under Leo X, in the Lateran Council the question of revising the ecclesiastical calendar was discussed, it then remained unsettled, simply because the length of the years and months, and the motions of the sun and moon were held to have been not yet sufficiently determined. Since that time, I have given my attention to observing these more accurately, urged on by a very distinguished man, Paul, Bishop of Fossombrone, who at that time had charge of the matter. But what I may have accomplished herein I leave to the judgment of Your Holiness in particular, and to that of all other learned mathematicians; and lest I seem to Your Holiness to promise more regarding the usefulness of the work than I can perform, I now pass to the work itself.

[Footnote A: Nicolaus Copernicus was born in 1473 at Thorn in West Prussia, of a Polish father and a German mother. He attended the university of Cracow and Bologna, lectured on astronomy and mathematics at Rome, and later studied medicine at Padua and canon law at Ferrara. He was appointed canon of the cathedral of Frauenburg, and in this town he died in 1543, having devoted the latter part of his life largely to astronomy.

The book which was introduced by this dedication laid the foundations of modern astronomy. At the time when it was written, the earth was believed by all to be the fixed centre of the universe; and although many of the arguments used by Copernicus were invalid and absurd, he was the first modern to put forth the heliocentric theory as "a better explanation." It remained for Kepler, Galileo, and Newton, to establish the theory on firm grounds.]

They said I should find that the more absurd most men now thought this theory of mine concerning the motion of the Earth, the more admiration and gratitude it would command after they saw in the publication of my commentaries the mist of absurdity cleared away by most transparent proofs.

Model Practice 1

Model Practice 2

Model Practice 3

Before the Diet of Worms

by Martin Luther
from The World's Famous Orations
edited by William Jennings Bryan
edited by Francis W. Halsey
1520

Born in 1483, died in 1546; became a Monk at Erfurt in 1505; published, at Wittenberg in 1517, his thesis against indulgences; excommunicated and his writings burned in 1520; proscribed at Worms in 1521; published a translation of the Bible in 1534.

MOST SERENE EMPEROR, AND YOU ILLUSTRIOUS PRINCES AND GRACIOUS LORDS:—I this day appear before you in all humility, according to your command, and I implore your majesty and your august highnesses, by the mercies of God, to listen with favor to the defense of a cause which I am well assured is just and right. I ask pardon, if by reason of my ignorance, I am wanting in the manners that befit a court; for I have not been brought up in king's palaces, but in the seclusion of a cloister.

Two questions were yesterday put to me by his imperial majesty; the first, whether I was the author of the books whose titles were read; the second, whether I wished to revoke or defend the doctrine I have taught. I answered the first, and I adhere to that answer.

As to the second, I have composed writings on very different subjects. In some I have discussed Faith and Good Works, in a spirit at once so pure, clear, and Christian, that even my adversaries themselves, far from finding anything to censure, confess that these writings are profitable, and deserve to be perused by devout persons. The pope's bull, violent as it is, acknowledges this. What, then, should I be doing if I were now to retract these writings? Wretched man! I alone, of all men living, should be abandoning truths approved by the unanimous voice of friends and enemies, and opposing doctrines that the whole world glories in confessing!

I have composed, secondly, certain works against popery, wherein I have attacked such as by false doctrines, irregular lives, and scandalous examples, afflict the Christian world, and ruin the bodies and souls of men. And is not this confirmed by the grief of all who fear God? Is it not manifest that the laws and human doctrines of the popes entangle, vex, and distress the consciences of the faithful, while the crying and endless extortions of Rome engulf the property and wealth of Christendom, and more particularly of this illustrious nation?

If I were to revoke what I have written on that subject, what should I do.... but strengthen this tyranny, and open a wider door to so many and flagrant impieties? Bearing down all resistance with fresh fury, we should behold these proud men swell, foam, and rage more than ever! And not merely would the yoke which now weighs down Christians be made more grinding by my retractation—it would thereby become, so to speak, lawful,—for, by my retractation, it would receive confirmation from your most serene majesty, and all the States of the Empire. Great God! I should thus be like to an infamous cloak, used to hid and cover over every kind of malice and tyranny.

In the third and last place, I have written some books against private individuals, who had undertaken to defend the tyranny of Rome by destroying the faith. I freely confess that I may have attacked such persons with more violence than was consistent with my profession as an ecclesiastic: I do not think of myself as a saint; but neither can I retract these books. because I should, by so doing, sanction the impieties of my opponents, and they would thence take occasion to crush God's people with still more cruelty.

Yet, as I am a mere man, and not God, I will defend myself after the example of Jesus Christ, who said: "If I have spoken evil, bear witness against me." (John 18:23) How much more should I, who am but dust and ashes, and so prone to error, desire that everyone should bring forward what he can against my doctrine.

Therefore, most serene emperor, and you illustrious princes, and all, whether high or low, who hear me, I implore you by the mercies of God to prove to me by the writings of the prophets and apostles that I am in error. As soon as I shall be convinced, I will instantly retract all my errors, and will myself be the first to seize my writings, and commit them to the flames.

What I have just said I think will clearly show that I have well considered and weighed the dangers to which I am exposing myself; but far from being dismayed by them, I rejoice exceedingly to see the Gospel this day, as of old, a cause of disturbance and disagreement. It is the character and destiny of God's word. "I came not to send peace unto the earth, but a sword," said Jesus Christ. God is wonderful and awful in His counsels. Let us have a care, lest in our endeavors to arrest discords, we be bound to fight against the holy word of God and bring down upon our heads a frightful deluge of inextricable dangers, present disaster, and everlasting desolations.... Let us have a care lest the reign of the young and noble prince, the Emperor Charles, on whom, next to God, we build so many hopes, should not only commence, but continue and terminate its course under the most fatal auspices. I might cite examples drawn from the oracles of God. I might speak of Pharaohs, of kings of Babylon, or of Israel, who were never more contributing to their own ruin than when, by measures in appearances most prudent, they thought to establish their authority! "God removeth the mountains and they know not." (Job 9:5)

In speaking thus, I do not suppose that such noble princes have need of my poor judgment; but I wish to acquit myself of a duty that Germany has a right to expect from her children. And so commending myself to your august majesty, and your most serene highnesses, I beseech you in all humility, not to permit the hatred of my enemies to rain upon me an indignation I have not deserved. (2)

Since your most serene majesty and your high mightinesses require of me a simple, clear and direct answer, I will give one, and it is this: I cannot submit my faith either to the pope or to the council, because it is as clear as noonday that they have fallen into error and even into glaring inconsistency with themselves. If, then, I am not convinced by proof from Holy Scripture, or by cogent reasons, if I am not satisfied by the very text I have cited, and if my judgment is not in this way brought into subjection to God's word, I neither can nor will retract anything; for it cannot be right for a Christian to speak against his country. I stand here and can say no more. God help me. Amen.(3)

Note 1. From the version given in D'Aubigny's "History of the Reformation"—the American edition of 1845. This speech was delivered at Worms on April 18, 1520, in response to a summons from the emperor, Charles V., who had assured Luther of a safe conduct to and from Worms. When the chancellor had demanded of Luther, "Are you prepared to defend all that your writings contain, or do you wish to retract any part of them?" it is stated in the "Acts of Worms," that Luther "made answer in a low and humble voice, without any vehemence or violence, but with gentleness and mildness and in a manner full of respect and diffidence, yet with much joy and Christian firmness." D'Aubigny says he took this speech, word for word, from an authentic document.

Note 2. D'Aubigny says that after Luther had pronounced these words in German, "with modesty, yet with much earnestness and resolution he was desired to repeat them in Latin," the emperor being not fond of German. The splendid assembly which surrounded Luther, its noise and excitement, had exhausted him. ("I was bathed in sweat," said he, "and standing in the center of the princes.") But having taken a moment's breathing time. Luther began again "and repeated his address in Latin, with undiminished power." The chancellor spokesman of the Diet, then said, "You have not given any answer to the inquiry put to you. You are not to question the decisions of the councils—you are required to return a clear and distinct answer. Will you or will you not retract?" Luther then proceeded with the answer given in the final paragraph.

Note 3. A detailed report of this memorable scene describes how, at this point, Luther, after going out of the room, was again summoned, and asked whether he actually meant to say that councils had erred, to which he answered, they had erred many times, mentioning the Council of Constance.

Luther was then told if he did not retract, the emperor and the States of the Empire would proceed "to consider how to deal with an obstinate heretic," to which he answered, "May God be my helper, but I can retract nothing." Pressed once more, and reminded that he had not spoken "with that humility which befitted his condition," he said, "I have no other answer to give than that I have already given." The emperor then made a sign to end the matter, rose from his seat, and the whole assembly followed his example.

In the third and last place, I have written some books against private individuals, who had undertaken to defend the tyranny of Rome by destroying the faith. I freely confess that I may have attacked such persons with more violence than was consistent with my profession as an ecclesiastic: I do not think of myself as a saint; but neither can I retract these books.

Model Practice 1

Model Practice 2

Model Practice 3

The Autobiography of St. Ignatius

from The Account of his Life dictated to Father Gonzalez (excerpt)
by St. Ignatius Loyola
1555 AD

Up to his twenty-sixth year, the heart of Ignatius was enthralled by the vanities of the world. His special delight was in the military life, and he seemed led by a strong and empty desire of gaining for himself a great name. The citadel of Pampeluna was held in siege by the French. All the other soldiers were unanimous in wishing to surrender on condition of freedom to leave, since it was impossible to hold out any longer; but Ignatius so persuaded the commander, that, against the views of all the other nobles, he decided to hold the citadel against the enemy.

When the day of assault came, Ignatius made his confession to one of the nobles, his companion in arms. The soldier also made his to Ignatius. After the walls were destroyed, Ignatius stood fighting bravely until a cannon ball of the enemy broke one of his legs and seriously injured the other.

When he fell, the citadel was surrendered. When the French took possession of the town, they showed great admiration for Ignatius. After twelve or fifteen days at Pampeluna, where he received the best care from the physicians of the French army, he was borne on a litter to Loyola. His recovery was very slow, and doctors and surgeons were summoned from all parts for a consultation. They decided that the leg should be broken again, that the bones, which had knit badly, might be properly reset; for they had not been properly set in the beginning, or else had been so jostled on the journey that a cure was impossible. He submitted to have his flesh cut again. During the operation, as in all he suffered before and after, he uttered no word and gave no sign of suffering save that of tightly clenching his fists.

In the meantime, his strength was failing. He could take no food, and showed other symptoms of approaching death. On the feast of St. John, the doctors gave up hope of his recovery and advised him to make his confession. Having received the sacraments on the eve of the feasts of Sts. Peter and Paul, toward evening the doctors said that if by the middle of the night there were no change for the better, he would surely die. He had great devotion to St. Peter, and it so happened by the goodness of God that in the middle of the night he began to grow better.

His recovery was so rapid that in a few days he was out of danger. As the bones of his leg settled and pressed upon each other, one bone protruded below the knee. The result was that one leg was shorter than the other, and the bone causing a lump there, made the leg seem quite deformed. As he could not bear this, since he intended to live a life at court, he asked the doctors whether the bone could be cut away. They replied that it could, but it would cause him more suffering than all that had preceded, as everything was healed, and they would need space in order to cut it. He determined, however, to undergo this torture.

His elder brother looked on with astonishment and admiration. He said he could never have had the fortitude to suffer the pain which the sick man bore with his usual patience. When the flesh and the bone that protruded were cut away, means were taken to prevent the leg from becoming shorter than the other. For this purpose, in spite of sharp and constant pain, the leg was kept stretched for many days. Finally the Lord gave him health. He came out of the danger safe and strong with the exception that he could not easily stand on his leg, but was forced to lie in bed.

As Ignatius had a love for fiction, when he found himself out of danger, he asked for some romances to pass away the time. In that house there was no book of the kind. They gave him, instead, "The Life of Christ," by Rudolph, the Carthusian, and another book called the "Flowers of the Saints," both in Spanish. By frequent reading of these books, he began to acquire some love for spiritual things. This reading led his mind to meditate on holy things, yet sometimes it wandered to thoughts which he had been accustomed to dwell upon before.

Among these there was one thought which, above the others, so filled his heart that he became, as it were, immersed and absorbed in it. Unconsciously, it engaged his attention for three and four hours at a time. He pictured to himself what he should do in honor of an illustrious lady, how he should journey to the city where she was, in what words he would address her, and what bright and pleasant sayings he would make use of, what manner of warlike exploits he should perform to please her. He was so carried away by this thought that he did not even perceive how far beyond his power it was to do what he proposed, for she was a lady exceedingly illustrious and of the highest nobility.

In the meantime, the divine mercy was at work substituting for these thoughts others suggested by his recent readings. While perusing the life of Our Lord and the saints, he began to reflect, saying to himself: "What if I should do what St. Francis did?" "What if I should act like St. Dominic?" He pondered over these things in his mind, and kept continually proposing to himself serious and difficult things. He seemed to feel a certain readiness for doing them, with no other reason except this thought: "St. Dominic did this; I, too, will do it." "St. Francis did this; therefore I will do it." These heroic resolutions remained for a time, and then other vain and worldly thoughts followed. This succession of thoughts occupied him for a long while, those about God alternating with those about the world. But in these thoughts there was this difference. When he thought of worldly things it gave him great pleasure, but afterward he found himself dry and sad. However, when he thought of journeying to Jerusalem, and of living only on herbs, and practicing austerities, he found pleasure not only while thinking of them, but also when he had ceased.

This difference he did not notice or value, until one day the eyes of his soul were opened and he began to inquire the reason of the difference. He learned by experience that one train of thought left him sad, the other joyful. This was his first reasoning on spiritual matters. Afterward, when he began the Spiritual Exercises, he was enlightened, and understood what he afterward taught his children about the discernment of spirits. When gradually he recognized the different spirits by which he was moved, one, the spirit of God, the other, the devil, and when he had gained no little spiritual light from the reading of pious books, he began to think more seriously of his past life, and how much penance he should do to expiate his past sins.

Amid these thoughts, the holy wish to imitate saintly men came to his mind; his resolve was not more definite than to promise with the help of divine grace that what they had done, he also would do. After his recovery, his one wish was to make a pilgrimage to Jerusalem. He fasted frequently and scourged himself to satisfy the desire of penance that ruled in a soul filled with the spirit of God.

The vain thoughts were gradually lessened by means of these desires—desires that were not a little strengthened by the following vision. While watching one night, he plainly saw the image of the Blessed Mother of God with the Infant Jesus, at the sight of which, for a considerable time, he received abundant consolation, and felt such contrition for his past life that he thought of nothing else. From that time until August, 1555, when this was written, he never felt the least motion of concupiscence. This privilege we may suppose from this fact to have been a divine gift, although we dare not state it, nor say anything except confirm what has been already said. His brother and all in the house recognized from what appeared externally how great a change had taken place in his soul.

He continued his reading meanwhile, and kept the holy resolution he had made. At home his conversation was wholly devoted to divine things, and helped much to the spiritual advancement of others.

When the day of assault came, Ignatius made his confession to one of the nobles, his companion in arms. The soldier also made his to Ignatius. After the walls were destroyed, Ignatius stood fighting bravely until a cannon ball of the enemy broke one of his legs and seriously injured the other.

Model Practice 1

Model Practice 2

Model Practice 3

Columbus to the Lord Treasurer of Spain

by Christopher Columbus
Barcelona, 1493 AD

To Lord Raphael Sanchez:—

Knowing that it will afford you pleasure to learn that I have brought my undertaking to a successful termination, I have decided upon writing you this letter to acquaint you with all the events which have occurred in my voyage, and the discoveries which have resulted from it.

Thirty-three days after my departure from Cadiz, I reached the Indian sea, where I discovered many islands, thickly peopled, of which I took possession without resistance in the name of our most illustrious monarchs, by public proclamation and with unfurled banners. To the first of these islands, which is called by the Indians Guanahani, I gave the name of the blessed Saviour, relying upon whose protection I had reached this as well as the other islands.

As soon as we arrived at that, which as I have said was named Juana, I proceeded along its coast a short distance westward, and found it to be so large and apparently without termination, that I could not suppose it to be an island, but the continental province of Cathay.

In the meantime, I had learned, from some Indians whom I had seized, that the country was certainly an island. Therefore, I sailed toward the east, coasting to the distance of three hundred and twenty-two miles, which brought us to the extremity of it. From this point, I saw lying eastwards another island, fifty-four miles distant from Juana, to which I gave the name Española.

All these islands were very beautiful and distinguished by a diversity of scenery. They were filled with a great variety of trees of immense height, and which I believe to retain their foliage in all seasons. For when I saw them, they were as verdant and luxurious as they usually are in Spain in the month of May,—some of them were blossoming, some bearing fruit, and all flourishing in the greatest perfection, according to their respective stages of growth, and the nature and quality of each; yet the islands are not so thickly wooded as to be impassable. The nightingale and various birds were singing in countless numbers, and that in November, the month in which I arrived there.

The inhabitants are very simple and honest, and exceedingly liberal with all they have. None of them refusing anything he may possess when he is asked for it, but on the contrary inviting us to ask them. They exhibit great love toward all others in preference to themselves. They also give objects of great value for trifles, and content themselves with very little or nothing in return.

I, however, forbade that these trifles and articles of no value (such as pieces of dishes, plates, and glass, keys, and leather straps) should be given to them. Although, if they could obtain them, they imagined themselves to be in possession of the most beautiful trinkets in the world.

It even happened that a sailor received for a leather strap as much gold as was worth three golden nobles, and for things of more trifling value offered by our men, the Indian would give whatever the seller required.

On my arrival, I had taken some Indians by force from the first island that I came to, in order that they might learn our language. These men are still traveling with me, and although they have been with us now a long time, they continue to entertain the idea that I have descended from heaven. And on our arrival at any new place they published this, crying out immediately with a loud voice to the other Indians, "Come, come and look upon beings of a celestial race." Upon which both men and women, children and adults, young men and old, when they got rid of the fear they at first entertained, would come out in throngs, crowding the roads to see us, some bringing food, others drink, with astonishing affection and kindness.

Although all I have related may appear to be wonderful and unheard of, yet the results of my voyage would have been more astonishing if I had had at my disposal such ships as I required. But these great and marvelous results are not to be attributed to any merit of mine, but to the holy Christian faith, and to the piety and religion of our Sovereigns. For that which the unaided intellect of man could not compass, the spirit of God has granted to human exertions, for God is wont to hear the prayers of his servants who love his precepts even to the performance of apparent impossibilities.

Thus it has happened to me in the present instance, who have accomplished a task to which the powers of mortal men had never hitherto attained; for if there have been those who have anywhere written or spoken of these islands, they have done so with doubts and conjectures, and no one has ever asserted that he has seen them, on which account their writings have been looked upon as little else than fables.

Therefore let the king and queen, our princes and their most happy kingdoms, and all the other provinces of Christendom, render thanks to our Lord and Saviour Jesus Christ, who has granted us so great a victory and such prosperity.

Christopher Columbus.

In the meantime, I had learned, from some Indians whom I had seized, that the country was certainly an island. Therefore, I sailed toward the east, coasting to the distance of three hundred and twenty-two miles, which brought us to the extremity of it. From this point, I saw lying eastwards another island, fifty-four miles distant from Juana, to which I gave the name Espafola.

Model Practice 1

Model Practice 2

Model Practice 3

Queen Elizabeth's Address to her Army at Tilbury Fort

from Fox's Book of Martyrs
speech by Queen Elizabeth I of England
1588 AD

"My loving people, we have been persuaded by some that are careful of our safety, to take heed how we commit ourselves to armed multitudes, for fear of treachery. But, I assure you, I do not desire to live to distrust my faithful and loving people. Let tyrants fear: I have always so behaved myself, that under God, I have placed my chiefest strength and safeguard in the loyal hearts and good will of my subjects. And therefore I am come among you at this time, not as for my recreation or sport, but being resolved, in the midst and heat of the battle, to live or die among you all, to lay down, for my God and for my kingdom and for my people, my honor and my blood, even in the dust. I know I have but the body of a weak and feeble woman, but I have the heart of a king, and of a king of England too; and think foul scorn that Parma or Spain, or any prince of Europe, should dare to invade the borders of my realms: To which rather than any dishonor should grow by me, I myself will take up arms; I myself will be your general, judge, and rewarder of every one of your virtues in the field. I know already, by your forwardness, that you have deserved rewards and crowns; and I do assure you, on the word of a prince, they shall be duly paid you. In the mean time my lieutenant-general shall be in my stead, than whom never prince commanded a more noble and worthy subject; not doubting by your obedience to my general, by your concord in the camp, and your valour in the field, we shall shortly have a famous victory over those enemies of my God, of my kingdom, and of my people."

My loving people, we have been persuaded by some that are careful of our safety, to take heed how we commit ourselves to armed multitudes, for fear of treachery. But, I assure you, I do not desire to live to distrust my faithful and loving people.

Model Practice 1

Model Practice 2

Model Practice 3

CHAPTER III

Poetry from Medieval History

Note: Poetry models should be written in the same manner that the author wrote them, meaning indentions and punctuation.

Each line of poetry should begin on a new line. If the student cannot fit the line of the model on one line, he should continue the sentence on the next line with an indention at the beginning.

For examples, see the model to "Saint Bernard's Hymn" on page III-24 and the model to "The Vesper Hymn of Abelard" on page III-35.

The poetry selections do not lend themselves as easily to written summations; written summation pages are not included.

All Glory, Laud, and Honor (Gloria, Laus, et Honor)

from The Story of the Hymns and Tunes
edited by Theron Brown and Hezekiah Butterworth
by Theodulph, Bishop of Orleans
820 AD

This stately Latin hymn of the early part of the 9th century was composed in AD. 820, by Theodulph, Bishop of Orleans, while a captive in the cloister of Anjou. King Louis (le Debonnaire) son of Charlemagne, had trouble with his royal relatives, and suspecting Theodulph to be in sympathy with them, shut him up in prison. A pretty story told by Clichtovius, an old church writer of AD. 1518, relates how on Palm Sunday the king, celebrating the feast with his people, passed in procession before the cloister, where the face of the venerable prisoner at his cell window caused an involuntary halt, and, in the moment of silence, the bishop raised his voice and sang this 26 / 6 hymn; and how the delighted king released the singer, and restored him to his bishopric. This tale, told after seven hundred years, is not the only legend that grew around the hymn and its author, but the fact that he composed it in the cloister of Anjou while confined there is not seriously disputed.

Gloria, laus et honor Tibi sit, Rex Christe Redemptor,
Cui puerile decus prompsit Hosanna pium.
Israel Tu Rex, Davidis et inclyta proles,
Nomine qui in Domini Rex benedicte venis
Gloria, laus et honor.

Theodulph was born in Spain, but of Gothic pedigree, a child of the race of conquerors who, in the 5th century, overran Southern Europe. He died in 821, but whether a free man or still a prisoner at the time of his death is uncertain. Some accounts allege that he was poisoned in the cloister. The Roman church canonized him, and his hymn is still sung as a processional in Protestant as well as Catholic churches. The above Latin lines are the first four of the original seventy-eight. The following is J.M. Neale's translation of the portion now in use:

All glory, laud, and honor,
To Thee, Redeemer, King:
To whom the lips of children
Made sweet Hosannas ring.

Thou are the King of Israel,
Thou David's royal Son,
Who in the Lord's name comest,
The King and Blessed One. All glory, etc.
The company of angels
Are praising Thee on high;
And mortal men, and all things
Created, make reply. All glory, etc.
The people of the Hebrews
With palms before Thee went;
Our praise and prayer and anthems
Before Thee we present. All glory, etc.
To Thee before Thy Passion
They sang their hymns of praise;
To Thee, now high exalted
Our melody we raise. All glory, etc.
Thou didst accept their praises;
Accept the prayers we bring,
Who in all good delightest,
Thou good and gracious King. All glory, etc.

All glory, laud, and honor,
To Thee, Redeemer, King:
To whom the lips of children
Made sweet Hosannas ring.

Model Practice 1

Model Practice 2

Model Practice 3

Arnold von Winkleried

from Poems Every Child Should Know
by James Montgomery
1386 AD

"Make way for liberty!" he cried,
Make way for liberty, and died.

In arms the Austrian phalanx stood,
A living wall, a human wood,—
A wall, where every conscious stone
Seemed to its kindred thousands grown.
A rampart all assaults to bear,
Till time to dust their frames should wear;
So still, so dense the Austrians stood,
A living wall, a human wood.

Impregnable their front appears,
All horrent with projected spears.
Whose polished points before them shine,
From flank to flank, one brilliant line,
Bright as the breakers' splendours run
Along the billows to the sun.

Opposed to these a hovering band
Contended for their fatherland;
Peasants, whose new-found strength had broke
From manly necks the ignoble yoke,
And beat their fetters into swords,
On equal terms to fight their lords;
And what insurgent rage had gained,
In many a mortal fray maintained;
Marshalled, once more, at Freedom's call,
They came to conquer or to fall,
Where he who conquered, he who fell,
Was deemed a dead or living Tell,
Such virtue had that patriot breathed,
So to the soil his soul bequeathed,
That wheresoe'er his arrows flew,
Heroes in his own likeness grew,
And warriors sprang from every sod,
Which his awakening footstep trod.

And now the work of life and death
Hung on the passing of a breath;
The fire of conflict burned within,
The battle trembled to begin;
Yet, while the Austrians held their ground,
Point for attack was nowhere found;
Where'er the impatient Switzers gazed,
The unbroken line of lances blazed;
That line 'twere suicide to meet,
And perish at their tyrant's feet;
How could they rest within their graves,
And leave their homes, the homes of slaves!
Would not they feel their children tread,
With clanging chains, above their head?

It must not be; this day, this hour,
Annihilates the invader's power;
All Switzerland is in the field;
She will not fly,—she cannot yield,—
She must not fall; her better fate
Here gives her an immortal date.
Few were the numbers she could boast,
But every freeman was a host,
And felt as 'twere a secret known
That one should turn the scale alone,
While each unto himself was he
On whose sole arm hung victory.

It did depend on one indeed;
Behold him,—Arnold Winkelried;
There sounds not to the trump of fame
The echo of a nobler name.
Unmarked he stood amid the throng,
In rumination deep and long,
Till you might see, with sudden grace,
The very thought come o'er his face;
And, by the motion of his form,
Anticipate the bursting storm,
And, by the uplifting of his brow,
Tell where the bolt would strike, and how.

But 'twas no sooner thought than done!
The field was in a moment won;
"Make way for liberty!" he cried,
Then ran, with arms extended wide,
As if his dearest friend to clasp;
Ten spears he swept within his grasp.
"Make way for liberty!" he cried.
Their keen points crossed from side to side;
He bowed amidst them like a tree,
And thus made way for liberty.

Swift to the breach his comrades fly,
"Make way for liberty!" they cry,
And through the Austrian phalanx dart,
As rushed the spears through Arnold's heart.

While instantaneous as his fall,
Rout, ruin, panic, seized them all;
An earthquake could not overthrow
A city with a surer blow.

Thus Switzerland again was free;
Thus Death made way for Liberty!

DEFINITIONS.—2. Pha/lanx, *a body of troops formed in closarray.* Cttn'seiotis, *sensible, knowing.* Kln'dred, *those of like nature, relatives.* Ram'piirt, *that which defends from assault, a bulwark.* 3. Im-pr6g'na-ble, *that can not be moved or shaken.* H6r'rent, *standing out like bristles.* 4. In-sur'gent, *rising in opposition to authority.* 6. An-nl'hi-lates, *destroys.* 7. Ru-mi-na'tion, *the act of musing, meditation.* 9. Breach, *a gap or opening made by breaking.'*

NOTES.—The incident related in this poem is one of actual occurrence, and took place at the battle of Sempach, fought in 1386 A. D., between only 1,300 Swiss and a large army of Austrians. The latter had obtained possession of a narrow pass in the mountains, from which it seemed impossible to dislodge them until Arnold Struth von Winkelried made a breach in their line, as narrated.

Rinaldo is a knight in Tasso's "Jerusalem Delivered" (Canto xvm, 17-40), who enters an enchanted wood, and, by cutting down a tree in spite of the nymphs and phantoms that endeavor in every way to stop him, breaks the spell; the Christian army are thus enabled to enter the grove and obtain timber for their engines of war.

Impregnable their front appears,
All horrent with projected spears.
Whose polished points before them shine,
From flank to flank, one brilliant line,
Bright as the breakers' splendours run
Along the billows to the sun.

Model Practice 1

Model Practice 2

Model Practice 3

The Glove and the Lions

from an Ontario Reader
by Leigh Hunt
1515 – 1547 AD

King Francis was a hearty king, and loved a royal sport,
And one day, as his lions strove, sat looking on the court;
The nobles filled the benches round, the ladies by their side,
And 'mongst them Count de Lorge, with one he hoped to make his bride;
And truly 'twas a gallant thing to see that crowning show,
Valor and love, and a king above, and the royal beasts below.

Ramped and roared the lions, with horrid laughing jaws;
They bit, they glared, gave blows like beams, a wind went with their paws.
With wallowing might and stifled roar, they rolled one on another,
Till all the pit, with sand and mane, was in a thunderous smother;
The bloody foam above the bars came whizzing through the air;
Said Francis, then, "Good gentlemen, we're better here than there!"

De Lorge's love o'erheard the King, a beauteous, lively dame,
With smiling lips, and sharp bright eyes, which always seemed the same:
She thought, "The Count, my lover, is as brave as brave can be;
He surely would do desperate things to show his love of me!
King, ladies, lover, all look on; the chance is wond'rous fine;
I'll drop my glove to prove his love; great glory will be mine!"

She dropped her glove to prove his love: then looked on him and smiled;
He bowed and in a moment leaped among the lions wild:
The leap was quick; return was quick; he soon regained his place;
Then threw the glove, but not with love, right in the lady's face!
"In truth!" cried Francis, "rightly done!" and he rose from where he sat:
"No love," quoth he, "but vanity, sets love a task like that!"

With wallowing might and stifled roar, they rolled
one on another,
Till all the pit, with sand and mane, was in a
thunderous smother;
The bloody foam above the bars came whizzing
through the air;
Said Francis, then, "Good gentlemen, we're better
here than there!"

Model Practice 1

Model Practice 2

Model Practice 3

Hamlet's Soliloquy

from The Tragedy of Hamlet, Prince of Denmark (soliloquy)
by William Shakespeare
written between 1599 and 1601

To be, or not to be—that is the question:
Whether 'tis nobler in the mind to suffer
The slings and arrows of outrageous fortune
Or to take arms against a sea of troubles,
And by opposing end them. To die— to sleep—
No more; and by a sleep to say we end
The heartache, and the thousand natural shocks
That flesh is heir to. 'Tis a consummation
Devoutly to be wish'd. To die—to sleep—
To sleep—perchance to dream: ay, there's the rub!
For in that sleep of death what dreams may come
When we have shuffled off this mortal coil,
Must give us pause. There's the respect
That makes calamity of so long life.
For who would bear the whips and scorns of time,
Th' oppressor's wrong, the proud man's contumely,
The pangs of despis'd love, the law's delay,
The insolence of office, and the spurns
That patient merit of th' unworthy takes,
When he himself might his quietus make
With a bare bodkin? Who would these fardels bear,
To grunt and sweat under a weary life,
But that the dread of something after death-
The undiscover'd country, from whose bourn
No traveller returns- puzzles the will,
And makes us rather bear those ills we have
Than fly to others that we know not of?
Thus conscience does make cowards of us all,
And thus the native hue of resolution
Is sicklied o'er with the pale cast of thought,
And enterprises of great pith and moment
With this regard their currents turn awry
And lose the name of action.—Soft you now!
The fair Ophelia!— Nymph, in thy orisons
Be all my sins rememb'red.

To sleep— perchance to dream: ay, there's the
rub!
For in that sleep of death what dreams may
come
When we have shuffled off this mortal coil,
Must give us pause. There's the respect
That makes calamity of so long life.

Model Practice 1

Model Practice 2

Model Practice 3

The Ladder of St. Augustine

354 – 430 AD
from Poems Teachers Ask For, Book Two
by H.W. Longfellow

Saint Augustine! well hast thou said,
That of our vices we can frame
A ladder, if we will but tread
Beneath our feet each deed of shame!

All common things, each day's events,
That with the hour begin and end,
Our pleasures and our discontents,
Are rounds by which we may ascend.

The low desire, the base design,
That makes another's virtues less;
The revel of the ruddy wine,
And all occasions of excess;

The longing for ignoble things;
The strife for triumph more than truth;
The hardening of the heart, that brings
Irreverence for the dreams of youth;

All thoughts of ill; all evil deeds,
That have their root in thoughts of ill;
Whatever hinders or impedes
The action of the nobler will;—

All these must first be trampled down
Beneath our feet, if we would gain
In the bright fields of fair renown
The right of eminent domain.

We have not wings, we cannot soar;
But we have feet to scale and climb
By slow degrees, by more and more,
The cloudy summits of our time.

The mighty pyramids of stone
That wedge-like cleave the desert airs,
When nearer seen, and better known,
Are but gigantic flights of stairs,

The distant mountains, that uprear
Their solid bastions to the skies,
Are crossed by pathways, that appear
As we to higher levels rise.

The heights by great men reached and kept
Were not attained by sudden flight.
But they, while their companions slept,
Were toiling upward in the night.

Standing on what too long we bore
With shoulders bent and downcast eyes,
We may discern—unseen before—
A path to higher destinies.

Nor deem the irrevocable Past
As wholly wasted, wholly vain,
If, rising on its wrecks, at last
To something nobler we attain.

Saint Augustine! well hast thou said,
That of our vices we can frame
A ladder, if we will but tread
Beneath our feet each deed of shame!

All common things, each day's events,
That with the hour begin and end,
Our pleasures and our discontents,
Are rounds by which we may ascend.

Model Practice 1

Model Practice 2

Model Practice 3

Polonius' Advice

from The Tragedy of Hamlet, Prince of Denmark
by William Shakespeare
written between 1599 and 1601

See thou character. Give thy thoughts no tongue,
Nor any unproportion'd thought his act.
Be thou familiar, but by no means vulgar:
The friends thou hast, and their adoption tried,
Grapple them to thy soul with hoops of steel;
But do not dull thy palm with entertainment
Of each new-hatch'd, unfledg'd comrade. Beware
Of entrance to a quarrel; but, being in,
Bear 't that th' opposed may beware of thee.
Give every man thine ear, but few thy voice:
Take each man's censure, but reserve thy judgment.
Costly thy habit as thy purse can buy
But not expressed in fancy; rich, not gaudy:
For the apparel oft proclaims the man.
Neither a borrower nor a lender be;
For loan oft loses both itself and friend,
And borrowing dulls the edge of husbandry.
This above all: to thine own self be true;
And it must follow, as the night the day,
Thou canst not then be false to any man.

Give every man thine ear, but few thy voice:
Take each man's censure, but reserve thy judgment.
Costly thy habit as thy purse can buy
But not expressed in fancy; rich, not gaudy:
For the apparel oft proclaims the man.

Model Practice 1

Model Practice 2

Model Practice 3

Saint Bernard's Hymn

from The Library of the World's Best Literature, Ancient and Modern
1091-1153

Jesu! the very thought of thee
 With sweetness fills my breast,
But sweeter far thy face to see
 And in thy presence rest.

Nor voice can sing nor heart can frame,
 Nor can the memory find,
A sweeter sound than thy blest name,
 O Savior of mankind!

O hope of every contrite heart!
 O joy of all the meek!
To those who fall, how kind thou art,
 How good to those who seek!

But what to those who find? Ah, this
 Nor tongue nor pen can show.
The love of Jesus, what it is
 None but his loved ones know.

Jesu! our only joy be thou,
 As thou our prize wilt be!
Jesu! be thou our glory now
 And through eternity!

Jesu! the very thought of thee
With sweetness fills my breast,
But sweeter far thy face to see
And in thy presence rest.

Model Practice 1

Model Practice 2

Model Practice 3

The Sermon of St. Francis

from the De La Salle Series
by Henry Wadsworth Longfellow
1182 – 1226 AD

Up soared the lark into the air,
A shaft of song, a wingèd prayer,
As if a soul, released from pain,
Were flying back to heaven again.

St. Francis heard; it was to him
An emblem of the Seraphim;
The upward motion of the fire,
The light, the heat, the heart's desire.

Around Assisi's convent gate
The birds, God's poor who cannot wait,
From moor and mere and darksome wood
Came flocking for their dole of food.

"O brother birds," St. Francis said,
"Ye come to me and ask for bread,
But not with bread alone today
Shall ye be fed and sent away.

"Ye shall be fed, ye happy birds
With manna of celestial words;
Not mine, though mine they seem to be,
Not mine, though they be spoken through me.

"O, doubly are ye bound to praise
The great Creator in your lays;
He giveth you your plumes of down,
Your crimson hoods, your cloaks of brown.

"He giveth you your wings to fly
And breathe a purer air on high,
And careth for you everywhere,
Who for yourselves so little care!"

With flutter of swift wings and songs
Together rose the feathered throngs,
And singing scattered far apart;
Deep peace was in St. Francis' heart.

He knew not if the brotherhood
His homily had understood;
He only knew that to one ear
The meaning of his words was clear.

"O brother birds," St. Francis said,
"Ye come to me and ask for bread,
But not with bread alone today
Shall ye be fed and sent away.

"Ye shall be fed, ye happy birds
With manna of celestial words;
Not mine, though mine they seem to be,
Not mine, though they be spoken through me.

Model Practice 1

Model Practice 2

Model Practice 3

The Slaying of Owain

6th century AD
from Library Of The World's Best Literature, Ancient And Modern, Vol. 2
by Aneurin

Among the triad of singers--Llywarch, prince and bard, Aneurin, warrior and bard, and Taliessin, bard only--who were among the followers of the heroic British chief Urien, when he bravely but unsuccessfully resisted the invasion of the victorious Angles and Saxons, Aneurin was famous both as poet and warrior. He sang of the long struggle that eventually was to turn Briton into England, and celebrated in his 'Gododin' ninety of the fallen Cymric chiefs. The notes of his life are scanty, and are drawn chiefly from his allusion to himself in his poem. He was the son of Cwm Cawlwyd, a chief of the tribe of Gododin. He seems to have been educated at St. Cadoc's College at Llancarvan, and afterwards entered the bardic order. As appears from the 'Gododin,' he was present at the battle of Cattræth both as bard and as priest. He fled, but was taken prisoner. In his poem he refers to the hardships he endured in his captivity. After his release he returned to Llancarvan, Wales, and in his old age he went north to live with his brother in Galloway. Here he was murdered; his death is referred to as one of the "three accursed hatchet-strokes of the isle of Britain." His friendship with Taliessin is commemorated by both bards.

The 'Gododin' is at once the longest and the most important composition in early Welsh literature. It has been variously interpreted, but is thought to celebrate the battle of Cattræth. This battle was fought in 570 between the Britons, who had formed a league to defend their country, and their Teutonic invaders. It "began on a Tuesday, lasted for a week, and ended with great slaughter of the Britons, who fought desperately till they perished on the field." Three hundred and sixty chieftains were slain; only three escaped by flight, among whom was Aneurin, who afterwards commemorated the slaughter in the 'Gododin,' a lament for the dead. Ninety-seven of the stanzas remain. In various measures of alliterative and assonant verse they sing the praises of ninety of the fallen chiefs, usually giving one stanza to each hero. One of these stanzas is known to readers of Gray, who translated it under the name of 'The Death of Hoel.'

Again the 'Gododin' is assumed to be, like many early epic poems whose origin is wrapped in mystery, not the commemoration of one single, particular event, but a collection of lays composed at various times, which compresses into one battle the long and disastrous period of the Anglo-Saxon invasion, ending in the subjugation of the Britons.

But whatever its history, the 'Gododin' is one of the finest monuments of Cymric literature. "In the brevity of the narrative, the careless boldness of the actors as they present themselves, the condensed energy of the action, and the fierce exultation of the slaughter, together with the recurring elegiac note, this poem (or poems if it be the work of two authors) has some of the highest epic qualities. The ideas and manners are in harmony with the age and the country to which it is referred."

Like all early songs, the poem was handed down through centuries by oral tradition. It is now preserved in the 'Book of Aneurin,' a small quarto manuscript of nineteen leaves of vellum, of the end of the thirteenth century.

The 'Gododin' has been published with an English translation and notes by the Rev. J. Williams (1852); and by the Cymmrodorion Society, with a translation by Thomas Stevens, in 1885. Interesting information covering it may be found in Skene's 'Four Ancient Books of Wales' (1866), and in the article 'Celtic Literature' in this work.

The Slaying of Owain

[During the battle a conference was held, at which the British leaders demanded as a condition of peace that part of the land of Gododin be restored. In reply, the Saxons killed Owain, one of the greatest of the Cymric bards. Aneurin thus pictures him:--]

A man in thought, a boy in form,
He stoutly fought, and sought the storm
Of flashing war that thundered far.
His courser, lank and swift, thick-maned,
Bore on his flank, as on he strained,
The light-brown shield, as on he sped,
With golden spur, in cloak of fur,
His blue sword gleaming. Be there said
No word of mine that does not hold thee dear!
Before thy youth had tasted bridal cheer,
The red death was thy bride! The ravens feed
On thee yet straining to the front, to lead.
Owain, the friend I loved, is dead!
Woe is it that on him the ravens feed!

His courser, lank and swift, thick-maned,
Bore on his flank, as on he strained,
The light-brown shield, as on he sped,
With golden spur, in cloak of fur,
His blue sword gleaming. Be there said
No word of mine that does not hold thee
dear!

Model Practice 1

Model Practice 2

Model Practice 3

The Vesper Hymn of Abelard

from The Library of the World's Best Literature, Ancient and Modern, Vol. 1
edited by Charles Dudley Warner
translation of Dr. Samuel W. Duffield.
1079 – 1142 AD

Oh, what shall be, oh, when shall be that holy Sabbath day,
Which heavenly care shall ever keep and celebrate alway,
When rest is found for weary limbs, when labor hath reward,
When everything forevermore is joyful in the Lord?
The true Jerusalem above, the holy town, is there,
Whose duties are so full of joy, whose joy so free from care;
Where disappointment cometh not to check the longing heart,
And where the heart, in ecstasy, hath gained her better part.
O glorious King, O happy state, O palace of the blest!
O sacred place and holy joy, and perfect, heavenly rest!
To thee aspire thy citizens in glory's bright array,
And what they feel and what they know they strive in vain to say.
For while we wait and long for home, it shall be ours to raise
Our songs and chants and vows and prayers in that dear country's praise;
And from these Babylonian streams to lift our weary eyes,
And view the city that we love descending from the skies.
There, there, secure from every ill, in freedom we shall sing
The songs of Zion, hindered here by days of suffering,
And unto Thee, our gracious Lord, our praises shall confess
That all our sorrow hath been good, and Thou by pain canst bless.
There Sabbath day to Sabbath day sheds on a ceaseless light,
Eternal pleasure of the saints who keep that Sabbath bright;
Nor shall the chant ineffable decline, nor ever cease,
Which we with all the angels sing in that sweet realm of peace.

Oh, what shall be, oh, when shall be that holy
Sabbath day,
Which heavenly care shall ever keep and
celebrate alway,
When rest is found for weary limbs, when
labor hath reward,
When everything forevermore is joyful in the
Lord?

Model Practice 1

Model Practice 2

Model Practice 3

Where to Find True Joy

849 – 901 AD
from The Library of the World's Best Literature, Ancient and Modern, Vol. 1
by 'Boethius'

Oh! It is a fault of weight,
Let him think it out who will,
And a danger passing great
Which can thus allure to ill
Careworn men from the rightway,
Swiftly ever led astray.

Will ye seek within the wood
Red gold on the green trees tall?
None, I wot, is wise that could,
For it grows not there at all:
Neither in wine-gardens green
Seek they gems of glittering sheen.

Would ye on some hill-top set,
When ye list to catch a trout,
Or a carp, your fishing-net?
Men, methinks, have long found out
That it would be foolish fare,
For they know they are not there.

In the salt sea can ye find,
When ye list to start an hunt,
With your hounds, the hart or hind?
It will sooner be your wont
In the woods to look, I wot,
Than in seas where they are not.

Is it wonderful to know
That for crystals red or white
One must to the sea-beach go,
Or for other colors bright,
Seeking by the river's side
Or the shore at ebb of tide?

Likewise, men are well aware
Where to look for river-fish;
And all other worldly ware
Where to seek them when they wish;
Wisely careful men will know
Year by year to find them so.
But of all things 'tis most sad
That they foolish are so blind,
So besotted and so mad,

That they cannot surely find
Where the ever-good is nigh
And true pleasures hidden lie.

Therefore, never is their strife
After those true joys to spur;
In this lean and little life
They, half-witted, deeply err
Seeking here their bliss to gain,
That is God Himself in vain.

Ah! I know not in my thought
How enough to blame their sin,
None so clearly as I ought
Can I show their fault within;
For, more bad and vain are they
And more sad than I can say.

All their hope is to acquire
Worship goods and worldly weal;
When they have their mind's desire,
Then such witless Joy they feel,
That in folly they believe
Those True Joys they then receive.

Oh! It is a fault of weight,
Let him think it out who will,
And a danger passing great
Which can thus allure to ill
Careworn men from the rightway,
Swiftly ever led astray.

Model Practice 1

Model Practice 2

Model Practice 3

CHAPTER IV

Tales from Various Cultures

The Gods of the Teutons

from Famous Men of the Middle Ages
by John H. Haaren and A. B. Poland
Norse Myth

In the little volume called The Famous Men of Rome, you have read about the great empire, which the Romans established. Now we come to a time when the power of Rome was broken and tribes of barbarians who lived north of the Danube and the Rhine took possession of lands that had been part of the Roman Empire. These tribes were the Goths, Vandals, Huns, Franks and Anglo-Saxons. From them have come the greatest nations of modern times. All except the Huns belonged to the same race and are known as Teutons. They were warlike, savage, and cruel. They spoke the same language—though in different dialects—and worshiped the same gods. Like the old Greeks and Romans, they had many gods.

Woden, who was also called Odin, was the greatest of all. His name means "mighty warrior," and he was king of all the gods. He rode through the air mounted on Sleipnir, an eight-footed horse fleeter than the eagle. When the tempest roared, the Teutons said it was the snorting of Sleipnir. When their ships came safely into port, they said it was Woden's breath that had filled their sails and wafted their vessels over the blue waters.

Thor, a son of Woden, ranked next to him among the gods. He rode through the air in a chariot drawn by goats. The Germans called him Donar and Thunar, words which are like our word thunder. From this, we can see that he was the thunder god. In his hand, he carried a wonderful hammer which always came back to his hand when he threw it. Its head was so bright that as it flew through the air it made the lightning. When it struck the vast ice mountains, they reeled and splintered into fragments, and thus Thor's hammer made thunder.

Another great god of our ancestors was Tiew. He was a son of Woden and was the god of battle. He was armed with a sword which flashed like lightning when he brandished it. A savage chief named Attila routed the armies of the Romans and so terrified all the world that he was called "The Scourge of God." His people believed that he gained his victories because he had the sword of Tiew, which a herdsman chanced to find where the god had allowed it to fall. The Teutons prayed to Tiew when they went into battle.

Frija (free' ya) was the wife of Woden and the queen of the gods. She ruled the bright clouds that gleam in the summer sky, and caused them to pour their showers on meadow and forest and mountain.

Four of the days of the week are named after these gods. Tuesday means the day of Tiew; Wednesday, the day of Woden; Thursday, the day of Thor; and Friday, the day of Frija.

Frija's son was Baldur, who was the favorite of all the gods. Only Loki, the spirit of evil, hated him. Baldur's face was as bright as sunshine. His hair gleamed like burnished gold. Wherever he went, night was turned into day.

One morning, when he looked toward earth from his father Woden's palace, black clouds covered the sky, but he saw a splendid rainbow reaching down from the clouds to the earth. Baldur walked upon this rainbow from the home of the gods to the dwellings of men. The rainbow was a bridge upon which the gods used to come to earth.

When Baldur stepped from the rainbow bridge to the earth, he saw a king's daughter so beautiful that he fell in love with her.

But an earthly prince had also fallen in love with her. So he and Baldur fought for her hand. Baldur was a god and hence was very much stronger than the prince. But some of Baldur's magic food was given to the prince, and it made him as strong as Baldur.

Frija heard about this and feared that Baldur was doomed to be killed. So she went to every beast on the land and every fish of the sea and every bird of the air and to every tree of the wood and every plant of the field and made each promise not to hurt Baldur.

But she forgot the mistletoe. So Loki, who always tried to do mischief, made an arrow of mistletoe, and gave it to the prince who shot and killed Baldur with it.

Then all the gods wept, the summer breeze wailed, the leaves fell from the sorrowing trees, the flowers faded and died from grief, and the earth grew stiff and cold. Bruin, the bear, and his neighbors, the hedgehogs and squirrels, crept into holes and refused to eat for weeks and weeks.

The pleasure of all living things in Baldur's presence means the happiness that the sunlight brings. The sorrow of all living things at his death means the gloom of northern countries when winter comes.

The Valkyries were beautiful female warriors. They had some of Woden's own strength and were armed with helmet and shield and spear. Like Woden, they rode unseen through the air and their horses were almost as swift as Sleipnir himself. They swiftly carried Woden's favorite warriors to Valhalla, the hall of the slain. The walls of Valhalla were hung with shields; its ceiling glittered with polished spearheads. From its five hundred and forty gates, each wide enough for eight hundred men abreast to march through, the warriors rushed every morning to fight a battle that lasted till nightfall and began again at the break of each day. When the heroes returned to Valhalla, the Valkyries served them with goblets of mead such as Woden drank himself.

The Teutons believed that before there were any gods or any world there was a great empty space where the world now is. It was called by the curious name Ginnungagap, which means a yawning abyss.

To the north of Ginnungagap it was bitterly cold. Nothing was there but fields of snow and mountains of ice. To the south of Ginnungagap was a region where frost and snow were never seen. It was always bright, and was the home of light and heat. The sunshine from the South melted the ice mountains of the North so that they toppled over and fell into Ginnungagap. There they were changed into a frost giant whose name was Ymir (e'mir). He had three sons. They and their father were so strong that the gods were afraid of them.

So Woden and his brothers killed Ymir. They broke his body in pieces and made the world of them. His bones and teeth became mountains and rocks; his hair became leaves for trees and plants; out of his skull was made the sky.

But Ymir was colder than ice, and the earth that was made of his body was so cold that nothing could live or grow upon it. So the gods took sparks from the home of light and set them in the sky. Two big ones were the sun and moon and the little ones were the stars. Then the earth became warm. Trees grew and flowers bloomed, so that the world was a beautiful home for men.

Of all the trees the most wonderful was a great ash tree, sometimes called the "world tree." Its branches covered the earth and reached beyond the sky until they almost touched the stars. Its roots ran in three directions, to heaven, to the frost giants' home and to the underworld, beneath the earth.

Near the roots in the dark underworld sat the Norns, or fates. Each held a bowl with which she dipped water out of a sacred spring and poured it upon the roots of the ash tree. This was the reason why this wonderful tree was always growing, and why it grew as high as the sky.

When Woden killed Ymir, he tried to kill all Ymir's children too; but one escaped, and ever after he and his family, the frost giants, tried to do mischief and fought against gods and men.

According to the belief of the Teutons, these wicked giants will some day destroy the beautiful world. Even the gods themselves will be killed in a dreadful battle with them. First of all will come three terrible winters without any spring or summer. The sun and moon will cease to shine and the bright stars will fall from the sky. The earth will be shaken as when there is a great earthquake; the waves of the sea will roar, and the highest mountains will totter and fall. The trees will be torn up by the roots, and even the "world tree" will tremble from its roots to its topmost boughs. At last the quivering earth will sink beneath the waters of the sea.

Then Loki, the spirit of evil, will break loose from the fetters with which the gods have bound him. The frost giants will join him. They will try to make a secret attack on the gods. But Heimdall, the sentry of heaven, will be on guard at the end of the rainbow-bridge. He needs no more sleep than a bird and can see for a hundred miles either by day or by night. He only can sound the horn whose blast can be heard through heaven and earth and the underworld. Loki and his army will be seen by him. His loud alarm will sound and bring the gods together. They will rush to meet the giants. Woden will wield his spear, Tiew his glittering sword and Thor his terrible hammer. These will all be in vain. The gods must die. But so must the giants and Loki.

And then a new earth will rise from the sea. The leaves of its forests will never fall; its fields will yield harvests unsown. And in a hall far brighter than Woden's Valhalla, the brave and good will be gathered forever.

Written Summation

In the little volume called The Famous Men of Rome, you have read about the great empire, which the Romans established. Now we come to a time when the power of Rome was broken and tribes of barbarians who lived north of the Danube and the Rhine took possession of lands that had been part of the Roman Empire.

Model Practice 1

Model Practice 2

Model Practice 3

The Nibelungs

from The Famous Men of the Middle Ages
by John H. Haaren, LL.D. and A. B. Poland, Ph.D.
Norse Myth

The time came when the people of Western Europe learned to believe in one God and were converted to Christianity, but the old stories about the gods and Valkyries and giants and heroes, who were half-gods and half-men, were not forgotten.

These stories were repeated from father to son for generations, and in the twelfth century a poet, whose name we do not know, wrote them in verse. He called his poem the Nibelungenlied (song of the Nibelungs). It is the great national poem of the Germans. The legends told in it are the basis of Wagner's operas.

"Nibelungs" was the name given to some northern dwarfs whose king had once possessed a great treasure of gold and precious stones but had lost it. Whoever got possession of this treasure was followed by a curse. The Nibelungenlied tells the adventures of those who possessed the treasure.

In the grand old city of Worms, in Burgundy, there lived long ago the princess Kriemhilda. Her eldest brother Gunther was king of Burgundy.

And in the faraway Netherlands, where the Rhine pours its waters into the sea, dwelt a prince named Siegfried, son of Siegmund, the king.

Ere long, Sir Siegfried heard of the beauty of fair Kriemhilda. He said to his father, "Give me twelve knights, and I will ride to King Gunther's land. I must win the heart of Kriemhilda."

After seven days' journey, the prince and his company drew near to the gates of Worms. All wondered who the strangers were and whence they came. Hagen, Kriemhilda's uncle, guessed. He said, "I never have seen the famed hero of Netherlands, yet I am sure that yonder knight is none but Sir Siegfried."

"And who," asked the wondering people, "may Siegfried be?"

"Siegfried," answered Sir Hagen, "is a truly wonderful knight. Once when riding all alone, he came to a mountain, where lay the treasure of the king of the Nibelungs. The king's two sons had brought it out from the cave in which it had been hidden, to divide it between them. But they did not agree about the division. So when Seigfied drew near, both princes said, 'Divide for us, Sir Siegfried, our father's hoard.' There were so many jewels that one hundred wagons could not carry them, and of ruddy gold there was even more. Seigfied made the fairest division he could, and as a reward, the princes gave him their father's sword called Balmung. But although Siegfried had done his best to satisfy them with his division, they soon fell to quarreling and fighting, and when he tried to separate them, they attacked him. To save his own life he slew them both. Alberich, a mountain dwarf, who had long been guardian of the Nibelung hoard, rushed to avenge his masters; but Siegfried vanquished him and took from him his cap of darkness which made its wearer invisible and gave him the strength of twelve men. The hero then ordered Alberich to place the treasure again in the mountain cave and guard it for him."

Hagen then told another story of Siegfried:

"Once he slew a fierce dragon and bathed himself in its blood, and this turned the hero's skin to horn, so that no sword or spear could wound him."

When Hagen had told these tales, he advised King Gunther and the people of Burgundy to receive Siegfried with all honor.

So, as was the fashion in those times, games were held in the courtyard of the palace in honor of Siegfried, and Kriemhilda watched the sport from her window.

For a full year, Siegfried stayed at the court of King Gunther, but never in all that time told why he had come and never once saw Kriemhilda.

At the end of the year, sudden tidings came that the Saxons and Danes, as was their habit, were pillaging the lands of Burgundy. At the head of a thousand Burgundian knights, Siegfried conquered both Saxons and Danes. The king of the Danes was taken prisoner and the Saxon king surrendered.

The victorious warriors returned to Worms, and the air was filled with glad shouts of welcome. King Gunther asked Kriemhilda to welcome Siegfried and offer him the thanks of all the land of Burgundy.

Siegfried stood before her, and she said, "Welcome, Sir Siegfried, welcome; we thank you one and all." He bent before her and she kissed him.

Far over the sea from sunny Burgundy lived Brunhilda, queen of Iceland. Fair was she of face and strong beyond compare. If a knight would woo and win her, he must surpass her in three contests: leaping, hurling the spear and pitching the stone. If he failed in even one, he must forfeit his life.

King Gunther resolved to wed this strange princess and Siegfried promised to help him. "But," said Siegfried, "if we succeed, I must have as my wife thy sister Kriemhilda." To this Gunther agreed, and the voyage to Iceland began.

When Gunther and his companions neared Brunhilda's palace, the gates were opened and the strangers were welcomed.

Siegfried thanked the queen for her kindness and told how Gunther had come to Iceland in hope of winning her hand.

"If in three contests, he gain the mastery," she said, "I will become his wife. If not, both he and you who are with him must lose your lives."

Brunhilda prepared for the contests. Her shield was so thick and heavy that four strong men were needed to bear it. Three could scarcely carry her spear, and the stone that she hurled could only be lifted by twelve.

Siegfried now helped Gunther in a wonderful way. He put on his cap of darkness, so that no one could see him. Then he stood by Gunther's side and did the fighting. Brunhilda threw her spear against the king's bright shield and sparks flew from the steel. But the unseen knight dealt Brunhilda such blows that she confessed herself conquered.

In the second and third contests, she fared no better, so she had to become King Gunther's bride. But she said that before she would leave Iceland she must tell all her kinsmen. Daily her kinsfolk rode to the castle, and soon an army had assembled.

Then Gunther and his friends feared unfair play. So Siegfried put on his cap of darkness, stepped into a boat, and went to the Nibelung land where Alberich the dwarf was guarding the wonderful Nibelung treasure.

"Bring me here," he cried to the dwarf, "a thousand Nibelung knights." At the call of the dwarf, the warriors gathered around Sir Siegfried. Then they sailed with him to Brunhilda's isle and the queen and her kinsmen, fearing such warriors, welcomed them instead of fighting. Soon after their arrival King Gunther and his men, Siegfried and his Nibelungs, and Queen Brunhilda, with two thousand of her kinsmen, set sail for King Gunther's land.

As soon as they reached Worms, the marriage of Gunther and Brunhilda took place. Siegfried and Kriemhilda also were married, and after their marriage went to Siegfried's Netherlands castle. There they lived more happily than I can tell.

Now comes the sad part of the Nibelung tale.

Brunhilda and Gunther invited Siegfried and Kriemhilda to visit them at Worms. During the visit, the two queens quarreled and Brunhilda made Gunther angry with Siegfried. Hagen, too, began to hate Siegfried and wished to kill him.

But Siegfried could not be wounded except in one spot on which a falling leaf had rested when he bathed himself in the dragon's blood. Only Kriemhilda knew where this spot was. Hagen told her to sew a little silk cross upon Siegfried's dress to mark the spot, so that he might defend Siegfried in a fight.

No battle was fought, but Siegfried went hunting with Gunther and Hagen one day, and they challenged him to race with them. He easily won, but after running he was hot and thirsty and knelt to drink at a spring. Then Hagen seized a spear and plunged it through the cross into the hero's body. Thus the treasure of the Nibelungs brought disaster to Siegfried.

Gunther and Hagen told Kriemhilda that robbers in the wood had slain her husband, but she could not be deceived.

Kriemhilda determined to take vengeance on the murderers of Siegfried, and so she would not leave Worms. There, too, stayed one thousand knights who had followed Siegfried from the Nibelung land.

Soon after Siegfried's death, Kriemhilda begged her younger brother to bring the Nibelung treasure from the mountain cave to Worms.

When it arrived, Kriemhilda gave gold and jewels to rich and poor in Burgundy, and Hagen feared that soon she would win the love of all the people and turn them against him. So one day, he took the treasure and hid it in the Rhine. He hoped some day to enjoy it himself.

As Hagen now possessed the Nibelung treasure, the name "Nibelungs" was given to him and his companions.

Etzel, or as we call him, Attila, king of the Huns, heard of the beauty of Kriemhilda and sent one of his knights to ask the queen to become his wife.

At first, she refused. However, when she remembered that Etzel carried the sword of Tiew, she changed her mind, because, if she became his wife, she might persuade him to take vengeance upon Gunther and Hagen.

And so it came to pass.

Shortly after their marriage, Etzel and Kriemhilda invited Gunther and all his court to a grand midsummer festival in the land of the Huns.

Hagen was afraid to go, for he felt sure that Kriemhilda had not forgiven the murder of Siegfried. However, it was decided that the invitation should be accepted, but that ten thousand knights should go with Gunther as a bodyguard.

Shortly after Gunther and his followers arrived at Attila's court, a banquet was prepared. Nine thousand Burgundians were seated at the board when Attila's brother came into the banquet hall with a thousand well-armed knights. A quarrel arose and a fight followed.

Thousands of the Burgundians were slain. The struggle continued for days. At last, of all the knights of Burgundy, Gunther and Hagen alone were left alive. Then one of Kriemhilda's friends fought with them and overpowered both. He bound them and delivered them to Kriemhilda.

The queen ordered one of her knights to cut off Gunther's head, and she herself cut off the head of Hagen with "Balmung," Siegfried's wonderful sword. A friend of Hagen then avenged his death by killing Kriemhilda herself.

Of all the Nibelungs who entered the land of the Huns one only ever returned to Burgundy.

Written Summation

Brunhilda prepared for the contests. Her shield was so thick and heavy that four strong men were needed to bear it. Three could scarcely carry her spear, and the stone that she hurled could only be lifted by twelve.

Model Practice 1

Model Practice 2

Model Practice 3

Siegfried, the King's Son

from A Child's Story Garden
compiled by Elizabeth Heber
Norse Myth

Siegfried was the son of the good King Siegmund. He lived in the great palace with his father and the gentle queen, his mother.

Siegfried had everything his heart could desire. Every one about the palace loved him. He had many servants to wait upon him and beautiful clothes to wear at all times. More than this, the stables of the great palace were full of horses, and Siegfried could ride or drive whenever he wished to do so.

Now, the king was as wise as he was good, and he knew that if Siegfried would grow to be a good king he must learn to work with his hands. The king and queen talked of it, and, although they disliked to part with their son, they decided to send Siegfried to Mimer, the wonderful blacksmith.

Mimer was a queer little man. His back was bent and his hair was long and white. He had a long white beard and two very sharp, black eyes. Mimer's shop was out in the great, dark forest, and many boys came to learn of this wonderful master, for Mimer, you must know, was the best blacksmith in all the king's country.

To this shop, Siegfried was sent. At first, he was very lonely and unhappy. There were no servants now to wait upon him. His soft, beautiful clothing had been exchanged for a suit of the coarsest material and a huge leather apron. There was no soft bed waiting for him at night, only a pile of straw in the corner. But Siegfried was a brave boy, and lost no time complaining. He worked patiently at his anvil, day after day, learning from his master to make strong chains of iron, as well as dainty chains of gold and silver, for the queen to wear. One day Mimer came into the shop and sat down beside Siegfried's anvil. The boys could see that he was troubled, and they left their anvils and came to the master, begging him to tell them what troubled him.

Slowly he raised his head and looked at them all. Then he said, "A giant has come into the country, who says he is the most wonderful smith of all. He says he has made a coat of armor that no sword can pierce. I have worked day and night, and cannot make a strong sword. Who is willing to try for me?"

The boys all hung their heads, for they knew not how to help Mimer. Then Siegfried stood before his master and said, "Let me try, oh, Mimer!" And the master was willing. Siegfried went to work at once, and for seven long days, he did not leave his place at the anvil.

At the end of the time, he brought to Mimer a sword that was strong and bright. "We will try it," said Mimer, called together all the boys, and took them to a little stream near the shop. Mimer then took a single thread of wool and threw it into the water. As it was carried along, Mimer took the sword and held it before the thread. The water carried the thread along until it reached the sword. Then one-half of the thread passed to the right of the sword and the other to the left, and the thread did not move from its course.

"This is a good blade," said Mimer proudly. But Siegfried was not satisfied. He took the sword, broke it in pieces, and put it into the fire again. For three long weeks, Siegfried worked patiently at the anvil. Then he brought to Mimer a sword that was sharper, brighter, and stronger than the first.

Again, the boys were taken to the little stream, and this time a handful of wool was thrown into the water. When it reached the edge of the sword, half of the wool passed to the right and half to the left of the sword, and not one single thread moved from its place. Siegfried, however, was not satisfied, and again broke the sword into pieces and put it back into the fire.

Patiently and faithfully, he worked for seven long weeks. The sword that he brought to Mimer now was stronger and brighter and more beautiful than either of the others. The handle was wound with flowers, and the edge was as bright as the lightning.

This time, when the boys gathered at the little stream, a pack of wool was thrown into the water. When the wool reached the edge of the blade, half passed to one side and half to the other, and not one thread moved from its place.

"We will give it another trial," said Siegfried. He ran quickly to the shop and paused a moment before the great anvil. Then he swung the sword, once, twice, thrice, about his head, and then brought it down onto the iron. There was no noise, but the great anvil fell apart, and the sword was as sharp and bright as ever.

"This is the best I can do," said Siegfried. "Good master, my sword is done!" Then Mimer sent his swiftest messenger to the king to tell him that he was ready to meet the giant.

The day of the contest came. Mimer's friends sat on one side of the road, the giant's friends on the other. At the top of the hill, the two masters were to meet, the giant with his armor, Mimer with his sword. Soon a mighty shout arose! The giant, wearing the wonderful coat of glittering steel, came up the hill. He sat down on a huge rock at the top of the hill. As the people waited, a queer little man was seen coming slowly up the hill. His back was bent, and his white hair hung about his shoulders. At his side, he carried a sword so bright that the lightning seemed to play about its edge, as he walked.

Slowly he went to the top of the hill and stood before the giant. It was Mimer, the master. He loosed the sword from his side and raised it above his head.

"Are you ready?" he asked.

"Yes; strike," said the giant, laughing, for he was not afraid.

One, two, three times the sword flashed about Mimer's head. Then it fell again at his side.

"I do not wish to hurt you," he said, "but if you will take off your armor and place it on that stone, I will show you what this wonderful blade can do."

The giant only laughed again—laughed so loud and so long that the very earth seemed to tremble. Then he took off the armor and laid it on the rock. Mimer stepped back, raised the sword again, swung it about his head until the light seemed to blind the people. Then it came down. The people waited. There was no clash of iron. All was still.

Then Mimer stepped up to the armor and touched it with his foot. It fell apart, and the rock beneath it fell apart, too. Half the rock started to roll down the hill. On, on it went, faster and faster, and fell with a mighty splash into the river at the foot of the hill, and if you should go to that far-away country you could see it lying there, far down below the surface of the water.

Then a mighty shout arose! Mimer's friends, and the great king, too, joined in the applause. The giant, no longer boastful, stooped down, gathered up the two parts of the armor, and went with his friends into a far country. Mimer took the wonderful sword and went back to his place in the blacksmith shop, still the master of all the smiths.

Very few people, however, knew that it was the king's own son, Siegfried, who had made the wonderful sword.

Written Summation

Mimer was a queer little man. His back was bent and his hair was long and white. He had a long white beard and two very sharp, black eyes. Mimer's shop was out in the great, dark forest, and many boys came to learn of this wonderful master, for Mimer, you must know, was the best blacksmith in all the king's country.

Model Practice 1

Model Practice 2

Model Practice 3

The Story of the Merchant and the Genie (pt. 1)

from Arabian Nights
by Andrew Lang

Sire, there was once upon a time a merchant who possessed great wealth, in land and merchandise, as well as in ready money. He was obliged from time to time to take journeys to arrange his affairs. One day, having to go a long way from home, he mounted his horse, taking with him a small wallet in which he had put a few biscuits and dates, because he had to pass through the desert where no food was to be got. He arrived without any mishap, and, having finished his business, set out on his return. On the fourth day of his journey, the heat of the sun being very great, he turned out of his road to rest under some trees. He found, at the foot of a large walnut tree, a fountain of clear and running water. He dismounted, fastened his horse to a branch of the tree, and sat by the fountain, after having taken from his wallet some of his dates and biscuits. When he had finished this frugal meal, he washed his face and hands in the fountain.

When he was thus employed. he saw an enormous genie, white with rage, coming towards him, with a scimitar in his hand.

"Arise," he cried in a terrible voice, "and let me kill you as you have killed my son!"

As he uttered these words, he gave a frightful yell. The merchant, quite as much terrified at the hideous face of the monster as at his words, answered him tremblingly, "Alas, good sir, what can I have done to you to deserve death?"

"I shall kill you," repeated the genie, "as you have killed my son."

"But," said the merchant, "how can I have killed your son? I do not know him, and I have never even seen him."

"When you arrived here did you not sit down on the ground?" asked the genie, "and did you not take some dates from your wallet, and whilst eating them did not you throw the stones about?"

"Yes," said the merchant, "I certainly did so."

"Then," said the genie, "I tell you; you have killed my son, for whilst you were throwing about the stones, my son passed by, and one of them struck him in the eye and killed him. So I shall kill you."

"Ah, sir, forgive me!" cried the merchant.

"I will have no mercy on you," answered the genie.

"But I killed your son quite unintentionally, so I implore you to spare my life."

"No," said the genie, "I shall kill you as you killed my son," and so saying, he seized the merchant by the arm, threw him on the ground, and lifted his saber to cut off his head.

The merchant, protesting his innocence, bewailed his wife and children, and tried pitifully to avert his fate. The genie, with his raised scimitar, waited until he had finished, but was not in the least touched.

Scheherazade, at this point, seeing that it was day and knowing that the Sultan always rose very early to attend the council, stopped speaking.

"Indeed, sister," said Dinarzade, "this is a wonderful story."

"The rest is still more wonderful," replied Scheherazade, "and you would say so, if the sultan would allow me to live another day, and would give me leave to tell it to you the next night."

Schahriar, who had been listening to Scheherazade with pleasure, said to himself, "I will wait till tomorrow; I can always have her killed when I have heard the end of her story."

All this time the grand-vizier was in a terrible state of anxiety. But he was much delighted when he saw the Sultan enter the council-chamber without giving the terrible command that he was expecting.

The next morning, before the day broke, Dinarzade said to her sister, "Dear sister, if you are awake I pray you to go on with your story."

The Sultan did not wait for Scheherazade to ask his leave. "Finish," said he, "the story of the genie and the merchant. I am curious to hear the end."

So Scheherazade went on with the story. This happened every morning. The Sultana told a story, and the Sultan let her live to finish it.

When the merchant saw that the genie was determined to cut off his head, he said, "One word more, I entreat you. Grant me a little delay, just a short time to go home and bid my wife and children farewell, and to make my will. When I have done this I will come back here, and you shall kill me."

"But," said the genie, "if I grant you the delay you ask, I am afraid that you will not come back."

"I give you my word of honor," answered the merchant, "that I will come back without fail."

"How long do you require?" asked the genie.

"I ask you for a year's grace," replied the merchant. "I promise you that tomorrow twelvemonth; I shall be waiting under these trees to give myself up to you."

On hearing this, the genie left him near the fountain and disappeared.

The merchant, having recovered from his fright, mounted his horse and went on his road.

When he arrived home, his wife and children received him with the greatest joy. But instead of embracing them, he began to weep so bitterly that they soon guessed that something terrible was the matter.

"Tell us, I pray you," said his wife, "what has happened?"

"Alas!" answered her husband, "I have only a year to live."

Then he told them what had passed between him and the genie, and how he had given his word to return at the end of a year to be killed. When they heard this sad news, they were in despair and wept much.

The next day the merchant began to settle his affairs and, first of all, to pay his debts. He gave presents to his friends, and large alms to the poor. He set his slaves at liberty, and provided for his wife and children. The year soon passed away, and he was obliged to depart. When he tried to say goodbye, he was quite overcome with grief and, with difficulty, tore himself away. At length he reached the place where he had first seen the genie, on the very day that he had appointed. He dismounted, and sat down at the edge of the fountain, where he awaited the genie in terrible suspense.

Whilst he was thus waiting an old man leading a hind came towards him. They greeted one another, and then the old man said to him, "May I ask, brother, what brought you to this desert place, where there are so many evil genii about? To see these beautiful trees one would imagine it was inhabited, but it is a dangerous place to stop long in."

The merchant told the old man why he was obliged to come there. He listened in astonishment.

"This is a most marvelous affair. I should like to be a witness of your interview with the genie." So saying he sat down by the merchant.

While they were talking another old man came up, followed by two black dogs. He greeted them, and asked what they were doing in this place. The old man who was leading the hind told him the adventure of the merchant and the genie. The second old man had not sooner heard the story than he, too, decided to stay there to see what would happen. He sat down by the others, and was talking, when a third old man arrived. He asked why the merchant who was with them looked so sad. They told him the story, and he also resolved to see what would pass between the genie and the merchant, so waited with the rest.

They soon saw in the distance a thick smoke, like a cloud of dust. This smoke came nearer and nearer, and then, all at once, it vanished, and they saw the genie, who, without speaking to them, approached the merchant, sword in hand, and, taking him by the arm, said, "Get up and let me kill you as you killed my son."

The merchant and the three old men began to weep and groan.

Then the old man leading the hind threw himself at the monster's feet and said, "O Prince of the Genii, I beg of you to stay your fury and to listen to me. I am going to tell you my story and that of the hind I have with me, and if you find it more marvelous than that of the merchant whom you are about to kill, I hope that you will do away with a third part of his punishment?"

The genie considered some time, and then he said, "Very well, I agree to this."

Written Summation

"But," said the genie, "if I grant you the delay you ask, I am afraid that you will not come back."

"I give you my word of honor," answered the merchant, "that I will come back without fail."

"How long do you require?" asked the genie.

Model Practice 1

Model Practice 2

Model Practice 3

The Story of the First Old Man and of the Hind (pt. 2)

from Arabian Nights
by Andrew Lang

I am now going to begin my story (said the old man), so please attend.

This hind that you see with me is my wife. We have no children of our own; therefore I adopted the son of a favorite slave, and determined to make him my heir.

My wife, however, took a great dislike to both mother and child, which she concealed from me till too late. When my adopted son was about ten years old, I was obliged to go on a journey. Before I went I entrusted to my wife's keeping both the mother and child, and begged her to take care of them during my absence, which lasted a whole year. During this time, she studied magic in order to carry out her wicked scheme. When she had learned enough, she took my son into a distant place and changed him into a calf. Then she gave him to my steward, and told him to look after the calf she had bought. She also changed the slave into a cow, which she sent to my steward.

When I returned I inquired after my slave and the child. "Your slave is dead," she said, "and as for your son, I have not seen him for two months, and I do not know where he is."

I was grieved to hear of my slave's death, but as my son had only disappeared, I thought I should soon find him. Eight months, however, passed, and still no tidings of him; then the feast of Bairam came.

To celebrate it I ordered my steward to bring me a very fat cow to sacrifice. He did so. The cow that he brought was my unfortunate slave. I bound her, but just as I was about to kill her she began to low most piteously, and I saw that her eyes were streaming with tears. It seemed to me most extraordinary, and, feeling a movement of pity, I ordered the steward to lead her away and bring another. My wife, who was present, scoffed at my compassion, which made her malice of no avail. "What are you doing?" she cried. "Kill this cow. It is the best we have to sacrifice."

To please her, I tried again, but again the animal's lows and tears disarmed me.

"Take her away," I said to the steward, "and kill her; I cannot."

The steward killed her, but on skinning her found that she was nothing but bones, although she appeared so fat. I was vexed.

"Keep her for yourself," I said to the steward, "and if you have a fat calf, bring that in her stead."

In a short time, he brought a very fat calf, which, although I did not know it, was my son. It tried hard to break its cord and come to me. It threw itself at my feet, with its head on the ground, as if it wished to excite my pity, and to beg me not to take away its life.

I was even more surprised and touched at this action than I had been at the tears of the cow.

"Go," I said to the steward, "take back this calf, take great care of it, and bring me another in its place instantly."

As soon as my wife heard me speak this, she at once cried out, "What are you doing, husband? Do not sacrifice any calf, but this."

"Wife," I answered, "I will not sacrifice this calf," and in spite of all her remonstrances, I remained firm.

I had another calf killed; this one was led away. The next day the steward asked to speak to me in private.

"I have come," he said, "to tell you some news which I think you will like to hear. I have a daughter who knows magic. Yesterday, when I was leading back the calf which you refused to sacrifice, I noticed that she smiled, and then directly afterwards began to cry. I asked her why she did so."

"Father," she answered, "this calf is the son of our master. I smile with joy at seeing him still alive, and I weep to think of his mother, who was sacrificed yesterday as a cow. These changes have been wrought by our master's wife, who hated the mother and son."

"At these words," continued the old man, "I leave you to imagine my astonishment. I went immediately with the steward to speak with his daughter myself. First of all, I went to the stable to see my son, and he replied in his dumb way to all my caresses. When the steward's daughter came, I asked her if she could change my son back to his proper shape."

"Yes, I can," she replied, "on two conditions. One is that you will give him to me for a husband, and the other is that you will let me punish the woman who changed him into a calf."

"To the first condition," I answered, "I agree with all my heart, and I will give you an ample dowry. To the second I also agree, I only beg you to spare her life."

"That I will do," she replied; "I will treat her as she treated your son."

Then she took a vessel of water and pronounced over it some words I did not understand. Then, on throwing the water over him, he became immediately a young man once more.

"My son, my dear son," I exclaimed, kissing him in a transport of joy. "This kind maiden has rescued you from a terrible enchantment, and I am sure that out of gratitude you will marry her."

He consented joyfully, but before they were married, the young girl changed my wife into a hind, and it is she whom you see before you. I wished her to have this form rather than a stranger one, so that we could see her in the family without repugnance.

Since then my son has become a widower and has gone traveling. I am now going in search of him, and not wishing to confide my wife to the care of other people, I am taking her with me. Is this not a most marvelous tale?

"It is indeed," said the genie, "and because of it, I grant to you the third part of the punishment of this merchant."

When the first old man had finished his story, the second, who was leading the two black dogs, said to the genie, "I am going to tell you what happened to me, and I am sure that you will find my story even more astonishing than the one to which you have just been listening. But when I have related it, will you grant me also the third part of the merchant's punishment?"

"Yes," replied the genie, "provided that your story surpasses that of the hind."

With this agreement the second old man began in this way.

Written Summation

"Father," she answered, "this calf is the son of our master. I smile with joy at seeing him still alive, and I weep to think of his mother, who was sacrificed yesterday as a cow. These changes have been wrought by our master's wife, who hated the mother and son."

Model Practice 1 (adapted from the original)

Model Practice 2

Model Practice 3

The Story of the Second Old Man, and of the Two Black Dogs (pt. 3)

from Arabian Nights
by Andrew Lang

Great prince of the genii, you must know that we are three brothers—these two black dogs and myself. Our father died, leaving us each a thousand sequins. With this sum, we all three took up the same profession and became merchants. A short time after we had opened our shops, my eldest brother, one of these two dogs, resolved to travel in foreign countries for the sake of merchandise. With this intention, he sold all he had and bought merchandise suitable for the voyages he was about to make. He set out, and was away a whole year. At the end of this time, a beggar came to my shop.

"Good day," I said.

"Good day," he answered. "Is it possible that you do not recognize me?" Then I looked at him closely and saw he was my brother. I made him come into my house, and asked him how he had fared in his enterprise.

"Do not question me," he replied. "When you see me, you see all I have. It would but renew my trouble to tell of all the misfortunes that have befallen me in a year, and have brought me to this state."

I shut up my shop, paid him every attention, taking him to the bath, giving him my most beautiful robes. I examined my accounts, and found that I had doubled my capital—that is, that I now possessed two thousand sequins. I gave my brother half, saying: "Now, brother, you can forget your losses." He accepted them with joy, and we lived together as we had before.

Some time afterwards, my second brother wished also to sell his business and travel. My eldest brother and I did all we could to dissuade him, but it was of no use. He joined a caravan and set out. He came back at the end of a year in the same state as his elder brother. I took care of him, and as I had a thousand sequins to spare I gave them to him, and he reopened his shop.

One day, my two brothers came to me to propose that we should make a journey and trade. At first, I refused to go. "You traveled," I said, "and what did you gain?" But they came to me repeatedly, and after having held out for five years, I at last gave way. But when they had made their preparation, and they began to buy the merchandise we needed, they found they had spent every piece of the thousand sequins I had given them. I did not reproach them. I divided my six thousand sequins with them, giving a thousand to each and keeping one for myself, and the other three I buried in a corner of my house. We bought merchandise, loaded a vessel with it, and set forth with a favorable wind.

After two months' sailing, we arrived at a seaport, where we disembarked and did a great trade. Then we bought the merchandise of the country, and were just going to sail once more, when I was stopped on the shore by a beautiful though poorly dressed woman. She came up to me, kissed my hand, and implored me to marry her, and take her on board. At first, I refused, but she begged so hard and promised to be such a good wife to me, that at last I consented. I got her some beautiful dresses, and after having married her, we embarked and set sail. During the voyage, I discovered so many good qualities in my wife that I began to love her more and more. But my brothers began to be jealous of my prosperity, and set to work to plot against my life. One night when we were sleeping they threw my wife and myself into the sea. My wife, however, was a fairy, and so she did not let me drown, but transported me to an island. When the day dawned, she said to me, "When I saw you on the seashore I took a great fancy to you, and wished to try your good nature, so I presented myself in the disguise you saw. Now I have rewarded you by saving your life. But I am very angry with your brothers, and I shall not rest till I have taken their lives."

I thanked the fairy for all that she had done for me, but I begged her not to kill my brothers.

I appeased her wrath, and in a moment she transported me from the island, where we were, to the roof of my house, and she disappeared a moment afterwards. I went down, opened the doors, and dug up the three thousand sequins, which I had buried. I went to my shop, opened it, and, received from my fellow-merchants congratulations on my return. When I went home, I saw two black dogs who came to meet me with sorrowful faces. I was much astonished, but the fairy who reappeared said to me, "Do not be surprised to see these dogs; they are your two brothers. I have condemned them to remain for ten years in these shapes." Then having told me where I could hear news of her, she vanished.

The ten years are nearly passed, and I am on the road to find her. As in passing I met this merchant and the old man with the hind, I stayed with them.

This is my history, O prince of genii! Do you not think it is a most marvelous one?

"Yes, indeed," replied the genie, "and I will give up to you the third of the merchant's punishment."

Then the third old man made the genie the same request as the other two had done, and the genie promised him the last third of the merchant's punishment, if his story surpassed both the others.

So he told his story to the genie, but I cannot tell you what it was, as I do not know.

But I do know that it was even more marvelous than either of the others, so that the genie was astonished, and said to the third old man, "I will give up to you the third part of the merchant's punishment. He ought to thank all three of you for having interested yourselves in his favor. But for you, he would be here no longer."

So saying, he disappeared, to the great joy of the company. The merchant did not fail to thank his friends, and then each went on his way. The merchant returned to his wife and children, and passed the rest of his days happily with them.

Written Summation

"Good day," I said.

"Good day," he answered. "Is it possible that you do not recognize me?" Then I looked at him closely and saw he was my brother. I made him come into my house, and asked him how he had fared in his enterprise.

Model Practice 1 (adapted from the original)

Model Practice 2

Model Practice 3

The Fairy

from The Fairy Tales of Charles Perrault
by Charles Perrault

There was, once upon a time, a widow, who had two daughters. The eldest was so much like her in the face and humor that whoever looked upon the daughter saw the mother. They were both so disagreeable, and so proud, that there was no living with them. The youngest, who was the very picture of her father, for courtesy and sweetness of temper, was withal one of the most beautiful girls ever seen. As people naturally love their own likeness, this mother doted on her eldest daughter, and at the same time had a horrible aversion for the youngest. She made her eat in the kitchen, and work continually.

Among other things, this poor child was forced twice a day to draw water a mile and a half from the house and bring home a pitcher full of it. One day, as she was at this fountain, there came to her a poor woman, who begged of her to let her drink.

"O yes, with all my heart, Goody," said this pretty maid, immediately. After rinsing the pitcher, she took up some water from the clearest place of the fountain and gave it to her, holding up the pitcher all the while that she might drink the easier.

The good woman having drank, said to her:

"You are so very pretty, my dear, so good and so mannerly, that I cannot help giving you a gift." (For this was a Fairy, who had taken the form of a poor countrywoman, who desired to see how far the civility and good manners of this pretty girl would go). "At every word you speak," continued the Fairy, "there shall come out of your mouth either a flower or a jewel."

When this pretty girl came home, her mother scolded her for staying so long at the fountain.

"I beg your pardon, mamma," said the poor girl, "for not making more haste." And, in speaking these words, there came out of her mouth two roses, two pearls, and two diamonds.

"What is this I see?" said her mother quite astonished. "I think I see pearls and diamonds come out of the girl's mouth! How happens this, child?" (This was the first time she had ever called her child.)

The poor creature told her what had happened, but not without dropping out infinite numbers of diamonds.

"In good faith," cried the mother, "I must send my child thither. Come hither, Fanny, look what comes out of thy sister's mouth when she speaks! Would not thou be glad, my dear, to have the same gift given to thee? Thou hast nothing else to do but go and draw water out of the fountain, and when a certain poor woman asks thee to let her drink, to give it her very civilly."

"It would be a very fine sight indeed," said this ill-bred minx, "to see me go draw water!"

"You shall go," said the mother, "and this minute."

So away she went, grumbling all the way, taking with her the best silver tankard in the house.

She was no sooner at the fountain, than she saw coming out of the wood a lady most gloriously dressed, who came up to her, and asked to drink. This was, you must know, the very Fairy who appeared to her sister, but had now taken the air and dress of a princess, to see how far this girl's rudeness would go.

"Am I come hither," said the proud sister, "to serve you with water, pray? I suppose the silver tankard was brought purely for your ladyship, was it? However, you may drink out of it, if you have a fancy."

"You are not over and above mannerly," answered the Fairy, without putting herself in a passion. "Well then, since you have so little breeding, and are so disobliging, I give you a gift, that at every word you speak there shall come out of your mouth a snake or a toad."

So soon as her mother saw her coming, she cried out: "Well, daughter?"

"Well, mother?" answered the pert child, throwing out of her mouth two vipers and two toads.

"O mercy!" cried the mother. "What is it I see? O, it is that wretch, her sister, who has occasioned all this; but she shall pay for it", and immediately she ran to beat her. The poor child fled away from her and went to hide herself in the forest, not far from thence.

The King's son, then on his return from hunting, met her and, seeing her so very pretty, asked her what she did there alone and why she cried.

"Alas! Sir, my mamma has turned me out of doors."

The King's son, who saw five or six pearls, and as many diamonds, come out of her mouth, desired her to tell him how that happened. She thereupon told him the whole story; and so the King's son fell in love with her; and, considering with himself that such a gift was worth more than any marriage portion whatsoever in another, conducted her to the palace of the King his father, and there married her.

As for her sister, she made herself so much hated that her own mother turned her off; and the miserable wretch, having wandered about a good while without finding anybody to take her in, went to a corner in the wood and there died.

Written Summation

Among other things, this poor child was forced twice a day to draw water a mile and a half from the house and bring home a pitcher full of it. One day, as she was at this fountain, there came to her a poor woman, who begged of her to let her drink.

Model Practice 1

Model Practice 2

Model Practice 3

Little Red Riding Hood

from Old-Time Stories
by Charles Perrault

Once upon a time there was a little village girl, the prettiest that had ever been seen. Her mother doted on her. Her grandmother was even fonder, and made her a little red hood, which became her so well that everywhere she went by the name of Little Red Riding Hood.

One day her mother, who had just made and baked some cakes, said to her, "Go and see how your grandmother is, for I have been told that she is ill. Take her a cake and this little pot of butter."

Little Red Riding Hood set off at once for the house of her grandmother, who lived in another village.

On her way through a wood, she met old Father Wolf. He would have very much liked to eat her, but dared not do so on account of some woodcutters who were in the forest. He asked her where she was going. The poor child, not knowing that it was dangerous to stop and listen to a wolf, said, "I am going to see my grandmother, and am taking her a cake and a pot of butter which my mother has sent to her."

"Does she live far away?" asked the Wolf.

"Oh yes," replied Little Red Riding Hood; "it is yonder by the mill which you can see right below there, and it is the first house in the village."

"Well now," said the Wolf, "I think I shall go and see her too. I will go by this path, and you by that path, and we will see who gets there first."

The Wolf set off running with all his might by the shorter road, and the little girl continued on her way by the longer road. As she went, she amused herself by gathering nuts, running after the butterflies, and making nosegays of the wild flowers which she found.

The Wolf was not long in reaching the grandmother's house.

He knocked. *Toc Toc.*

"Who is there?"

"It is your little daughter, Red Riding Hood," said the Wolf, disguising his voice, "and I bring you a cake and a little pot of butter as a present from my mother."

The worthy grandmother was in bed, not being very well, and cried out to him, "Pull out the peg, and the latch will fall."

The Wolf drew out the peg, and the door flew open. Then he sprang upon the poor old lady and ate her up in less than no time, for he had been more than three days without food.

After that, he shut the door, lay down in the grandmother's bed, and waited for Little Red Riding Hood.

Presently she came and knocked. *Toc Toc.*

"Who is there?"

Now Little Red Riding Hood on hearing the Wolf's gruff voice was at first frightened, but thinking that her grandmother had a bad cold, she replied, "It is your little daughter, Red Riding Hood, and I bring you a cake and a little pot of butter from my mother."

Softening his voice, the Wolf called out to her, "Pull out the peg, and the latch will fall."

Little Red Riding Hood drew out the peg, and the door flew open.

When he saw her enter, the Wolf hid himself in the bed beneath the counterpane.

"Put the cake and the little pot of butter on the bin," he said, "and come up on the bed with me."

Little Red Riding Hood took off her little red hood, but when she climbed up on the bed, she was astonished to see how her grandmother looked in her nightgown.

"Grandmother dear!" she exclaimed, "what big arms you have!"

"The better to embrace you, my child!"

"Grandmother dear, what big legs you have!"

"The better to run with, my child!"

"Grandmother dear, what big ears you have!"

"The better to hear with, my child!"

"Grandmother dear, what big eyes you have!"

"The better to see with, my child!"

"Grandmother dear, what big teeth you have!"

"The better to eat you with!"

With these words, the wicked Wolf leapt upon Little Red Riding Hood and gobbled her up.

Written Summation

"It is your little daughter, Red Riding Hood," said the Wolf, disguising his voice, "and I bring you a cake and a little pot of butter as a present from my mother."

The worthy grandmother was in bed, not being very well, and cried out to him, "Pull out the peg, and the latch will fall."

Model Practice 1

Model Practice 2

Model Practice 3

The Master Cat or Puss in Boots

from The Fairy Tales of Charles Perrault
by Charles Perrault

There was a miller, who left no more estate to the three sons he had, than his Mill, his donkey, and his Cat. The partition was soon made. Neither the scrivener nor attorney were sent for. They would soon have eaten up all the poor patrimony. The eldest had the Mill, the second the Donkey, and the youngest nothing but the Cat.

The poor young fellow was quite comfortless at having so poor a lot.

"My brothers," said he, "may get their living handsomely enough, by joining their stocks together; but for my part, when I have eaten up my Cat, and made me a muff of his skin, I must die with hunger."

The Cat, who heard all this, but made as if he did not, said to him with a grave and serious air, "Do not thus afflict yourself, my good master; you have only to give me a bag, and get a pair of boots made for me, that I may scamper thro' the dirt and the brambles, and you shall see that you have not so bad a portion of me as you imagine."

Tho' the Cat's master did not build very much upon what he said, he had, however, often seen him play a great many cunning tricks to catch rats and mice; as when he used to hang by the heels, or hide himself in the meal, and make as if he were dead; so that he did not altogether despair of his affording him some help in his miserable condition.

When the Cat had what he asked for, he booted himself very gallantly. And putting his bag about his neck, he held the strings of it in his two fore paws and went into a warren where there was great abundance of rabbits. He put bran and sow-thistle into his bag, and stretching himself out at length, as if he had been dead, he waited for some young rabbit, not yet acquainted with the deceits of the world, to come and rummage his bag for what he had put into it.

Scarce was he lain down, but he had what he wanted; a rash and foolish young rabbit jumped into his bag, and Monsieur Puss, immediately drawing close the strings, took and killed him without pity. Proud of his prey, he went with it to the palace and asked to speak with his Majesty. He was shown up stairs into the King's apartment and, making a low reverence, said to him, "I have brought you, sir, a rabbit of the warren which my noble lord the Marquis of Carabas" (for that was the title which Puss was pleased to give his master) "has commanded me to present to your Majesty from him."

"Tell thy master," said the King, "that I thank him, and that he does me a great deal of pleasure."

Another time he went and hid himself among some standing corn, holding still his open bag. When a brace of partridges ran into it, he drew the strings and caught them both. He went and made a present of these to the King, as he had done before with the rabbit. The King in like manner received the partridges with great pleasure, and ordered him something to drink.

The Cat continued for two or three months, thus to carry his Majesty, from time to time, game of his master's taking. One day in particular, when he knew for certain that the King was to take the air, along the river side, with his daughter, the most beautiful Princess in the world, he said to his master, "If you will follow my advice, your fortune is made. You have nothing else to do, but go and wash yourself in the river, in that part I shall shew you, and leave the rest to me."

The Marquis of Carabas did what the Cat advised him to, without knowing why or wherefore.

While he was washing, the King passed by, and the Cat began to cry out, as loud as he could, "Help, help, my lord Marquis of Carabas is drowning."

At this noise, the King put his head out of his coach window, and finding it was the Cat who had so often brought him such good game, he commanded his guards to run immediately to the assistance of his lordship the Marquis of Carabas.

While they were drawing the poor Marquis out of the river, the Cat came up to the coach, and told the King that while his master was washing, there came by some rogues, who went off with his clothes, tho' he had cried out "Thieves, thieves," several times, as loud as he could. This cunning Cat had hidden them under a great stone. The King immediately commanded the officers of his wardrobe to run and fetch one of his best suits for the lord Marquis of Carabas.

The King received him with great kindness, and as the fine clothes he had given him extremely set off his good appearance (for he was well made, and very handsome in his person), the King's daughter took a secret inclination to him, and the Marquis of Carabas had no sooner cast two or three respectful and somewhat tender glances, but she fell in love with him to distraction.

The King would needs have him come into his coach, and take part of the airing. The Cat, quite overjoyed to see his project begin to succeed, marched on before, and meeting with some countrymen, who were mowing a meadow, he said to them, "Good people, you who are mowing, if you do not tell the King, that the meadow you mow belongs to my lord Marquis of Carabas, you shall be chopped as small as mincemeat."

The King did not fail asking of the mowers to whom the meadow they were mowing belonged.

"To my lord Marquis of Carabas," answered they all together; for the Cat's threats had made them terribly afraid.

"Truly a fine estate," said the King to the Marquis of Carabas.

"You see, sir," said the Marquis, "this is a meadow which never fails to yield a plentiful harvest every year."

The Master Cat, who still went on before, met with some reapers, and said to them, "Good people, you who are reaping, if you do not tell the King that all this corn belongs to the Marquis of Carabas, you shall be chopped as small as mince-meat."

The King, who passed by a moment after, would needs know to whom all that corn, which he then saw, did belong. "To my lord Marquis of Carabas," replied the reapers; and the King again congratulated the Marquis.

The Master Cat, who went always before, said the same words to all he met; and the King was astonished at the vast estates of my lord Marquis of Carabas.

Monsieur Puss came at last to a stately castle, the master of which was an Ogre, the richest had ever been known; for all the lands which the King had then gone over belonged to this castle. The Cat, who had taken care to inform himself who this Ogre was, and what he could do, asked to speak with him, saying, he could not pass so near his castle, without having the honor of paying his respects to him.

The Ogre received him as civilly as an Ogre could do, and made him sit down.

"I have been assured," said the Cat, "that you have the gift of being able to change yourself into all sorts of creatures you have a mind to; you can, for example, transform yourself into a lion, or elephant, and the like."

"This is true," answered the Ogre very briskly, "and to convince you, you shall see me now become a lion."

Puss was so sadly terrified at the sight of a lion so near him, that he immediately got into the gutter, not without abundance of trouble and danger, because of his boots, which were ill-suited for walking upon the tiles. A little while after, when Puss saw that the Ogre had resumed his natural form, he came down, and owned he had been very much frightened.

"I have been moreover informed," said the Cat, "but I know not how to believe it, that you have also the power to take on you the shape of the smallest animals; for example, to change yourself into a rat or a mouse; but I must own to you, I take this to be impossible."

"Impossible?" cried the Ogre. "You shall see that presently," and at the same time changed into a mouse, and began to run about the floor.

Puss no sooner perceived this, but he fell upon him, and ate him up.

Meanwhile the King, who saw, as he passed, this fine castle of the Ogre's, had a mind to go into it. Puss, who heard the noise of his Majesty's coach running over the drawbridge, ran out and said to the King:

"Your Majesty is welcome to this castle of my lord Marquis of Carabas."

"What! My lord Marquis?" cried the King. "And does this castle also belong to you? There can be nothing finer than this court, and all the stately buildings which surround it; let us go into it, if you please."

The Marquis gave his hand to the Princess, and followed the King, who went up first. They passed into a spacious hall, where they found a magnificent collation which the Ogre had prepared for his friends, who were that very day to visit him, but dared not to enter knowing the King was there. His Majesty was perfectly charmed with the good qualities of my lord Marquis of Carabas, as was his daughter who was fallen violently in love with him; and seeing the vast estate he possessed, said to him, after having drank five or six glasses, "It will be owing to yourself only, my lord Marquis, if you are not my son-in-law."

The Marquis making several low bows, accepted the honor which his Majesty conferred upon him, and forthwith, that very same day, married the Princess.

Puss became a great lord, and never ran after mice any more, but only for his diversion.

Written Summation

Another time he went and hid himself among some standing corn, holding still his open bag. When a brace of partridges ran into it, he drew the strings and caught them both. He went and made a present of these to the King, as he had done before with the rabbit. The King in like manner received the partridges with great pleasure, and ordered him something to drink.

Model Practice 1

Model Practice 2

Model Practice 3

Mr. and Mrs. Vinegar

from English Fairy Tales
by Flora Annie Steel

Mr. and Mrs. Vinegar, a worthy couple, lived in a glass pickle jar. The house, though small, was snug, and so light that each speck of dust on the furniture showed like a mole-hill; so while Mr. Vinegar tilled his garden with a pickle-fork and grew vegetables for pickling, Mrs. Vinegar, who was a sharp, bustling, tidy woman, swept, brushed, and dusted, brushed and dusted and swept to keep the house clean as a new pin. Now one day she lost her temper with a cobweb and swept so hard after it that bang! Bang! The broom-handle went right through the glass, and crash! Crash! Clatter! Clatter! There was the pickle-jar house about her ears all in splinters and bits.

She picked her way over these as best she might, and rushed into the garden.

"Oh, Vinegar, Vinegar!" she cried. "We are clean ruined and done for! Quit these vegetables! They won't be wanted! What is the use of pickles if you haven't a pickle jar to put them in, and—I've broken ours—into little bits!" And with that she fell to crying bitterly.

But Mr. Vinegar was of different mettle; though a small man, he was a cheerful one, always looking at the best side of things, so he said, "Accidents will happen, lovely! But there are as good pickle bottles in the shop as ever came out of it. All we need is money to buy another. So let us go out into the world and seek our fortunes."

"But what about the furniture?" sobbed Mrs. Vinegar.

"I will take the door of the house with me, lovey," quoth Mr. Vinegar stoutly. "Then no one will be able to open it, will they?"

Mrs. Vinegar did not quite see how this fact would mend matters, but, being a good wife, she held her peace. So off they trudged into the world to seek fortune, Mr. Vinegar bearing the door on his back like a snail carries its house.

Well, they walked all day long, but not a brass farthing did they make, and when night fell, they found themselves in a dark, thick forest. Now Mrs. Vinegar, for all she was a smart, strong woman, was tired to death, and filled with fear of wild beasts, so she began once more to cry bitterly; but Mr. Vinegar was cheerful as ever.

"Don't alarm yourself, lovely," he said. "I will climb into a tree, fix the door firmly in a fork, and you can sleep there as safe and comfortable as in your own bed."

So he climbed the tree, fixed the door, and Mrs. Vinegar lay down on it, and being dead tired was soon fast asleep. But her weight tilted the door sideways, so, after a time, Mr. Vinegar, being afraid she might slip off, sat down on the other side to balance her and keep watch.

Now in the very middle of the night, just as he was beginning to nod, what should happen but that a band of robbers should meet beneath that very tree in order to divide their spoils. Mr. Vinegar could hear every word said quite distinctly, and began to tremble like an aspen as he listened to the terrible deeds the thieves had done to gain their ends.

"Don't shake so!" murmured Mrs. Vinegar, half asleep. "You'll have me off the bed."

"I'm not shaking, Lovey," whispered back Mr. Vinegar in a quaking voice. "It is only the wind in the trees."

But for all his cheerfulness he was not really *very* brave *inside*, so he went on trembling and shaking, and shaking and trembling, till, just as the robbers were beginning to parcel out the money, he actually shook the door right out of the tree-fork, and down it came—with Mrs. Vinegar still asleep upon it—right on top of the robbers' heads!

As you may imagine, they thought the sky had fallen, and made off as fast as their legs would carry them, leaving their booty behind them. But Mr. Vinegar, who had saved himself from the fall by clinging to a branch, was far too frightened to go down in the dark to see what had happened. So up in the tree he sat like a big bird until dawn came.

Then Mrs. Vinegar woke, rubbed her eyes, yawned, and said, "Where am I?"

"On the ground, Lovey," answered Mr. Vinegar, scrambling down.

And when they lifted up the door, what do you think they found? One robber squashed flat as a pancake, and forty golden guineas all scattered about! My goodness! How Mr. and Mrs. Vinegar jumped for joy!

"Now, Vinegar!" said his wife when they had gathered up all the gold pieces, "I will tell you what we must do. You must go to the next market town and buy a cow; for, see you, money makes the mare to go, truly; but it also goes itself. Now a cow won't run away, but will give us milk and butter, which we can sell. So we shall live in comfort for the rest of our days."

"What a head you have, lovey!" said Mr. Vinegar admiringly, and started off on his errand.

"Mind you make a good bargain," bawled his wife after him.

"I always do," bawled back Mr. Vinegar. "I made a good bargain when I married such a clever wife, and I made a better one when I shook her down from the tree. I am the happiest man alive!"

So he trudged on, laughing and jingling the forty gold pieces in his pocket.

Now the first thing he saw in the market was an old red cow.

"I am in luck today," he thought. "That is the very beast for me. I shall be the happiest of men if I get that cow." So he went up to the owner, jingling the gold in his pocket.

"What will you take for your cow?" he asked.

And the owner of the cow, seeing he was a simpleton, said, "What you've got in your pocket."

"Done!" said Mr. Vinegar, handed over the forty guineas, and led off the cow, marching her up and down the market, much against her will, to show off his bargain.

Now, as he drove it about, proud as punch, he noticed a man who was playing the bagpipes. He was followed about by a crowd of children who danced to the music, and a perfect shower of pennies fell into his cap every time he held it out.

"Ho, ho!" thought Mr. Vinegar. "That is an easier way of earning a livelihood than by driving about a beast of a cow! Then the feeding, and the milking, and the churning! Ah, I should be the happiest man alive if I had those bagpipes!"

So he went up to the musician and said, "What will you take for your bagpipes?"

"Well," replied the musician, seeing he was a simpleton, "it is a beautiful instrument, and I make so much money by it, that I cannot take anything less than that red cow."

"Done!" cried Mr. Vinegar in a hurry, lest the man should repent of his offer.

So the musician walked off with the red cow, and Mr. Vinegar tried to play the bagpipes. But, alas and alack! Though he blew till he almost burst, not a sound could he make at first, and when he did at last, it was such a terrific squeal and screech that all the children ran away frightened, and the people stopped their ears.

But he went on and on, trying to play a tune, and never earning anything, save hootings and peltings, until his fingers were almost frozen with the cold, when of course the noise he made on the bagpipes was worse than ever.

Then he noticed a man who had on a pair of warm gloves, and he said to himself, "Music is impossible when one's fingers are frozen. I believe I should be the happiest man alive if I had those gloves."

So he went up to the owner and said, "You seem, sir, to have a very good pair of gloves." And the man replied, "Truly, sir, my hands are as warm as toast this bitter November day."

That quite decided Mr. Vinegar, and he asked at once what the owner would take for them; and the owner, seeing he was a simpleton, said, "As your hands seem frozen, sir, I will, as a favor, let you have them for your bagpipes."

"Done!" cried Mr. Vinegar, delighted, and made the exchange.

Then he set off to find his wife, quite pleased with himself. "Warm hands, warm heart!" he thought. "I'm the happiest man alive!"

But as he trudged he grew very, very tired, and at last began to limp. Then he saw a man coming along the road with a stout stick.

"I should be the happiest man alive if I had that stick," he thought. "What is the use of warm hands if your feet ache!" So he said to the man with the stick, "What will you take for your stick?" and the man, seeing he was a simpleton, replied, "Well, I don't want to part with my stick, but as you are so pressing, I'll oblige you, as a friend, for those warm gloves you are wearing."

"Done for you!" cried Mr. Vinegar delightedly; and trudged off with the stick, chuckling to himself over his good bargain.

But as he went along a magpie fluttered out of the hedge and sat on a branch in front of him, and chuckled and laughed as magpies do. "What are you laughing at?" asked Mr. Vinegar.

"At you, forsooth!" chuckled the magpie, fluttering just a little further. "At you, Mr. Vinegar, you foolish man—you simpleton—you blockhead! You bought a cow for forty guineas when she wasn't worth ten, you exchanged her for bagpipes you couldn't play—you changed the bagpipes for a pair of gloves, and the pair of gloves for a miserable stick. Ho, ho! Ha, ha! So you've nothing to show for your forty guineas save a stick you might have cut in any hedge. Ah, you fool! You simpleton! You blockhead!"

And the magpie chuckled, and chuckled, and chuckled in such guffaws, fluttering from branch to branch as Mr. Vinegar trudged along, that at last he flew into a violent rage and flung his stick at the bird. And the stick stuck in a tree out of his reach; so he had to go back to his wife without anything at all.

But he was glad the stick had stuck in a tree, for Mrs. Vinegar's hands were quite hard enough.

When it was all over, Mr. Vinegar said cheerfully, "You are too violent, lovey. You broke the pickle-jar, and now you've nearly broken every bone in my body. I think we had better turn over a new leaf and begin afresh. I shall take service as a gardener, and you can go as a housemaid, until we have enough money to buy a new pickle jar. There are as good ones in the shop as ever came out of it."

And that is the story of Mr. and Mrs. Vinegar.

Written Summation

"Don't shake so!" murmured Mrs. Vinegar, half-asleep. "You'll have me off the bed."

"I'm not shaking, Lovey," whispered back Mr. Vinegar in a quaking voice. "It is only the wind in
the trees."

Model Practice 1 (adapted from the original)

Model Practice 2

Model Practice 3

The Three Wishes

From More English Fairy Tales
by Joseph Jacobs

Once upon a time, and be sure it was a long time ago, there lived a poor woodman in a great forest, and every day of his life he went out to fell timber. So one day he started out, and the goodwife filled his wallet and slung his bottle on his back that he might have meat and drink in the forest. He had marked out a huge old oak, which, thought he, would furnish many and many a good plank. And when he was come to it, he took his axe in his hand and swung it round his head as though he were minded to fell the tree at one stroke. But he hadn't given one blow, when what should he hear but the pitifullest entreating, and there stood before him a fairy who prayed and beseeched him to spare the tree. He was dazed, as you may fancy, with wonderment and affright, and he couldn't open his mouth to utter a word. But he found his tongue at last, and, "Well," said he, "I'll e'en do as thou wishest."

"You've done better for yourself than you know," answered the fairy, "and to show I'm not ungrateful, I'll grant you your next three wishes, be they what they may." And therewith the fairy was no more to be seen, and the woodman slung his wallet over his shoulder and his bottle at his side, and off he started home.

But the way was long, and the poor man was regularly dazed with the wonderful thing that had befallen him. When he got home, there was nothing in his noodle but the wish to sit down and rest. Maybe, too, it was a trick of the fairy's. Who can tell? Anyhow down he sat by the blazing fire, and as he sat he waxed hungry, though it was a long way off suppertime yet.

"Hasn't thou naught for supper, dame?" said he to his wife.

"Nay, not for a couple of hours yet," said she.

"Ah!" groaned the woodman, "I wish I'd a good link of black pudding here before me."

No sooner had he said the word, when clatter, clatter, rustle, rustle, what should come down the chimney but a link of the finest black pudding the heart of man could wish for.

If the woodman stared, the goodwife stared three times as much. "What's all this?" says she.

Then all the morning's work came back to the woodman, and he told his tale right out, from beginning to end, and as he told it the goodwife glowered and glowered, and when he had made an end of it she burst out, "Thou bee'st but a fool, Jan, thou bee'st but a fool; and I wish the pudding were at thy nose, I do indeed."

And before you could say Jack Robinson, there the goodman sat and his nose was the longer for a noble link of black pudding.

He gave a pull but it stuck, and she gave a pull but it stuck, and they both pulled till they had nigh pulled the nose off, but it stuck and stuck.

"What's to be done now?" said he.

"'T isn't so very unsightly," said she, looking hard at him.

Then the woodman saw that if he wished, he must need wish in a hurry; and wish he did, that the black pudding might come off his nose. Well! there it lay in a dish on the table, and if the goodman and goodwife didn't ride in a golden coach, or dress in silk and satin, why, they had at least as fine a black pudding for their supper as the heart of man could desire.

Written Summation

But the way was long, and the poor man was regularly dazed with the wonderful thing that had befallen him. When he got home, there was nothing in his noodle but the wish to sit down and rest. Maybe, too, it was a trick of the fairy's. Who can tell? Anyhow down he sat by the blazing fire, and as he sat he waxed hungry, though it was a long way off suppertime yet.

Model Practice 1 (adapted from the original)

Model Practice 2

Model Practice 3

Schippeitaro

from Tales of Wonder Every Child Should Know
edited by Kate Douglas Wiggin and Nora Archibald Smith
Japanese Tale

Long, long ago, in the days of fairies and giants, ogres, and dragons, valiant knights and distressed damsels; in those good old days, a brave young warrior went out into the wide world in search of adventures.

For some time, he went on without meeting with anything out of the common, but at length, after journeying through a thick forest, he found himself, one evening, on a wild and lonely mountainside. No village was in sight, no cottage, not even the hut of a charcoal burner, so often to be found on the outskirts of the forest. He had been following a faint and much overgrown path, but at length, even that was lost sight of. Twilight was coming on, and in vain he strove to recover the lost track. Each effort seemed only to entangle him more hopelessly in the briers and tall grasses which grew thickly on all sides. Faint and weary, he stumbled on in the fast gathering darkness, until suddenly he came upon a little temple, deserted and half ruined, but which still contained a shrine. Here at least was shelter from the chilly dews, and here he resolved to pass the night. Food he had not, but wrapped in his mantle, and with his good sword by his side, he lay down, and was soon fast asleep.

Toward midnight he was awakened by a dreadful noise, At first he thought it must be a dream, but the noise continued, the whole place resounding with the most terrible shrieks and yells. The young warrior raised himself cautiously, and seizing his sword, looked through a hole in the ruined wall. He beheld a strange and awful sight. A horde of hideous cats was engaged in a wild and horrible dance, their yells meanwhile echoing through the night. Mingled with their unearthly cries the young warrior could clearly distinguish the words:

Tell it not to Schippeitaro!
Listen for his bark!
Tell it not to Schippeitaro!
Keep it close and dark!

A beautiful clear full moon shed its light upon this gruesome scene, which the young warrior watched with amazement and horror. Suddenly, the midnight hour being passed, the phantom cats disappeared, and all was silence once more. The rest of the night passed undisturbed, and the young warrior slept soundly until morning.

When he awoke, the sun was already up, and he hastened to leave the scene of last night's adventure. By the bright morning light, he presently discovered traces of a path which the evening before had been invisible. This he followed, and found to his great joy, that it led, not as he had feared to the forest through which he had come the day before, but in the opposite direction toward an open plain.

There he saw one or two scattered cottages, and, a little farther on, a village. Pressed by hunger, he was making the best of his way toward the village, when he heard the tones of a woman's voice loud in lamentation and entreaty. No sooner did these sounds of distress reach the warrior's ears, than his hunger was forgotten, and he hurried on to the nearest cottage to find out what was the matter and if he could give any help. The people listened to his questions, and shaking their heads sorrowfully, told him that all help was vain.

"Every year," said they, "the mountain spirit claims a victim. The time has come, and this very night will he devour our loveliest maiden. This is the cause of the wailing and lamentation."

When the young warrior, filled with wonder, inquired further, they told him that at sunset the victim would be put into a cage, carried to the ruined temple where he had passed the night, and left there alone. In the morning, she would have vanished. So it was each year, and so it would be now; there was no help for it.

As he listened, the young warrior was filled with an earnest desire to deliver the maiden. And, the mention of the ruined shrine having brought back to his mind the adventure of the night before, he asked the people whether they had ever heard the name of Schippeitaro, and who and what he was.

"Schippeitaro is a strong and beautiful dog," was the reply; "he belongs to the head man of our Prince who lives only a little way from here. We often see him following his master; he is a fine, brave fellow."

The young knight did not stop to ask more questions, but hurried off to Schippeitaro's master and begged him to lend his dog for one night. At first the man was unwilling, but at length agreed to lend Schippeitaro on condition that he should be brought back the next day. Overjoyed, the young warrior led the dog away.

Next he went to see the parents of the unhappy maiden, and told them to keep her in the house and watch her carefully until his return. He then placed the dog Schippeitaro in the cage which had been prepared for the maiden; and, with the help of some of the young men of the village, carried it to the ruined temple, and there set it down. The young men refused to stay one moment on that haunted spot, but hurried down the mountain as if the whole troop of hobgoblins had been at their heels. The young warrior, with no companion but the dog, remained to see what would happen. At midnight, when the full moon was high in the heaven and shed her light over the mountain, came the phantom cats once more. This time they had in their midst a huge black tomcat, fiercer and more terrible than all the rest, which the young warrior had no difficulty in knowing as the frightful mountain fiend himself. No sooner did this monster catch sight of the cage than he danced and sprang round it, with yells of triumph and hideous joy, followed by his companions. When he had long enough jeered at and taunted his victim, he threw open the door of the cage.

But this time he met his match. The brave Schippeitaro sprang upon him, and seizing him with his teeth, held him fast, while the young warrior with one stroke of his good sword laid the monster dead at his feet. As for the other cats, too much astonished to fly, they stood gazing at the dead body of their leader and were made short work of by the knight and Schippeitaro. The young warrior brought back the brave dog to his master, with a thousand thanks, and told the father and mother of the maiden that their daughter was free and the people of the village that the fiend had claimed his last victim and would trouble them no more.

"You owe all this to the brave Schippeitaro," he said as he bade them farewell, and went his way in search of fresh adventures.

Written Summation

A beautiful clear full moon shed its light upon this gruesome scene, which the young warrior watched with amazement and horror. Suddenly, the midnight hour being passed, the phantom cats disappeared, and all was silence once more. The rest of the night passed undisturbed, and the young warrior slept soundly until morning.

Model Practice 1 (adapted from the original)

Model Practice 2

Model Practice 3

A Tale of a Penny

from Mediaeval Tales
by Various
editor Henry Morley

There was an emperor whose porter was very shrewd. He earnestly besought his master that he might have the custody of a city for a single month, and receive, by way of tax, one penny from every crook-backed, one-eyed, scabby, leprous, or ruptured person. The emperor admitted his request, and confirmed the gift under his own seal.

Accordingly, the porter was installed in his office. And as the people entered the city, he took note of their defects and charged them in accordance with the grant. It happened that a hunchbacked fellow entered, and the porter made his demand. The hunchbacked fellow protested that he would pay nothing.

The porter immediately laid hands upon him and, accidentally raising his cap, discovered that he was *one-eyed* also. He demanded two pennies forthwith.

The other still more vehemently opposed, and would have fled; but the porter catching hold of his head, the cap came off, and disclosed a bald *scab*; whereupon he required three pennies.

The hunchbacked fellow, very much enraged, persisted in his refusal and began to struggle with the porter. This caused an exposure of his arms, by which it became manifest that he was *leprous*. The porter immediately demanded a fourth penny. Refusing to pay, the hunchbacked fellow continued to struggle, revealing a *rupture*, which made a fifth.

Thus, a fellow unjustly refusing to pay a rightful demand of *one* penny, was necessitated, much against his inclination, to pay *five*.

Written Summation

Accordingly, the porter was installed in his office. And as the people entered the city, he took note of their defects and charged them in accordance with the grant. It happened that a hunchbacked fellow entered, and the porter made his demand. The hunchbacked fellow protested that he would pay nothing.

Model Practice 1 (adapted from the original)

Model Practice 2

Model Practice 3

As You Like It

from Beautiful Stories from Shakespeare
by Edith Nesbit

There was once a wicked Duke named Frederick, who took the dukedom that should have belonged to his brother, sending him into exile. His brother went into the Forest of Arden, where he lived the life of a bold forester, as Robin Hood did in Sherwood Forest in merry England.

The banished Duke's daughter, Rosalind, remained with Celia, Frederick's daughter, and the two loved each other more than most sisters. One day there was a wrestling match at Court, and Rosalind and Celia went to see it. Charles, a celebrated wrestler, was there, who had killed many men in contests of this kind. Orlando, the young man he was to wrestle with, was so slender and youthful, that Rosalind and Celia thought he would surely be killed, as others had been; so they spoke to him, and asked him not to attempt so dangerous an adventure; but the only effect of their words was to make him wish more to come off well in the encounter, so as to win praise from such sweet ladies.

Orlando, like Rosalind's father, was being kept out of his inheritance by his brother, and was so sad at his brother's unkindness that, until he saw Rosalind, he did not care much whether he lived or died. But now the sight of the fair Rosalind gave him strength and courage, so that he did marvelously, and at last, threw Charles to such a tune, that the wrestler had to be carried off the ground. Duke Frederick was pleased with his courage, and asked his name.

"My name is Orlando, and I am the youngest son of Sir Rowland de Boys," said the young man.

Now Sir Rowland de Boys, when he was alive, had been a good friend to the banished Duke, so that Frederick heard with regret whose son Orlando was, and would not befriend him. But Rosalind was delighted to hear that this handsome young stranger was the son of her father's old friend, and as they were going away, she turned back more than once to say another kind word to the brave young man.

"Gentleman," she said, giving him a chain from her neck, "wear this for me. I could give more, but that my hand lacks means."

Rosalind and Celia, when they were alone, began to talk about the handsome wrestler, and Rosalind confessed that she loved him at first sight.

"Come, come," said Celia, "wrestle with thy affections."

"Oh," answered Rosalind, "they take the part of a better wrestler than myself. Look, here comes the Duke."

"With his eyes full of anger," said Celia.

"You must leave the Court at once," he said to Rosalind.

"Why?" she asked.

"Never mind why," answered the Duke, "you are banished. If within ten days you are found within twenty miles of my Court, you die."

So Rosalind set out to seek her father, the banished Duke, in the Forest of Arden. Celia loved her too much to let her go alone, and as it was rather a dangerous journey, Rosalind, being the taller, dressed up as a young countryman, and her cousin as a country girl, and Rosalind said that she would be called Ganymede, and Celia, Aliena. They were very tired when at last they came to the Forest of Arden, and as they were sitting on the grass a countryman passed that way, and Ganymede asked him if he could get them food. He did so, and told them that a shepherd's flocks and house were to be sold. They bought these and settled down as shepherd and shepherdess in the forest.

In the meantime, Oliver having sought to take his brother Orlando's life, Orlando also wandered into the forest, and there met with the rightful Duke, and being kindly received, stayed with him. Now, Orlando could think of nothing but Rosalind, and he went about the forest carving her name on trees, and writing love sonnets and hanging them on the bushes, and there Rosalind and Celia found them. One day Orlando met them, but he did not know Rosalind in her boy's clothes, though he liked the pretty shepherd youth, because he fancied a likeness in him to her he loved.

"There is a foolish lover," said Rosalind, "who haunts these woods and hangs sonnets on the trees. If I could find him, I would soon cure him of his folly."

Orlando confessed that he was the foolish lover, and Rosalind said, "If you will come and see me everyday, I will pretend to be Rosalind, and I will take her part, and be wayward and contrary, as is the way of women, till I make you ashamed of your folly in loving her."

And so every day he went to her house, and took a pleasure in saying to her all the pretty things he would have said to Rosalind; and she had the fine and secret joy of knowing that all his love words came to the right ears. Thus many days passed pleasantly away.

One morning, as Orlando was going to visit Ganymede, he saw a man asleep on the ground, and that there was a lioness crouching near, waiting for the man who was asleep to wake: for they say that lions will not prey on anything that is dead or sleeping. Then Orlando looked at the man, and saw that it was his wicked brother, Oliver, who had tried to take his life. He fought with the lioness and killed her, and saved his brother's life.

While Orlando was fighting the lioness, Oliver woke to see his brother, whom he had treated so badly, saving him from a wild beast at the risk of his own life. This made him repent of his wickedness, and he begged Orlando's pardon, and from thenceforth they were dear brothers. The lioness had wounded Orlando's arm so much, that he could not go on to see the shepherd, so he sent his brother to ask Ganymede to come to him.

Oliver went and told the whole story to Ganymede and Aliena, and Aliena was so charmed with his manly way of confessing his faults, that she fell in love with him at once. But when Ganymede heard of the danger Orlando had been in she fainted; and when she came to herself, said truly enough, "I should have been a woman by right."

Oliver went back to his brother and told him all this, saying, "I love Aliena so well that I will give up my estates to you and marry her, and live here as a shepherd."

"Let your wedding be tomorrow," said Orlando, "and I will ask the Duke and his friends."

When Orlando told Ganymede how his brother was to be married on the morrow, he added, "Oh, how bitter a thing it is to look into happiness through another man's eyes."

Then answered Rosalind, still in Ganymede's dress and speaking with his voice, "If you do love Rosalind so near the heart, then when your brother marries Aliena, shall you marry her."

Now the next day the Duke and his followers, and Orlando, and Oliver, and Aliena, were all gathered together for the wedding.

Then Ganymede came in and said to the Duke, "If I bring in your daughter Rosalind, will you give her to Orlando here?"

"That I would," said the Duke, "if I had all kingdoms to give with her."

"And you say you will have her when I bring her?" she said to Orlando.

"That would I," he answered, "were I king of all kingdoms."

Then Rosalind and Celia went out, and Rosalind put on her pretty woman's clothes again, and after a while came back.

She turned to her father. "I give myself to you, for I am yours."

"If there be truth in sight," he said, "you are my daughter."

Then she said to Orlando, "I give myself to you, for I am yours."

"If there be truth in sight," he said, "you are my Rosalind."

"I will have no father, if you be not he," she said to the Duke, and to Orlando, "I will have no husband, if you be not he."

So Orlando and Rosalind were married, and Oliver and Celia, and they lived happy ever after, returning with the Duke to the kingdom. For Frederick had been shown by a holy hermit the wickedness of his ways, and so gave back the dukedom of his brother, and himself went into a monastery to pray for forgiveness.

The wedding was a merry one, in the mossy glades of the forest. A shepherd and shepherdess who had been friends with Rosalind, when she was herself disguised as a shepherd, were married on the same day, and all with such pretty feastings and merrymakings as could be nowhere within four walls, but only in the beautiful green wood.

Written Summation

There was once a wicked Duke named Frederick, who took the dukedom that should have belonged to his brother, sending him into exile. His brother went into the Forest of Arden, where he lived the life of a bold forester, as Robin Hood did in Sherwood Forest in merry England.

Model Practice 1 (adapted from the original)

Model Practice 2

Model Practice 3

King Lear

from Beautiful Stories from Shakespeare
by Edith Nesbit

King Lear was old and tired. He was aweary of the business of his kingdom, and wished only to end his days quietly near his three daughters. Two of his daughters were married to the Dukes of Albany and Cornwall; and the Duke of Burgundy and the King of France were both suitors for the hand of Cordelia, his youngest daughter.

Lear called his three daughters together, and told them that he proposed to divide his kingdom between them. "But first," said he, "I should like to know much you love me."

Goneril, who was really a very wicked woman, and did not love her father at all, said she loved him more than words could say; she loved him dearer than eyesight, space or liberty, more than life, grace, health, beauty, and honor.

"I love you as much as my sister and more," professed Regan, "since I care for nothing but my father's love."

Lear was very much pleased with Regan's professions, and turned to his youngest daughter, Cordelia. "Now, our joy, though last not least," he said, "the best part of my kingdom have I kept for you. What can you say?"

"Nothing, my lord," answered Cordelia.

"Nothing can come of nothing. Speak again," said the King.

And Cordelia answered, "I love your Majesty according to my duty—no more, no less."

And this she said, because she was disgusted with the way in which her sisters professed love, when really they had not even a right sense of duty to their old father.

"I am your daughter," she went on, "and you have brought me up and loved me, and I return you those duties back as are right and fit, obey you, love you, and most honor you."

Lear, who loved Cordelia best, had wished her to make more extravagant professions of love than her sisters. "Go," he said, "be for ever a stranger to my heart and me."

The Earl of Kent, one of Lear's favorite courtiers and captains, tried to say a word for Cordelia's sake, but Lear would not listen. He divided the kingdom between Goneril and Regan, and told them that he should only keep a hundred knights at arms, and would live with his daughters by turns.

When the Duke of Burgundy knew that Cordelia would have no share of the kingdom, he gave up his courtship of her. But the King of France was wiser, and said, "Thy dowerless daughter, King, is Queen of us—of ours, and our fair France."

"Take her, take her," said the King; "for I will never see that face of hers again."

So Cordelia became Queen of France, and the Earl of Kent, for having ventured to take her part, was banished from the kingdom. The King now went to stay with his daughter Goneril, who had got everything from her father that he had to give, and now began to grudge even the hundred knights that he had reserved for himself. She was harsh and undutiful to him, and her servants either refused to obey his orders or pretended that they did not hear them.

Now the Earl of Kent, when he was banished, made as though he would go into another country, but instead he came back in the disguise of a serving man and took service with the King. The King had now two friends—the Earl of Kent, whom he only knew as his servant, and his Fool, who was faithful to him. Goneril told her father plainly that his knights only served to fill her Court with riot and feasting; and so she begged him only to keep a few old men about him such as himself.

"My train are men who know all parts of duty," said Lear. "Goneril, I will not trouble you further—yet I have left another daughter."

And his horses being saddled, he set out with his followers for the castle of Regan. But she, who had formerly outdone her sister in professions of attachment to the King, now seemed to outdo her in undutiful conduct, saying that fifty knights were too many to wait on him, and Goneril (who had hurried thither to prevent Regan showing any kindness to the old King) said five were too many, since her servants could wait on him.

Then when Lear saw that what they really wanted was to drive him away, he left them. It was a wild and stormy night, and he wandered about the heath half mad with misery, and with no companion but the poor Fool. But presently his servant, the good Earl of Kent, met him, and at last persuaded him to lie down in a wretched little hovel. At daybreak the Earl of Kent removed his royal master to Dover, and hurried to the Court of France to tell Cordelia what had happened.

Cordelia's husband gave her an army and with it she landed at Dover. Here she found poor King Lear, wandering about the fields, wearing a crown of nettles and weeds. They brought him back and fed and clothed him, and Cordelia came to him and kissed him.

"You must bear with me," said Lear; "forget and forgive. I am old and foolish."

And now he knew at last which of his children it was that had loved him best, and who was worthy of his love.

Goneril and Regan joined their armies to fight Cordelia's army, and were successful; and Cordelia and her father were thrown into prison. Then Goneril's husband, the Duke of Albany, who was a good man, and had not known how wicked his wife was, heard the truth of the whole story; and when Goneril found that her husband knew her for the wicked woman she was, she killed herself, having a little time before given a deadly poison to her sister, Regan, out of a spirit of jealousy.

But they had arranged that Cordelia should be hanged in prison, and though the Duke of Albany sent messengers at once, it was too late. The old King came staggering into the tent of the Duke of Albany, carrying the body of his dear daughter Cordelia, in his arms.

And soon after, with words of love for her upon his lips, he fell with her still in his arms, and died.

Written Summation

And Cordelia answered, "I love your Majesty according to my duty—no more, no less."

And this she said, because she was disgusted with the way in which her sisters professed love, when really they had not even a right sense of duty to their old father.

Model Practice 1 (adapted from the original)

Model Practice 2

Model Practice 3

APPENDIX

Models Only

For Teacher Use

Note: Paragraph-sized models from Chapters I and IV are treated as independent models and are indented.

Oral Narration Questions

(Your student may not need these questions, if he can retell the story easily.)

Questions for Chapter I, historical narratives, or Chapter IV, cultural tales.

1. Who was the main character?
2. What was the character like?
3. Where was the character?
4. What time was it in the story? Time of day? Time of year?
5. Who else was in the story?
6. Does the main character have an enemy? What is the enemy's name?
   (The enemy may also be self or nature.)
7. Does the main character want something? If not, does the main character have a problem?
8. What does the main character do? What does he say? If there are others, what do they do or say?
9. Why does the character do what he does?
10. What happens to the character as he tries to solve his problem?
11. Does the main character solve his problem? How does he solve his problem?
12. What happens at the end of the story?
13. Is there a moral to the story? If so, what was it?

Questions for Chapter II, primary source documents.

(This may be difficult for grammar stage students, help them to answer the questions. Over time, it will become easier.)

1. Who is speaking?
2. To whom is he speaking?
3. What is the main idea from the speaker?
4. Does he give facts to support his message?
5. Why is he telling this information?

Questions for Chapter III, poetry.

1. Is the poem about a character, an event, or an idea?
2. Does this poem express a feeling of happiness, sadness, anger, excitement, joy, hope, determination, or fear?
3. How does the poem make you feel?
4. Do you think the author of the poem had a message?
5. What do you think the message of the poem is?

Written Summations

(Have your student sum up the story in no more than six sentences—two for each question. Less is best)

1. What happened at the beginning of the story?
2. What happened at the middle of the story?
3. What happened at the end of the story?

Principle of Praise

Encourage, build up, praise, and celebrate your student's successes.

Let no corrupt communication
proceed out of your mouth, but
that which is good to the use of edifying,
that it may minister grace
unto the hearers.

Using the Grammar Guide

The Grammar Guide only provides an overview with definitions and a few examples of the grammar concepts. For 3rd – 5th graders, this will more than likely be enough, since the students are working with the grammar in context. But for some, this may not be enough. To supplement, you may use a separate yearlong grammar curriculum, or you, as the teacher, may purchase a guide to provide you with further explanations to pass on to your student. If you use the guide in this book, please note that the guide is not all inclusive. More advanced grammar terms, such as relative pronouns and indefinite adjectives, are not included.

1. Have your student read the model.
2. Have your student copy the selection before he marks up the model.
3. Return to the model and circle the part of speech being learned in the proper color. See page 4.
4. **For older students, have them label the parts of speech according to the definitions and abbreviations below.**
5. For adjectives, adverbs, and prepositional phrases, have your student draw an arrow to the word being modified.

	Label	**Definition**
nouns	**DO, IO, PN**	**direct object, indirect object, or predicate nominative**

Subject is the noun that is or does something. (Who ran? What stinks?)	**I** ran. **The dog** stinks.
Direct objects answers what. (I ate what?)	I ate **the cookie**.
Indirect objects tell for whom the action of the verb was done.	I gave **her** the cookie.
Predicate Nominative (Noun LinkingVerb Noun.)	John is my **dad**.

verbs	**AV, SB, LV**	**action verb, state of being, or linking verb**

Action verbs with a direct object are transitive verbs.	(He kicked the ball.)
Action verbs without a direct object are intransitive.	(He kicked.)
State of being verbs are the "to be" verbs.	(am, are, is, was, were, be, being, been)
Helping verbs help the main verb express time and mood.	(do run, can clean, am eating, might hit)
Linking verbs link the subject to the predicate.	(The wind grew chilly. The wind was chilly.)
	(If I can replace grew with was, it is a LV.)

pronouns	**SP, OP, PP, DP**	**Subject, Object, Possessive, Demonstrative**

Subject Pronouns	I, you, he, she, it, we, they	We love to read. It was outside.
Object Pronouns	me, you, him, her, it, us, them	She took it. I handed them the candy.
Possessive Pronouns	mine, yours, his, hers, theirs, ours, its, whose	That is **mine**! Ours is blue.
Demonstrative Pronouns	this, that, these, those	**That** is mine! We love that.

adjectives	**AA, PA, DA**	**Attributive, Predicate, or Demonstrative Adjectives**

Attributive Adjectives modify the noun and are right next to it.	(The **big** car.)
Predicate Adjectives follow linking verbs.	(The car is **big**.)
Demonstrative Adjectives (This, that, these, those)	**That** flower grew.

adverbs	**where, how, when, extent**

Adverbs that tell where, how, and when modify an adverb.	(up, down, quickly, softly, yesterday, now)
Adverbs that tell extent modify an adverb or adjective.	(almost, also, only, very, enough, rather, too)

prepositions	**OP**	**object of the preposition**

GRAMMAR GUIDE

Month 1

Memorize the definitions for each part of speech. Review Weekly.
Teach the following with copywork. Circle the nouns in the copywork.

Nouns **circle blue** a word that names a person, place, thing, or idea

Common nouns	**man, city, car, happiness**	
Proper nouns	**David, Lake Charles, Mustang**	
Subject	**Children** should appreciate their pastor.	
Direct object	My parents bought **a birthday present**.	(noun phrase)
Indirect object	My parents gave **the pastor** the present.	(noun phrase)
Predicate Nominative	The queen is a **pilot**.	(A noun that renames a noun, queen = **pilot**.)

Capitalization Beginning of a sentence, I, proper nouns.

Month 2

Teach everything in month one and the following. Color-code the nouns and verbs in the copywork.

Verbs **circle red** a word that expresses action, state of being, or links two words together

Action verbs	**jump, run, think, have, skip, throw, say, dance, smell**
State of being	any form of to be = **am, are, is, was, were, be, being, been**
Linking verbs	**any "to be" verb** and any verb that can logically be replaced by a "to be" verb She **seems** nice. She is nice. The flower **smells** stinky. The flower is stinky.
Helping verbs	am, are, is, was, were, be, being, been, do, does, did, has, have, had, may, might, must shall, will, can, should, would, could

Month 3

Teach everything previous and the following.

Pronouns **circle green** a word that replaces the noun

Jack ran.	**He** ran.
Ike hit Al and Mary.	Ike hit **them**
The car is very nice.	**That** is very nice.

Types of sentences and punctuation

Declarative or statement	I have a blue dress. The ground is wet from the rain.
Interrogative or question	Will we have dessert today? What time is it?
Imperative or demand	Come here. Sit down. Mop the floor at 2:00.
Exclamation	I sold my painting for ten million dollars!

Month 4

Teach everything previous and the following.

Adjectives **circle yellow** a word that describes a noun or a pronoun
(When studying adverbs, you may have your student draw an arrow to the word being modified.)

I want candy.	I want **five** candies.	
the car	the **red** car	
I like shoes.	I like **those** shoes.	
The tall girl	The girl is **tall**.	Predicate adjectives (tall, stinky, angry)
The stinky dog	The dog smells **stinky**.	
The angry man	The man appeared **angry**.	

Month 5

Adverbs **circle orange** a word that describes a verb, another adverb, or an adjective

		Modifies the verb
Don't run.	Don't run **inside**.	tells where
The man ran.	The man ran **swiftly.**	tells how
It will rain.	It will rain **soon**.	tells when
		Modifies adjectives or other adverbs
The dog is hairy.	The dog is **very** hairy.	tells extent (modifies hairy)

Possessives words that show ownership

Mine, yours, his, hers, ours, theirs, whose	possessive pronouns (used alone)
My car, **your** house, **his** shirt, **her** computer	possessive pronouns (used with a noun)
Jane**'**s car, Mike**'**s shoes, Jesus**'** parables,	singular possessive nouns
Mom and Dad**'**s sons, my sisters**'** names, children**'**s books	plural possessive nouns

Month 6

Preposition **circle purple** a word that shows relationship between one noun and another word in the sentence

(Prepositional phrases are to be underlined)

He is **on** the box. He is **under** the box. He went **around** the box. He is **in** the box.

Commas 3 items or more in a series

The elephant**,** the mouse**,** and the gnat are best friends.

I like red, green**,** and orange vegetables.

Month 7

Conjunction **circle brown** a word that links words, phrases, or clauses (and, but, or, nor, so, for, yet)

Jamie **and** I left.
(words)

The blue sky, the warm sun, **and** the rainbow of flowers brightened my spirits.
(phrases)

He is tall, **for** both of his parents are tall.
(independent clauses, must have a comma when combining main clauses)

Quotation Marks Use quotation marks to set off direct quotations.

"No, I don't like peas,**"** answered the little boy.	beginning of a sentence
The little boy answered**, "**I don't like peas.**"**	end of a sentence
"No,**"** answered the little boy**, "**I don't like peas.**"**	middle of a sentence

Month 8

Interjection **circle black** a word that expresses emotion, sometimes but not always, sudden or intense.

Yes! I want ice cream too! **Well**, we're late because the car broke down.

Semi-colons replace commas and conjunction when combining two independent clauses

My family is going to the farm**, and** we are going to have a grand time riding horses.

My family is going to the farm**;** we are going to have a grand time riding horses.

Models from Chapter I

from **Alaric the Visigoth**
from Famous Men of the Middle Ages
by John H. Haaren, LL.D. and A. B. Poland, Ph.D.

One night, not long after he became king, Alaric had a very strange dream. He thought he was driving in a golden chariot through the streets of Rome amid the shouts of the people who hailed him as emperor. This dream made a deep impression on his mind. He was always thinking of it, and soon he had the idea that he could make the dream come true.

Then began the work of destruction. The Goths ran in crowds through the city, wrecked private houses and public buildings, and seized everything of value they could find. Alaric gave orders that no injury should be done to the Christian churches, but other splendid buildings of the great city were stripped of the beautiful and costly articles that they contained.

from **Attila the Hun**
from Famous Men of the Middle Ages
by John H. Haaren, LL.D. and A. B. Poland, Ph.D.

The army, which Attila saw, was an army of 300,000 Romans and Visigoths. It was led by a Roman general name Aëtius and the Visigoth king Theodoric. The Visigoths, after the death of Alaric, had settled in parts of Gaul, and their king had now agreed to join the Romans against the common enemy—the terrible Huns.

The Huns mourned their king in a barbarous way. They shaved their heads and cut themselves on their faces with knives, so that their blood, instead of their tears, flowed for the loss of their great leader. They enclosed his body in three coffins—one of gold, one of silver, and one of iron—and they buried him at night, in a secret spot in the mountains.

from **Clovis**
from Famous Men of the Middle Ages
by John H. Haaren, LL.D. and A. B. Poland, Ph.D.

When Clovis stepped out in front of his own army, accompanied by some of his savage warriors, Syagrius also came forward. But the moment he saw the king of the Franks, he laughed loudly and exclaimed, "A boy! A boy has come to fight me! The Franks with a boy to lead them have come to fight the Romans."

When Clovis returned home, he did not forget his promise. He told Clotilde how he had prayed to her God for help and how his prayer had been heard. He said he was now ready to become a Christian. Clotilde was very happy on hearing this, and she arranged that her husband should be baptized in the church of Rheims on the following Christmas Day.

from **Justinian the Great**

from Famous Men of the Middle Ages
by John H. Haaren, LL.D. and A. B. Poland, Ph.D.

He had many wars during his reign, but he himself did not take part in them. He was not experienced as a soldier, for he had spent most of his time in study. He was fortunate enough, however, to have two great generals to lead his armies. One of them was named Belisarius and the other Narses.

To the last year of his life, Justinian was strong and active and a hard worker. He often worked or studied all day and all night without eating or sleeping. He died in 565 at the age of eighty-three years.

from **Mohammed**

from Famous Men of the Middle Ages
by John H. Haaren, LL.D. and A. B. Poland, Ph.D.

When Mohammed returned home after the angel had first spoken to him, he told his wife of what he had seen and heard. She at once believed and became a convert to the new religion. She fell upon her knees at the feet of her husband and cried out, "There is but one God. Mohammed is God's prophet."

Often while speaking in public, Mohammed had what he called a "vision of heavenly things." At such times, his face grew pale as death, his eyes became red and staring, he spoke in a loud voice, and his body trembled violently. Then he would tell what he had seen in his vision.

from **Charles Martel and Pepin**

from Famous Men of the Middle Ages
by John H. Haaren, LL.D. and A. B. Poland, Ph.D.

After the parade, the king was escorted to the great hall of the palace, which was filled with nobles. Seated on a magnificent throne, he saluted the assemblage and made a short speech. The speech was prepared beforehand by Pepin and committed to memory by the king. At the close of the ceremony, the royal "nobody" retired to his country house and was not heard of again for a year.

Charles Martel is especially celebrated as the hero of this battle. It is said that the name Martel was given to him because of his bravery during the fight. Marteau is the French word for hammer, and one of the old French historians says that as a hammer breaks and crushes iron and steel, so Charles broke and crushed the power of his enemies in the Battle of Tours.

from **Charlemagne**
from Famous Men of the Middle Ages
by John H. Haaren, LL.D. and A. B. Poland, Ph.D.

Pepin had two sons Charles and Carloman. After the death of their father, they ruled together, but in a few years Carloman died, and Charles became sole king.

This Charles was the most famous of the kings of the Franks. He did so many great and wonderful things that he is called Charlemagne, which means Charles the Great.

On Christmas day, he went to the church of St. Peter, and as he knelt before the altar, the Pope placed a crown upon his head, saying, "Long live Charles Augustus, Emperor of the Romans."

The people assembled in the church shouted the same words; and so Charlemagne was now emperor of the Western Roman Empire, as well as king of the Franks.

from **Egbert**
from Famous Men of the Middle Ages
by John H. Haaren, LL.D. and A. B. Poland, Ph.D.

After the Roman legions had left Britain, the Jutes, led by two great captains named Hengist and Horsa, landed upon the southeastern coast and made a settlement.

Britain proved a pleasant place to live in, and soon the Angles and Saxons also left the North Sea shores and invaded the beautiful island.

The new invaders met with brave resistance. The Britons were headed, legend says, by King Arthur, about whom many marvelous stories are told. His court was held at Caerleon, in North Wales, where his hundred and fifty knights banqueted at their famous "Round Table."

from **Alfred the Great**
from Famous Men of the Middle Ages
by John H. Haaren, LL.D. and A. B. Poland, Ph.D.

"Oh, what a lovely book!" exclaimed the boys.

"Yes, it is lovely," replied the mother. "I will give it to whichever of you children can read it the best in a week."

At the end of the week, the boys read the book to their mother, one after the other. Much to the surprise of his brothers, Alfred proved to be the best reader, and his mother gave him the book.

While still very young, Alfred was sent by his father to Rome to be anointed by His Holiness, the Pope. It was a long and tiresome journey, made mostly on horseback.

from **Rollo the Viking**

from Famous Men of the Middle Ages

by John H. Haaren, LL.D. and A. B. Poland, Ph.D.

These Vikings were the first European discoverers of the North American continent. Ancient books found in Iceland tell the story of the discovery. According to these writings, a Viking ship was driven during a storm to a strange coast, which is now known as Labrador. One such book detailing early Viking explorations is titled Book of the Icelanders. (modified)

Rollo now granted parts of Normandy to his leading men on condition that they would bring soldiers to his army and fight under him. They became his vassals, as he was the king's vassal.

The lands granted to vassals in this way were called feuds, and this plan of holding lands was called the Feudal System.

from **Canute the Great**

from Famous Men of the Middle Ages

by John H. Haaren, LL.D. and A. B. Poland, Ph.D.

Canute, however, went to Denmark and raised one of the largest armies of Danes that had ever been assembled. With this powerful force, he sailed to England. When he landed, Northumberland and Wessex acknowledged him as king. Shortly after this Ethelred died.

"You say I can do anything," he said to the courtiers. "Very well, I who am king and the lord of the ocean now command these rising waters to go back and not dare wet my feet."

But the tide was disobedient and steadily rose and rose, until the feet of the king were in the water.

from **El Cid**

from Famous Men of the Middle Ages

by John H. Haaren, LL.D. and A. B. Poland, Ph.D.

The vision replied, "I am St. Lazarus, the leper to whom you were so kind. Because I have breathed upon you, you shall accomplish whatever you shall undertake in peace or in battle. All shall honor you. Therefore, go on and evermore do good."

With that, the vision vanished.

Then on June 15, 1094, the governor went to the camp of El Cid and delivered to him the keys of the city. El Cid placed his men in all the forts and took the citadel as his own dwelling. His banner floated from the towers. He called himself the Prince of Valencia.

from Edward the Confessor

from Famous Men of the Middle Ages

by John H. Haaren, LL.D. and A. B. Poland, Ph.D.

These pirates were mostly Norwegians, whose leader was a barbarian named Kerdric. They would come sweeping down upon the Kentish coast in many ships, make a landing where there were no soldiers, and fall upon the towns and plunder them. Then, as swiftly and suddenly as they had come, they would sail away homeward before they could be captured.

When the king learned the number of soldiers Malcolm would probably need, he gave orders for double that number to march into Scotland. Malcolm, with this support, attacked Macbeth, and after several well-fought battles drove the usurper from Scotland and took possession of the throne.

from Peter the Hermit

from Famous Men of the Middle Ages

by John H. Haaren, LL.D. and A. B. Poland, Ph.D.

The council was so roused by his words that they broke forth into loud cries, “God wills it! God wills it!”

“It is, indeed, His will,” said the Pope, “and let these words be your war cry when you meet the enemy.”

Peter listened with deep attention. Immediately after the council, he began to preach in favor of a war against the Turks. With head and feet bare, and clothed in a long, coarse robe tied at the waist with a rope, he went through Italy from city to city, riding on a donkey. He preached in churches and on the streets—wherever he could secure an audience.

from William the Conqueror

from Famous Men of the Middle Ages

by John H. Haaren, LL.D. and A. B. Poland, Ph.D.

On the morning of October 14, 1066, the two armies met. The Norman foot soldiers opened the battle by charging on the English stockades. They ran over the plain to the low hills, singing a war song at the top of their voices, but they could not carry the stockades although they tried again and again. They therefore attacked another part of the English forces.

He made a law that all lights should be put out and fires covered with ashes at eight o'clock every evening, so that the people would have to go to bed then. A bell was rung in all cities and towns throughout England to warn the people of the hour. The bell was called the curfew. (modified)

from **Frederick Barbarossa**

from Famous Men of the Middle Ages
by John H. Haaren, LL.D. and A. B. Poland, Ph.D.

Frederick now devoted himself to making Germany a united nation. Two of his nobles had been quarreling for a long time. And as a punishment for their conduct, each was condemned, with ten of his counts and barons, to carry dogs on his shoulders from one country to another.

Frederick finally succeeded in keeping the nobles in the different provinces of Germany at peace with one another. He persuaded them to work together for the good of the whole empire. He had no more trouble with them. And for many years, his reign was peaceful and prosperous.

from **Henry the Second**

from Famous Men of the Middle Ages
by John H. Haaren, LL.D. and A. B. Poland, Ph.D.

His chief assistant in the management of public affairs was Thomas Becket, whom he made chancellor of the kingdom. Becket was fond of pomp and luxury, and lived in a more magnificent manner than even the king himself.

At this time, the clergy had become almost independent of the king. To bring them under his authority, Henry made Becket Archbishop of Canterbury, thus putting him at the head of the Church in England. The king expected that Becket would carry out all his wishes.

from **Marco Polo**

from Famous Men of the Middle Ages
by John H. Haaren, LL.D. and A. B. Poland, Ph.D.

Eight hundred years before Marco Polo's birth, some of the people of North Italy had fled before Attila to the muddy islands of the Adriatic and founded Venice upon them. Since then the little settlement had become the most wealthy and powerful city of Europe. Venice was the queen of the Adriatic and her merchants were princes.

One of his fellow prisoners was a skillful penman and Marco dictated to him an account of his experiences in China, Japan, and other Eastern countries. This account was carefully written out. Copies of the manuscript The Travels of Marco Polo exist to this day. One of these is in a library in Paris. It was carried into France in the year 1307. (modified)

from **William Tell and Arnold von Winkelried**
from Famous Men of the Middle Age
by John H. Haaren, LL.D. and A. B. Poland, Ph.D.

At this time, a famous mountaineer named William Tell lived in one of the Forest Cantons. He was tall and strong. In all Switzerland, no man had a foot as sure as his on the mountains or a hand as skilled in the use of a bow. He was determined to resist the Austrians.

A few years later, the duke himself came with a large army, determined to conquer the mountaineers. He had to march through a narrow pass, with mountains rising abruptly on either side. The Swiss were expecting him and hid along the heights above the pass. As soon as the Austrians appeared in the pass, the mountaineers hurled rocks and trunks of trees down upon them.

from **King Robert Bruce**
from Famous Men of the Middle Ages
by John H. Haaren, LL.D. and A. B. Poland, Ph.D.

Bruce said to his wife, "Henceforth you are the queen, and I am the king of our country."

"I fear," said his wife, "that we are only playing at being king and queen, like children in their games."

"Nay, I shall be king in earnest," said Bruce.

However, many brave patriots joined them, until after a while Bruce had a small army. Five times, he attacked the English, and five times, he was beaten. After his last defeat, he fled from Scotland and took refuge in a wretched hut on an island off the north coast of Ireland. Here he stayed all alone during one winter.

from **Edward the Black Prince**
from Famous Men of the Middle Ages
by John H. Haaren, LL.D. and A. B. Poland, Ph.D.

"Is my son dead or unhorsed or so wounded that he cannot help himself?" asked the king.

"No, Sire," was the reply; "but he is hard pressed."

"Return to your post, and come not to me again for aid so long as my son lives," said the king. "Let the boy prove himself a true knight and win his spurs."

Early on the morning of September 14, 1356, the battle began. The English were few in number, but they were determined to contest every inch of ground and not surrender while a hundred of them remained to fight. For hours, they withstood the onset of the French. At last a body of English horsemen charged furiously on one part of the French line, while the Black Prince attacked another part.

from **Henry V**

from Famous Men of the Middle Ages

by John H. Haaren, LL.D. and A. B. Poland, Ph.D.

"I would not have a single man more," said Henry. "If god give us victory, it will be plain we owe it to His grace. If not, the fewer we are the less loss for England."

The men drew courage from their king. The English archers poured arrows into the ranks of their opponents; and although the French fought bravely, they were completely routed. Eleven thousand Frenchmen fell.

Strangely, the king against whom he had been fighting and over whom he was triumphing sat by his side as he rode through the streets. What did this mean? It meant that the French were so terrified by the many victories of Henry that all—king and people—were willing to give him whatever he asked.

from **Joan of Arc**

from Famous Men of the Middle Ages

from John H. Haaren, LL.D. and A. B. Poland, Ph.D.

"Father, I must do what God has willed, for this is no work of my choosing," she replied. "Mother, I would far rather sit and spin by your side than take part in war. My mission is no dream. I know that I have been chosen by the Lord to fulfill His purpose and nothing can prevent me from going where He purposes to send me."

When Joan arrived at Chinon, a force of French soldiers was preparing to go to the south of France to relieve the city of Orleans, which the English were besieging.

King Charles received Joan kindly and listened to what she had to say with deep attention. The girl spoke modestly, but with a calm belief that she was right.

from **Gutenberg**

from Famous Men of the Middle Ages

by John H. Haaren, LL.D. and A. B. Poland, Ph.D.

While Joan of Arc was busy rescuing France from the English, another wonderful worker was busy in Germany. This was John Gutenberg, who was born in Mainz.

The Germans—and most other people—think that he was the inventor of the art of printing with movable types. So in the cities of Dresden and Mainz, his countrymen have put up statues in his memory.

All his neighbors wondered what became of him when he left his home in the early morning, and where he had been when they saw him coming back late in the twilight. Some felt sure that he must be a wizard, and that he had meetings somewhere with the devil, and that the devil was helping him to do some strange business.

from **Warwick the Kingmaker**

from Famous Men of the Middle Ages

by John H. Haaren, LL.D. and A. B. Poland, Ph.D.

Most people though this was a wise arrangement; but Queen Margaret, Henry's wife, did not like it at all, because it took from her son the right to reign after his father's death. So she went to Scotland and the North of England, where she had many friends, and raised an army.

His army grew larger and larger every day. People had been very dissatisfied with Edward and had rejoiced when Henry replaced him as king, because if Henry was not clever he was good. But in a short time, they learned that England needed a king who was not only good but capable.

from **Christopher Columbus**

from Famous men of Modern times

by John H. Haaren, LL.D. and A. B. Poland, Ph.D.

Two wealthy gentlemen added a third ship to the two supplied by the king and queen; and the wonderful voyage began. The Santa Maria with a crew of fifty men was commanded by Columbus himself; the Pinta with thirty men was in the charge of Martin Pinzon; and the Nina or "Baby" with twenty-four men was commanded by Martin's brother, Vincente Pinzon.

On the shore of Haiti, the Santa Maria went ashore and became a wreck. With the two remaining vessels, Columbus soon afterwards set sail for Spain, and on the 15th of March, 1493, he dropped anchor in the port of Palos.

from **Vasco da Gama**

from Famous men of Modern times

by John H. Haaren, LL.D. and A. B. Poland, Ph.D.

Three ships, not larger than the schooners which sail up and down our rivers, were lying at anchor in the harbor of Lisbon. They were named Michael, Gabriel, and Raphael after the three archangels. They were laden with everything which the king and Vasco thought might be useful on a voyage of discovery.

After the treaty had been made, Vasco wished at once to sail to India. But he had to cross the great Indian Ocean, and favorable winds would not blow until August, and it was now only May. So for three months the Portuguese remained at Melinda.

from **Sir Walter Raleigh**

from Famous men of Modern times

by John H. Haaren, LL.D. and A. B. Poland, Ph.D.

Returning to England at the age of thirty, he became one of Queen Elizabeth's courtiers. He constantly sought to please her. A story is told that one day when Elizabeth was out walking at Greenwich, she came to a muddy place. Raleigh was in attendance upon her, and quickly took off his costly coat and spread it over the mud so that it formed a carpet for the queen to walk on.

In return for his services in quelling the Irish rebellion, the queen gave him a large grant of land in Ireland. The most interesting fact about this Irish property is that Raleigh raised there the first potatoes grown in Europe.

from **Galileo**

from Famous men of Modern times

by John H. Haaren, LL.D. and A. B. Poland, Ph.D.

Galileo, like everybody else, could look at the star only with the naked eye. He tried to contrive something that would show both it and the other stars more plainly. He had seen spectacles. His grandfather wore a pair. He had also read somewhere that if two eyeglasses are placed one above the other, things seen through them would appear nearer and larger.

Galileo had an old friend called Kepler, who was the greatest astronomer then living. Galileo wrote to him, "Oh, my dear Kepler, how I wish we could have one good laugh together. Why are you not here? What shouts of laughter we should have at their glorious folly!"

Models from Chapter II

from The Confessions of Saint Augustine (excerpt)

by Saint Augustine

Now, behold, let my heart tell Thee what it sought there, that I should be gratuitously evil, having no temptation to ill, but the ill itself. It was foul, and I loved it. I loved to perish. I loved mine own fault, not that for which I was faulty, but my fault itself.

Fair were those pears, but not them did my wretched soul desire; for I had store of better, and those I gathered, only that I might steal. For, when gathered, I flung them away, my only feast therein being my own sin, which I was pleased to enjoy.

Of The Greatest Good (excerpt)

from Consolations of Philosophy
from Library Of The World's Best Literature, Ancient And Modern, Vol. 5
by Boëtius

Every mortal is troubled with many and various anxieties, and yet all desire, through various paths, to arrive at one goal. That is, they strive by different means to attain one happiness—in a word, God. He is the beginning and the end of every good, and He is the highest happiness.

I know, however, that earthly power never sows the virtues, but collects and gathers vices; and when it has gathered them, then it nevertheless shows and does not conceal them. For the vices of great men many men see; because many know them and many are with them. Therefore we always lament concerning power, and also despise it, when we see that it comes to the worst, and to those who are to us most unworthy.

from Institutes of Justinian (excerpt)

by Caesar Flavius Justinian or Justinian the Great

4. The study of law consists of two branches—law public and law private. The former relates to the welfare of the Roman State; the latter to the advantage of the individual citizen. Of private law then we may say that it is of threefold origin, being collected from the precepts of nature, from those of the law of nations, or from those of the civil law of Rome.

11. But the laws of nature, which are observed by all nations alike, are established by divine providence and remain ever fixed and immutable. But the municipal laws of each individual state are subject to frequent change, either by the tacit consent of the people, or by the subsequent enactment of another statute.

from A Letter from Alcuin to Charlemagne

from Library of the World's Best Literature, Ancient and Modern, Vol. I
edited by Charles Dudley Warner

I am eager that others should drink deep of the old wine of ancient learning. I shall presently begin to nourish still others with the fruits of grammatical ingenuity. And some of them I am eager to enlighten with a knowledge of the order of the stars, that seem painted, as it were, on the dome of some mighty palace.

I have noted that your zeal, which is pleasing to God and praiseworthy, is always advancing toward this wisdom and takes pleasure in it. And that you are adorning the magnificence of your worldly rule with still greater intellectual splendor.

from The Life of King Alfred, (excerpt)

by E. A. Wallis Budge

His noble nature implanted in him from his cradle a love of wisdom above all things. But by the unworthy neglect of his parents and nurses, he remained illiterate even till he was twelve years old or more. He, however, listened with serious attention to the Saxon poems which he often heard recited, and easily retained them in his docile memory.

When he was young and had the capacity for learning, he could not find teachers; however, when he was more advanced in life, he was harassed by so many diseases unknown to all the physicians of this island, as well as by the internal and external anxieties of sovereignty, and by continual invasions of the pagans that there was no time for reading.

from Pope Urban II Plea for a Crusade 1095 (excerpt)

from The First Crusade: The Accounts of Eyewitnesses and Participants
by August C. Krey

Hence it is that you murder and devour one another, that you wage war, and that frequently you perish by mutual wounds. Let therefore hatred depart from among you, let your quarrels end, let wars cease, and let all dissensions and controversies slumber. Enter upon the road to the Holy Sepulcher; wrest that land from the wicked race, and subject it to yourselves.

And we do not command or advise that the old or the feeble, or those unfit for bearing arms, undertake this journey. Nor ought women to set out at all without their husbands or brothers or legal guardians. For such are more of a hindrance than aid, more of a burden than an advantage.

from **How Can the Absolute Be a Cause?**
from Library Of The World's Best Literature, Ancient And Modern, Vol. 2
by Thomas Aquinas
edited by Charles Dudley Warner

Each created thing resembles and manifests the Deity. Not as a being of the same species or genus with itself, but as a supereminent source from which are derived its effects. They represent Him, in a word, just as the energy of the terrestrial elements represents the energy of the sun.

What we call goodness in creatures preexists in God in a far higher way. Whence it follows, not that God is good because He is the source of good, but rather, because He is good, He imparts goodness to all things else; as St. Augustine says, "Inasmuch as He is good, we are."

from **The Decameron, (On the Black Death) Volume I**
by Giovanni Boccacci
translated by J.M. Rigg

Nay, the evil went yet further. For not merely by speech or association with the sick was the malady communicated to the healthy; but any that touched the cloth of the sick, or aught else that had been touched or used by them, seemed to contract the disease.

Many died daily or nightly in the public streets. Of many others who died at home, the departure was hardly observed by their neighbors, until the stench of their putrefying bodies carried the tidings. And with their corpses and the corpses of others who died on every hand, the whole place was a sepulcher.

from **The Imitation of Christ**
by Thomas a Kempis
translated by Rev. William Benham

He that followeth me shall not walk in darkness saith the Lord. These are the words of Christ; and they teach us how far we must imitate His life and character, if we seek true illumination and deliverance from all blindness of heart. Let it be our most earnest study, therefore, to dwell upon the life of Jesus Christ.

The greater and more complete thy knowledge, the more severely shalt thou be judged. Therefore, be not lifted up by any skill or knowledge that thou hast; but rather fear concerning the knowledge which is given to thee. If it seemeth to thee that thou knowest many things, know also that there are many more things which thou knowest not. (modified)

from Joan of Arc (excerpt)

by Ronald Sutherland Gower

taken from the transcripts of the trials of Joan of Arc

If this is not done, King of England, I, as a leader in war, whenever I shall meet with your people in France, will oblige them to go whether they be willing or not. And if they go not, they will perish; but if they will depart, I will pardon them. I have come from the King of Heaven to drive you out of France.

And do not imagine that you will ever permanently hold France, for the true heir, King Charles, shall possess it; for it is God's wish that it should belong to him. And this has been revealed to him by the Maid, who will enter Paris. If you will not obey, we shall make such a stir as hath not happened these thousand years in France.

from Dedication of the Revolutions of the Heavenly Bodies

from Prefaces and Prologues to Famous Books

by Nicolaus Copernicus

translated by G. C. Macaulay

They said I should find that the more absurd most men now thought this theory of mine concerning the motion of the Earth, the more admiration and gratitude it would command after they saw in the publication of my commentaries the mist of absurdity cleared away by most transparent proofs.

Therefore, I would not have it unknown to Your Holiness, that the only thing which induced me to look for another way of reckoning the movements of the heavenly bodies was that I knew that mathematicians by no means agree in their investigations thereof.

from Martin Luther Before the Diet of Worms

by Martin Luther

In the third and last place, I have written some books against private individuals, who had undertaken to defend the tyranny of Rome by destroying the faith. I freely confess that I may have attacked such persons with more violence than was consistent with my profession as an ecclesiastic: I do not think of myself as a saint; but neither can I retract these books.

Therefore, most serene emperor, and you illustrious princes, and all, whether high or low, who hear me, I implore you by the mercies of God to prove to me by the writings of the prophets and apostles that I am in error. As soon as I shall be convinced, I will instantly retract all my errors, and will myself be the first to seize my writings, and commit them to the flames.

from **The Autobiography of St. Ignatius**

from The Account of his Life dictated to Father Gonzalez (excerpt)

by St. Ignatius Loyola

When the day of assault came, Ignatius made his confession to one of the nobles, his companion in arms. The soldier also made his to Ignatius. After the walls were destroyed, Ignatius stood fighting bravely until a cannon ball of the enemy broke one of his legs and seriously injured the other.

His elder brother looked on with astonishment and admiration. He said he could never have had the fortitude to suffer the pain which the sick man bore with his usual patience. When the flesh and the bone that protruded were cut away, means were taken to prevent the leg from becoming shorter than the other.

from **Columbus to the Lord Treasurer of Spain**

by Christopher Columbus

In the meantime, I had learned, from some Indians whom I had seized, that the country was certainly an island. Therefore, I sailed toward the east, coasting to the distance of three hundred and twenty-two miles, which brought us to the extremity of it. From this point, I saw lying eastwards another island, fifty-four miles distant from Juana, to which I gave the name Española.

On my arrival, I had taken some Indians by force from the first island that I came to, in order that they might learn our language. These men are still traveling with me, and although they have been with us now a long time, they continue to entertain the idea that I have descended from heaven.

from **Queen Elizabeth's Address to her Army at Tilbury Fort**
AT TILBURY FORT

from Fox's Book of Martyrs

speech by Queen Elizabeth I of England

My loving people, we have been persuaded by some, that are careful of our safety, to take heed how we commit ourselves to armed multitudes, for fear of treachery. But, I assure you, I do not desire to live to distrust my faithful and loving people.

And therefore I am come among you at this time, not as for my recreation or sport, but being resolved, in the midst and heat of the battle, to live or die among you all, to lay down, for my God and for my kingdom and for my people, my honor and my blood, even in the dust.

Models from Chapter III

from All Glory, Laud, and Honor

from The Story of the Hymns and Tunes
edited by Theron Brown and Hezekiah Butterworth
by Theodulph, Bishop of Orleans

All glory, laud, and honor,
To Thee, Redeemer, King:
To whom the lips of children
Made sweet Hosannas ring.

Thou didst accept their praises;
Accept the prayers we bring,
Who in all good delightest,
Thou good and gracious King.

from Arnold von Winkleried

from Poems Every Child Should Know
by James Montgomery

Impregnable their front appears,
All horrent with projected spears.
Whose polished points before them shine,
From flank to flank, one brilliant line,
Bright as the breakers' splendours run
Along the billows to the sun.

But 'twas no sooner thought than done!
The field was in a moment won;
"Make way for liberty!" he cried,
Then ran, with arms extended wide,
As if his dearest friend to clasp;
Ten spears he swept within his grasp.

from The Glove and the Lions

from an Ontario Reader
by Leigh Hunt

With wallowing might and stifled roar, they rolled one on another,
Till all the pit, with sand and mane, was in a thunderous smother;
The bloody foam above the bars came whizzing through the air;
Said Francis, then, "Good gentlemen, we're better here than there!"

She dropped her glove to prove his love: then looked on him and smiled;
He bowed and in a moment leaped among the lions wild:
The leap was quick; return was quick; he soon regained his place;
Then threw the glove, but not with love, right in the lady's face!

from **Hamlet's Soliloquy**

from The Tragedy of Hamlet, Prince of Denmark (soliloquy)
by William Shakespeare

To sleep—perchance to dream: ay, there's the rub!
For in that sleep of death what dreams may come
When we have shuffled off this mortal coil,
Must give us pause. There's the respect
That makes calamity of so long life.

Thus conscience does make cowards of us all,
And thus the native hue of resolution
Is sicklied o'er with the pale cast of thought,
And enterprises of great pith and moment
With this regard their currents turn awry
And lose the name of action.

from **The Ladder of St. Augustine**

from Poems Teachers Ask For, Book Two
by H.W. Longfellow

Saint Augustine! well hast thou said,
That of our vices we can frame
A ladder, if we will but tread
Beneath our feet each deed of shame!

All common things, each day's events,
That with the hour begin and end,
Our pleasures and our discontents,
Are rounds by which we may ascend.

The heights by great men reached and kept
Were not attained by sudden flight.
But they, while their companions slept,
Were toiling upward in the night.

Standing on what too long we bore
With shoulders bent and downcast eyes,
We may discern—unseen before—
A path to higher destinies.

from **Polonius' Advice**

from The Tragedy of Hamlet, Prince of Denmark
by William Shakespeare

Give every man thine ear, but few thy voice:
Take each man's censure, but reserve thy judgment.
Costly thy habit as thy purse can buy
But not expressed in fancy; rich, not gaudy:
For the apparel oft proclaims the man.

Neither a borrower nor a lender be;
For loan oft loses both itself and friend,
And borrowing dulls the edge of husbandry.
This above all: to thine own self be true;
And it must follow, as the night the day,
Thou canst not then be false to any man.

from **Saint Bernard's Hymn**

from The Library of the World's Best Literature, Ancient and Modern, Vol. 2
translation by Andrew Lang
edited by Charles Dudley Warner

Jesu! the very thought of thee
With sweetness fills my breast,
But sweeter far thy face to see
And in thy presence rest.

O hope of every contrite heart!
O joy of all the meek!
To those who fall, how kind thou art,
How good to those who seek!

from **The Sermon of St. Francis**

by Henry Wadsworth Longfellow
from the De La Salle Series

"O brother birds," St. Francis said,
"Ye come to me and ask for bread,
But not with bread alone today
Shall ye be fed and sent away.

"Ye shall be fed, ye happy birds
With manna of celestial words;
Not mine, though mine they seem to be,
Not mine, though they be spoken through me.

With flutter of swift wings and songs
Together rose the feathered throngs,
And singing scattered far apart;
Deep peace was in St. Francis' heart.

He knew not if the brotherhood
His homily had understood;
He only knew that to one ear
The meaning of his words was clear.

from **The Slaying of Owain**

from Library Of The World's Best Literature, Ancient And Modern, Vol. 2
by Aneurin

His courser, lank and swift, thick-maned,
Bore on his flank, as on he strained,
The light-brown shield, as on he sped,
With golden spur, in cloak of fur,
His blue sword gleaming. Be there said
No word of mine that does not hold thee dear!

Before thy youth had tasted bridal cheer,
The red death was thy bride! The ravens feed
On thee yet straining to the front, to lead.
Owain, the friend I loved, is dead!
Woe is it that on him the ravens feed!

from **The Vesper Hymn of Abelard**

from The Library of the World's Best Literature, Ancient and Modern, Vol. 1

edited by Charles Dudley Warner

Oh, what shall be, oh, when shall be that holy Sabbath day,
Which heavenly care shall ever keep and celebrate alway,
When rest is found for weary limbs, when labor hath reward,
When everything forevermore is joyful in the Lord?

There, there, secure from every ill, in freedom we shall sing
The songs of Zion, hindered here by days of suffering,
And unto Thee, our gracious Lord, our praises shall confess
That all our sorrow hath been good, and Thou by pain canst bless.

from **Where to Find True Joy**

from The Library of the World's Best Literature, Ancient and Modern, Vol. 1

by 'Boethius'

Oh! It is a fault of weight,
Let him think it out who will,
And a danger passing great
Which can thus allure to ill
Careworn men from the rightway,
Swiftly ever led astray.

All their hope is to acquire
Worship goods and worldly weal;
When they have their mind's desire,
Then such witless Joy they feel,
That in folly they believe
Those True Joys they then receive.

Models from Chapter IV

from **The Gods of the Teutons**
from Famous Men of the Middle Ages
by John H. Haaren and A. B. Poland

In the little volume called The Famous Men of Rome, you have read about the great empire, which the Romans established. Now we come to a time when the power of Rome was broken and tribes of barbarians who lived north of the Danube and the Rhine took possession of lands that had been part of the Roman Empire.

Then all the gods wept, the summer breeze wailed, the leaves fell from the sorrowing trees, the flowers faded and died from grief, and the earth grew stiff and cold. Bruin, the bear, and his neighbors, the hedgehogs and squirrels, crept into holes and refused to eat for weeks and weeks.

from **The Nibelungs**
from Famous Men of the Middle Ages
by John H. Haaren and A. B. Poland

Brunhilda prepared for the contests. Her shield was so thick and heavy that four strong men were needed to bear it. Three could scarcely carry her spear, and the stone that she hurled could only be lifted by twelve.

In the second and third contests, she fared no better, so she had to become King Gunther's bride. But she said that before she would leave Iceland she must tell all her kinsmen. Daily her kinsfolk rode to the castle, and soon an army had assembled.

from **Siegfried, the King's Son**
from A Child's Story Garden
compiled by Elizabeth Heber

Mimer was a queer little man. His back was bent and his hair was long and white. He had a long white beard and two very sharp, black eyes. Mimer's shop was out in the great, dark forest, and many boys came to learn of this wonderful master, for Mimer, you must know, was the best blacksmith in all the king's country.

"This is a good blade," said Mimer proudly. But Siegfried was not satisfied. He took the sword, broke it in pieces, and put it into the fire again. For three long weeks, Siegfried worked patiently at the anvil. Then he brought to Mimer a sword that was sharper, brighter, and stronger than the first.

from **The Story of the Merchant and the Genie** (pt. 1)

from Arabian Nights

by Andrew Lang

"But," said the genie, "if I grant you the delay you ask, I am afraid that you will not come back."

"I give you my word of honor," answered the merchant, "that I will come back without fail."

"How long do you require?" asked the genie.

When he arrived home, his wife and children received him with the greatest joy. But instead of embracing them, he began to weep so bitterly that they soon guessed that something terrible was the matter.

"Tell us, I pray you," said his wife, "what has happened?"

from **The Story of the Merchant and the Genie** (pt. 2)

from Arabian Nights

by Andrew Lang

"Father," she answered, "this calf is the son of our master. I smile with joy at seeing him still alive, and I weep to think of his mother, who was sacrificed yesterday as a cow. These changes have been wrought by our master's wife, who hated the mother and son."

Then she took a vessel of water and pronounced over it some words I did not understand. Then, on throwing the water over him, he became immediately a young man once more.

"My son, my dear son," I exclaimed, kissing him in a transport of joy. "This kind maiden has rescued you from a terrible enchantment, and I am sure that out of gratitude you will marry her."

from **The Story of the Merchant and the Genie** (pt. 3)

from Arabian Nights

by Andrew Lang

"Good day," I said.

"Good day," he answered. "Is it possible that you do not recognize me?" Then I looked at him closely and saw he was my brother. I made him come into my house, and asked him how he had fared in his enterprise.

Some time afterwards, my second brother wished also to sell his business and travel. My eldest brother and I did all we could to dissuade him, but it was of no use. He joined a caravan and set out. He came back at the end of a year in the same state as his elder brother. I took care of him, and as I had a thousand sequins to spare I gave them to him, and he reopened his shop.

from **The Fairy**
from The Fairy Tales of Charles Perrault
by Charles Perrault

Among other things, this poor child was forced twice a day to draw water a mile and a half from the house and bring home a pitcher full of it. One day, as she was at this fountain, there came to her a poor woman, who begged of her to let her drink.

"What is this I see?" said her mother quite astonished. "I think I see pearls and diamonds come out of the girl's mouth! How happens this, child?" (This was the first time she had ever called her child.)

The poor creature told her what had happened, but not without dropping out infinite numbers of diamonds.

from **Little Red Riding Hood**
from Old-Time Stories
by Charles Perrault

"It is your little daughter, Red Riding Hood," said the Wolf, disguising his voice, "and I bring you a cake and a little pot of butter as a present from my mother."

The worthy grandmother was in bed, not being very well, and cried out to him, "Pull out the peg, and the latch will fall."

"Grandmother dear, what big ears you have!"
"The better to hear with, my child!"
"Grandmother dear, what big eyes you have!"
"The better to see with, my child!"

from **The Master Cat or Puss in Boots**
from The Fairy Tales of Charles Perrault
by Charles Perrault

Another time he went and hid himself among some standing corn, holding still his open bag. When a brace of partridges ran into it, he drew the strings and caught them both. He went and made a present of these to the King, as he had done before with the rabbit. The King in like manner received the partridges with great pleasure, and ordered him something to drink.

The Marquis making several low bows, accepted the honor which his Majesty conferred upon him, and that very same day married the Princess.

Puss became a great lord, and never ran after mice any more, but only for his diversion.

(modified from the original)

from **Mr. and Mrs. Vinegar**

from English Fairy Tales
by Flora Annie Steel

"Don't shake so!" murmured Mrs. Vinegar, half-asleep. "You'll have me off the bed."

"I'm not shaking, Lovey," whispered back Mr. Vinegar in a quaking voice. "It is only the wind in the trees."

Then Mrs. Vinegar woke, rubbed her eyes, yawned, and said, "Where am I?"

"On the ground, Lovey," answered Mr. Vinegar, scrambling down.

And when they lifted up the door, what do you think they found? One robber squashed flat as a pancake, and forty golden guineas all scattered about! My goodness! How Mr. and Mrs. Vinegar jumped for joy!

from **The Three Wishes**

from More English Fairy Tales
by Joseph Jacobs

But the way was long, and the poor man was regularly dazed with the wonderful thing that had befallen him. When he got home, there was nothing in his noodle but the wish to sit down and rest. Maybe, too, it was a trick of the fairy's. Who can tell? Anyhow down he sat by the blazing fire, and as he sat he waxed hungry, though it was a long way off suppertime yet.

He gave a pull but it stuck, and she gave a pull but it stuck, and they both pulled till they had nigh pulled the nose off, but it stuck and stuck.

"What's to be done now?" said he.

"It isn't so very unsightly," said she, looking hard at him.

from **Schippeitaro**

from Tales of Wonder Every Child Should Know
edited by Kate Douglas Wiggin and Nora Archibald Smith

A beautiful clear full moon shed its light upon this gruesome scene, which the young warrior watched with amazement and horror. Suddenly, the midnight hour being passed, the phantom cats disappeared, and all was silence once more. The rest of the night passed undisturbed, and the young warrior slept soundly until morning.

When the young warrior, filled with wonder, inquired further, they told him that at sunset the victim would be put into a cage, carried to the ruined temple where he had passed the night, and left there alone. In the morning, she would have vanished. So it was each year, and so it would be now; there was no help for it.

from A Tale of a Penny

from Medieval Tales
by Various
edited by Henry Morley

Accordingly, the porter was installed in his office. And as the people entered the city, he took note of their defects and charged them in accordance with the grant. It happened that a hunchbacked fellow entered, and the porter made his demand. The hunchbacked fellow protested that he would pay nothing.

The hunchbacked fellow, very much enraged, persisted in his refusal and began to struggle with the porter. This caused an exposure of his arms, by which it became manifest that he was leprous. The porter immediately demanded a fourth penny. Refusing to pay, the hunchbacked fellow continued to struggle, revealing a rupture, which made a fifth.

from As You Like It

from Beautiful Stories from Shakespeare
by Edith Nesbit

There was once a wicked Duke named Frederick, who took the dukedom that should have belonged to his brother, sending him into exile. His brother went into the Forest of Arden, where he lived the life of a bold forester, as Robin Hood did in Sherwood Forest in merry England.

And so every day he went to her house, and took a pleasure in saying to her all the pretty things he would have said to Rosalind; and she had the fine and secret joy of knowing that all his love words came to the right ears. Thus many days passed pleasantly away.

from King Lear

from Beautiful Stories from Shakespeare
by Edith Nesbit

And Cordelia answered, "I love your Majesty according to my duty—no more, no less."

And this she said, because she was disgusted with the way in which her sisters professed love, when really they had not even a right sense of duty to their old father.

"You must bear with me," said Lear; "forget and forgive. I am old and foolish."

And now he knew at last which of his children it was that had loved him best, and who was worthy of his love.

Made in the USA
San Bernardino, CA
29 August 2019